Contradiction
Contradicted

W. S. Gilbert in the 1870s.

Contradiction Contradicted

The Plays of W. S. Gilbert

Andrew Crowther

Madison • Teaneck
Fairleigh Dickinson University Press
London: Associated University Presses

Associated University Presses
440 Forsgate Drive
Cranbury, NJ 08512

Associated University Presses
16 Barter Street
London WC1A 2AH, England

Associated University Presses
P.O. Box 338, Port Credit
Mississauga, Ontario
Canada L5G 4L8

The paper used in this publication meets the requirements of the American National Standard for Permanence of Paper for Printed Library Materials Z39.48-1984.

Library of Congress Cataloging-in-Publication Data

Crowther, Andrew, 1969–
    Contradiction contradicted : the plays of W.S. Gilbert / Andrew Crowther.
        p. cm.
    Enlargement of author's thesis (M.A.)—University of Bradford.
    Includes bibliographical references (p.) and index.
    ISBN 0–8386–3839–2 (alk. paper)
    1. Gilbert, W. S. (William Schwenck), 1836–1911—Criticism and interpretation. I. Title.

PR4714 .C76 2000

00–025686

CONTENTS

Acknowledgments

THIS BOOK IS A REWRITTEN VERSION OF THE THESIS I WROTE FOR MY Master of Philosophy degree at the University of Bradford. I should like to thank, first of all, my supervisor, Dr. Lynda Prescott, for guiding me toward coherence and intelligibility. I am also indebted to Professor Michael Wheeler of the University of Lancaster, who suffered from my first attempts at writing about Gilbert and, more recently, was a vital catalyst in finding me a publisher.

The quotation from the letter by Sir W. S. Gilbert to William Archer, dated 5 October 1904, is published by kind permission of the Royal Theatrical Fund.

I am grateful to the Raymond Mander and Joe Mitchenson Theatre Collection for permission to use several illustrations, and to the Pierpont Morgan Library, New York, for permission to reproduce the Gilbert self-caricature.

I could not have written this book had it not been for the financial support of the British Department of Social Security, now called the Employment Service; those institutions that have been rash enough to employ me, notably the Library Service of the London Borough of Barnet, and the solicitors firm Hammond Suddards; and, last and most importantly, my long-suffering parents.

Special thanks are also due to my brother Mark for the use of his computer facilities.

During the past few years in which I have been immersed in Gilbert's works, I have gained many E-mail friends, whose sympathy and support have been vital to me: Ralph MacPhail Jr. (who has helped me also by providing me with some of Gilbert's less-accessible texts), Michael Walters, Fraser Charlton, John Baesch, Helga Perry, and all the SavoyNet gang. My apologies to all those whom I should have mentioned here but haven't: that is a measure of lack of space, not of lack of gratitude. Thanks also are due to Brian Jones and Philip Plumb for their friendship and advice.

The folk of the Document Management Department of Hammond Suddards in Bradford have a special place in this list, for succeeding, against all the odds, in reminding me that there is indeed life beyond Gilbert.

Finally, I must return to two people whom I have already thanked: my parents. I can never thank them enough. Their love and forbearance while I was being thoughtless, selfish, and stupid are quite staggering. This book is a small, inadequate token of my own love and gratitude.

Author's Note

I HAVE ASSUMED, FOR THE SAKE OF CONVENIENCE, THAT THE READER IS familiar with the plots of the main Savoy operas. However, I have not made the same assumption concerning Gilbert's less well-known works and therefore include brief plot summaries where required.

A matter of terminology must be mentioned here. The Gilbert and Sullivan operas are, strictly speaking, operettas, because song alternates with spoken dialogue. However, they are traditionally known as operas, and I have decided to follow tradition on this point.

Contradiction
Contradicted

Introduction: The Problem of Gilbert

Almost every aspect of the life and work of W. S. Gilbert (1836–1911) is dogged by paradox and contradiction. Gilbert is, as a writer, at the same time famous and unknown. His most famous works, the librettos for such pieces as *The Mikado* and *The Pirates of Penzance,* are an integral part of Britain's national culture, and yet their importance in its cultural history is often neglected, reduced to a footnote to Oscar Wilde. It is as if the operas were thought too popular to deserve serious examination. Gilbert and Sullivan are, as a combination, famous—they are sometimes considered the archetypal collaboration—but there are some, even many Savoy enthusiasts, who could not say which wrote the words and which the music; and the name "W. S. Gilbert" triggers no spark of recognition in most people, even the well educated. The fame of Gilbert and Sullivan lies almost entirely in their combination, and each, considered alone, is thought a negligible figure.

Isaac Goldberg asked in 1929: "Gilbert or Sullivan? As well debate the superiority of oxygen to hydrogen, when what we thirst for is water."[1] This has long been the accepted attitude, that the work of neither man is worth separate study. A. H. Godwin insisted that "Neither . . . was a genius himself, but the association of the two, a gifted dramatist with a gifted composer, gave the world an art-form that has undeniable genius."[2] Some of those who have expressed this view have at least gone to the trouble of studying Gilbert's other works. Goldberg is a good example. Others seem to have merely parroted the accepted opinion without making a proper effort to verify it.

It is very easy to see how the attitude arose. The second half of Gilbert's career was dominated by his work with Arthur Sullivan: within a few years the international fame of the Savoy operas entirely overwhelmed the smaller, more select celebrity of his early plays. By 1907, when Edith A. Browne's study of Gilbert's plays was published, the pattern was well established, and a short, grudging chapter on his fairy

13

comedies and "serious" plays was followed, with obvious relief, by two enthusiastic chapters on the Sullivan pieces. The operas certainly deserved their success, but the easy corollary that Gilbert's other works deserved their comparative failure does not follow. This is partly because many of these plays seem failures only when set alongside the operas, a phenomenon of international success that was entirely unique, and partly because the question of a play's immediate commercial success is not, and has never been, the only criterion by which its artistic worth can be judged (though it can be a good basic indicator).

It is, unfortunately, a natural human assumption that a writer's lesser-known works should be judged entirely by the standard set by the better-known ones, and any deviation from that standard, even if it merely implies working by a different standard, is dismissed as an artistic falling short. For instance, Gilbert's play *Charity* (1874) has long been derided for its un-Gilbertian seriousness and moralism, yet viewed from a slightly different angle it becomes a highly interesting anticipation of the "problem play" of the 1890s, as Jane W. Stedman has observed.[3] And even Gilbert at his most Gilbertian can easily be dismissed when Sullivan is absent, as in the following passage from *The Oxford History of English Literature:*

> For all its brilliance, [Gilbert's] *Engaged* was disliked in its day for its heartless cynicism; and satire so purely destructive needed something like the verse-form of the *Bab Ballads* to make it sympathetic. This was supplied by Sullivan's music in the Savoy Operas (1875–1896), where the spiteful and almost sadistic nature of Gilbert's wit was obscured by the warmth and gaiety of the musical settings.[4]

It is interesting to see such a view expressed as recently as 1989: one would have thought that, by comparison with the works of such dramatists as Joe Orton or Edward Bond, the "spiteful and almost sadistic nature of Gilbert's wit" might appear highly civilized, almost genteel. And yet it appears that, even now, the British public is too easily shocked to be able to cope with the Gilbertian world-view unsoftened by Sullivan.

There has always been a certain ambivalence in public attitudes to the Gilbert and Sullivan operas. The operas are undoubtedly satirical—they are highly critical of British institutions and British customs—yet the operas very quickly became, themselves, a British institution. Gilbert, writing to Sullivan on 19 February 1888, told him that "we are . . . as much an institution as Westminster Abbey."[5] When, at the turn of the century, the D'Oyly Carte Opera Company began a systematic process of reviving the operas, these operas were welcomed as a reminder of the solid artistic quality of a past time, as opposed to the new, meretricious musical comedy.[6] And ever since, they have been accepted as part of the English tendency to misty-eyed nostalgia, and their hard edges have been tacitly softened. So we find Ian Bradley writing in 1996:

> What are the reasons for the enduring popularity of the Savoy Operas? Undoubtedly the nostalgia factor is an important one. . . . Half the charm of the Savoy Operas is that they are so dated. They seem to breathe the innocence, the naïvety and the fun of a long-vanished age.[7]

This is indeed a true expression of what the general public perceives of the operas. But a proper study of the librettos, and of Gilbert's other plays, shows these works to be much more interesting than Bradley implies. If we put to one side the easy nostalgia for chocolate-box Victorianism— and, just as importantly, the easy scorn for the faults of that age—we shall soon discover that these operas were an intelligent and far from naive response to the concerns of the day, which are often still our concerns, and that Gilbert was skillfully using popular forms to serious ends: that, like Jack Point, he was gilding the philosophic pill.

The lightness of touch with which Gilbert's best librettos are written makes it all the more difficult to accept that they might stand up to proper critical examination. How could something that is so entertaining also have anything of any importance to say? Eric Midwinter, in his article "W. S. Gilbert: Victorian Entertainer" (1986), pours scorn on the idea that Gilbert might have been anything more than a shrewd commercial dramatist: he insists that Gilbert was simply what he calls "a Samuel Smiles of the theatre."[8] "His task was the provision of human enjoyment, and his hope was that he would make a pot of gold out of it."[9] He was nothing more profound than "the pre-eminent entertainer of the Victorian age and the brief Edwardian epoch."[10] Midwinter's portrait relies too much on the idea that Gilbert did nothing significant apart from the Savoy operas: for instance, his assertion that "Gilbert showed precious little interest in political questions and never risked the goodwill of his audiences by belligerent outspokenness"[11] fails to take into account Gilbert's involvement in *The Happy Land* (1873), and completely ignores the many plays in which his originality of thought certainly did risk offending audiences.

Of course, Midwinter's argument is not completely untenable, as far as it goes. Gilbert was a commercial dramatist, as all dramatists in that age had to be in order to keep their heads above water. But his plays were not simply moneymakers; their interest lies in what is happening in them as well as providing Gilbert with an income.

The fame of the Savoy operas has done much to prevent a balanced examination of Gilbert's achievement by obscuring the sixty or so plays that he wrote apart from Sullivan. These other plays are not simply insignificant satellites to the operas, of interest only when they contributed ideas to the later, famous pieces, which is what many Gilbert and Sullivan books seem to imply in their approach. Gilbert's stage works are all of a piece and deserve to be examined on more or less equal terms with each other. And that is what I shall be attempting to do in this book—though the Savoy operas are undeniably Gilbert's most mature and sophisticated achievement, and this fact will be reflected in the amount of attention I give to them. The important point is that all Gilbert's works should be judged by the same criteria.

Others have attempted such an assessment before me, sometimes with worrying success: Max Keith Sutton's *W. S. Gilbert* (1975) is a notable achievement in this respect, and a handful of dissertations have been written with the declared aim of making sense of the Gilbertian oeuvre. Some of these, such as Mary Watkins Waters's "W. S. Gilbert and the Discovery of a Satiric Method for the Victorian Stage" (1974), have taken the attractive line of Gilbert as an unflinching satirist of the beliefs of the age, while others, such as Alan Fischler's thesis and published book *Modified Rapture* (1987/1991), have viewed Gilbert as an apologist for the bourgeois establishment (more or less as argued by Midwinter). Clearly, there is no generally accepted consensus about Gilbert's works, and the line I shall be taking myself has not, as far as I know, been argued before, at least in any detail. I may describe it as steering a middle course between the extremes of Waters and Fischler.

This is not a "definitive" study of Gilbert's plays, nor would I pretend it could be. It simply examines the plays according to one person's perception of what is interesting about them and that same person's ideas of what themes might be seen as binding the plays together. Gilbert's works are, for all their apparent simplicity, complex works of art, and they have different truths to unfold to different people. When I have explained what things they say to me, my task is complete, and it is for others to bring their own distinctive perspectives to the debate.

1

1863–1875—Finding a Style

As a rule, writers do not find their creative voice easily or immediately. When they begin to practice their profession, they imitate, they ramble, they blunder. They can only discover where their creative strengths lie by testing their weaknesses. Naturally, Gilbert was no exception. It was in 1861 that he joined the comic paper *Fun* and there found a place where he was allowed to explore what he could do in terms of prose, verse, cartoons, and excruciating puns. But, important though this phase in his career was, we must skim over it and concentrate instead on his introduction to writing for the theater, the place where after much effort he was to find the fullest outlet for his talents.

In this first period of his career as a dramatist—roughly from 1863 to 1875—Gilbert experimented in many dramatic forms, trying to find the ideal style in which he could utilize his creative strengths. As to what those strengths were, that is one of the major concerns of this book as a whole, but for the moment it may be useful to define them as a flair for fantasy combined with a stern and almost brutal sense of reality.

During this period Gilbert enjoyed a remarkable explosion of creativity, writing plays that, while often lacking the final polish of the more famous Sullivan collaborations, make up for this in vitality, quickness of wit, and raw energy. They also take many more risks than Gilbert was later to find acceptable: as a result, those plays that fail fail badly, but those that succeed are invested with an irresistible note of daring. Though many of these plays may seem from our modern perspective mere creative dead ends, they have much to offer us if taken on their own terms and in any proper study of Gilbert's plays cannot decently be ignored.

Verse Extravaganzas

Gilbert's first extant play is *Uncle Baby,* a one-act comedietta premiered to no great acclaim in 1863. But his theatrical career really began three years later with the first performance of his extravaganza *Dulcamara*, the play that in later years he insisted was his first. It and its four successors established him as a popular dramatist, and, while they are not particularly good as drama, they do have points of interest.

It is important to notice that, from the very outset, Gilbert's work for the theater combined dialogue with song. Jane W. Stedman suggests that Gilbert may have contributed lyrics to several pantomimes by Charles Millward, performed in the 1865 Christmas season;[1] and in the extravaganzas, rhymed dialogue is capped with ebullient, frequently nonsensical, songs, with music taken from the popular operas and operettas of the time (particularly Offenbach's). From the beginning, Gilbert's theatrical talents displayed themselves not in the "straight" dramatic forms of the time—farce and melodrama—but in the mixed form of extravaganza/burlesque. This is obviously significant in the light of his later career. While I mean to discuss this in greater detail later, it may be useful to draw attention now to the fact that of all the popular theatrical genres this was the one that had the least direct relationship to reality. Farce depended on its characters being comic reflections of ordinary types, and melodrama often fed on the issues of the day, but burlesque and extravaganza were always avowedly fantastic. They gloried in the spectacular and the artificial. We should bear in mind Gilbert's immediate attraction to this atmosphere, particularly considering his surface commitment to naturalism on the stage, as popularized by Tom Robertson.

The extravaganza or burlesque of the 1860s was a vulgarized development from the fairy extravaganzas that James Robinson Planché wrote for the Olympic Theatre in the 1830s and 1840s. As Michael R. Booth has observed, "it is not easy to distinguish between extravaganza and burlesque,"[2] and the two terms were often used interchangeably. Gilbert called these plays extravaganzas, but they could with equal justice be called burlesques in that they rely heavily upon parody of melodramatic and operatic conventions—not to mention parody of the conventions of burlesque itself. Thus the following speech from *Dulcamara,* in response to the rash query, "But, tell me where I am, and who are these?":

> You're in a village during harvest time,
> Where all the humblest peasants talk in rhyme,
> And sing about their pleasures and their cares
> In parodies of all the well-known airs.
>
> They earn their bread by going in a crowd,
> To sing their humble sentiments aloud,
> In choruses of striking unanimity—

> (*Aside*) The only rhyme I know to that, is dimity.
> They never wear umbrellas—so they get
> Their dress of *watered* silk—or else *well wet.*
> Their dresses of *drawing rooms* is emblematic
> Although their mode of life is *upper-attic!*[3]

The first half of this speech is a very direct criticism of the genre and consists of the same kind of joke as that which Gilbert was also developing in his parody reviews in *Fun* at this time. (These page-long parodies of current London plays also made extensive use of this trick of making characters point out the absurdities of aspects of plot or characterization.)

But in the second half of the speech we seem to see Gilbert giving in to the demands of the form and dredging up those linguistic contortions that his audience might possibly recognize as puns. (The pun on *well wet*—velvet—is particularly tortuous.) The extreme demands of the burlesque form take a heavy toll and render these pieces extremely difficult to read today. Gilbert was later to write of the restrictions imposed by stage censorship that made the dramatist's work a hornpipe in fetters, but the fetters imposed by the burlesque form were much more cumbersome and did much more to prevent the results from being real works of art. Because these five pieces are written in rhymed couplets, punctuated at regular intervals with puns of wildly varying quality, the reader is constantly aware that the work's form is intruding itself between him and the meaning of the words.

This is not to say that all the puns are as bad as the ones above. For instance, the following, also from *Dulcamara,* is reasonably amusing and in its way rather charming:

> *Adina.* It's true, Belcore's got a lot of money—
>   But if you'll have me I'll be sweet as honey!
> *Nemorino.* I'm sage enough to know you love this money 'un.
> *Adina.* You're sage; but what is sage without a *honey 'un?*[4]

The pun here is not gratuitous but accords with plot and character.

In many other instances throughout these pieces, the puns are all too clearly the result of desperation, as in this from *La Vivandière:*

> I let it when he first paid nature's debts
> At Austerlitz, and now the *'ouse to let's!*[5]

I now wish to examine, in greater detail, one of Gilbert's later extravaganzas: *Robert the Devil* (1868). We can see in this, more clearly than in most of the others, Gilbert beginning to use his comic techniques to serious ends—though the atmosphere of enforced frivolity still remains.

It, like all Gilbert's other verse extravaganzas, is a frivolous reworking of an established opera—in this case, Meyerbeer's *Robert le Diable*. The hero, Robert, becomes a "breeches role" for Nellie Farren, who had a specialism in this kind of thing: Robert is played as an insouciant "swell." He is tempted by a devil, Bertram, who turns out to be his dissolute father, now damned in hell. More space is given to the whimsicalities of pun and bon mot than to the development of plot, but Bertram does tempt Robert to steal "the magic branch / That's planted in the Nun's Enchanted Bower"[6]—exactly as in the original opera. The Bower turns out to be the Chamber of Horrors in Madame Tussaud's:

> *Robert.* A kind of treat for butchers only, meet!
> *Bertram.* A treat for *butchers?* Nonsense! *Baker's treat!*[7]

This provides a chance for the waxworks to have a scene in which they come alive at the stroke of midnight. The waxwork of King John bewails his comedown since the time he was Bishop Wilberforce: "It's hard to saddle one, who saints has passed for, / With all the vices of a part he's *cast* for?"[8] This small suggestion that people may not be entirely responsible for their own vices reflects back to a passage in the first scene:

> *Bertram.* I don't indulge in crimes by choice;
>   In perpetrating them I have no voice.
>   And after perpetration comes revulsion.
>   A saint by choice, a devil by compulsion!
> *Ferdidando.* Oh, a policeman.[9]

(Which is, apparently, not the right answer.)

Bertram comments on the waxworks, "These are all statues, raised from time to time, / To people who're remarkable for crime"; and when Robert asks, "Why give them statues?" he replies, "'Cause they don't deserve one! / That's our strict rule—a rule we never garble— / 'Good deeds we write in sand—bad deeds in marble!'"[10] Even at this early stage in his career Gilbert was beginning to express a distinctively satirical view of the world.

To return to the Madame Tussaud's scene, the "magic branch" turns out to be *"a policeman's staff,"*[11] with a scroll attached, reading in part:

> . . . in all kind of modern high-way danger,
>   Invisibility it will afford—

> If street-rows should be rife, or thieves abroad,
> Or beery ruffians, brave with half-and-half,
> *No eye can see the man who bears this staff!*[12]

Robert, possessed with this magic staff (which also freezes people in their places), speculates:

> . . . only think,
> How useful it would be to Government!
> A First Lord might employ it to prevent
> His restive steeds from kicking o'er the traces,
> And keep small members in their proper places!
> What would some agents give, that we could name,
> If they could only use this little game,
> To fix, now our new legislature meets,
> Corrupting members safely in their seats![13]

This is evidently topical satire, but the references, though obscure, are clear enough in general outline. Gilbert was already becoming bold in his satirical ideas, and if the above passages seem a little scattershot, there is a real feeling of bitterness in them that sets them apart from the mere professional frivolity of most burlesque. And the ending of the piece, in which Bertram descends through a trap to become a part of the Madame Tussaud's exhibits (while Robert sings, "Among the dead men down you go"),[14] is distinctly dark, for surely no one would be fooled by that trivializing euphemism for hell.

These extravaganzas are most commonly dismissed as the worst kind of hackwork, unworthy of Gilbert, but at the time they were very well received, and, as Stedman notes, "critics praised Gilbert for reforming burlesque."[15] We can see in these pieces the seeds of his later works. Distinctive Gilbertian ideas periodically struggle to the surface through the necessary clinker of puns.

The last of the conventional extravaganzas, *The Pretty Druidess* (1869), is comparatively restrained in tone: a burlesque of *Norma*, in which the story is apparently retained with reasonable fidelity (except for getting rid of the original tragic ending), it feels almost serious, despite the obligatory puns. The central conflict between the druid priestesses of Gaul and the Roman soldiers looks forward to *The Princess, The Wicked World,* and *Iolanthe.* The sudden decision not to burn Norma at the stake in the final scene but to allow her to pass harmlessly through theatrical "red fire" seems to recall a similar reversal at the end of Planché's *The Golden Fleece* (1845). Indeed *The Pretty Druidess* is much closer in atmosphere to

Planché than were any of its predecessors. The similarity may be defined as a sense of respect for the thing parodied.

The most interesting passage in *The Pretty Druidess* is Norma's final address to the audience. It has often been quoted but only because it deserves quotation.

> . . . I come to speak the tag,
>   With downcast eyes, and faltering steps, that lag,
> I'm cowed and conscience-stricken—for tonight
> We have, no doubt, contributed our mite
> To justify that topic of the age,
> The degradation of the English stage.
> . . . the piece is common-place, grotesque,
> A solemn folly—a proscribed burlesque!
> So for burlesque I plead. Forgive our rhymes;
> Forgive the jokes you've heard five thousand times;
> Forgive each breakdown, cellar-flap, and clog,
> Our low-bred songs—our slangy dialogue;
> And, above all—oh, ye with double-barrel—
> Forgive the scantiness of our apparel![16]

Stedman points out that *The Pretty Druidess* actually was costumed with unusual "respectability" and that there were none of the energetic dances ("breakdown, cellar-flap, and clog") that were normally considered obligatory.[17]

This speech exhibits an ambivalence that will become a familiar note in Gilbert's later work. This was his last burlesque/extravaganza, and we may take the speech as a deliberate goodbye to all that. In his extravaganzas he often seems to despise the idiocies he perpetrates, and this note is loudly sounded in Norma's apology. His extravaganzas hark back to the old elegant burlesques of Planché, and in his "fairy comedies" he would soon make further steps in that direction. Having started his theatrical career in this vulgar genre, he was searching for a more refined, literary style, in which he could be more seriously regarded as a dramatist. Norma's words sound like an apology for past follies.

Yet these words also strike a note of defiance. "So for burlesque I plead": that sounds defensive. And when "ye with double-barrel" are asked to "Forgive the scantiness of our apparel," the sardonic tone can scarcely be ignored. As if the young aristocrats in the audience would have objected to scant apparel, had it been there! Gilbert seems to be saying that he is above the popular crudities of burlesque, and yet he regards them with affection. Throughout his career the same ambivalence is visible: giving the audience what it wants, and yet despising such tricks; hankering for a more refined style of drama that will earn the respect of the critics, and yet scorning the exclusive and the effete, and always in the end revolting against the approval of authority. Perhaps the easiest image for his situation is that he was torn between two sets of values—a surface adherence to the middle-class virtues of respectability, and, underneath this, an earthier sense of the ignobility of such respectability. At heart, I believe, his instincts were vulgar in the best sense of that word, in that he understood the beliefs, enthusiasms, and antipathies of ordinary people. But he could only express that vulgarity in a way that would satisfy his intellect and prevent him from despising himself as a mercenary hack. His dramatic range was expanding rapidly now, and he was no longer able to say all he wanted to say within the tight framework imposed by the form of the rhymed extravaganza/burlesque.

Gilbert's development as a dramatist is not easy to describe in terms of linear narrative: around the time of *The Pretty Druidess* he was beginning to experiment in several directions at once. In March 1869, three months before the premiere of *The Pretty Druidess, No Cards* was produced at the Gallery of Illustration. This was his first libretto with prose dialogue and was the start of an association with the Gallery of Illustration that was to bring forth the first of Gilbert's dramatic works that are recognizably Gilbertian in style. Just one month after *The Pretty Druidess*'s premiere, the Gaiety produced *An Old Score*, which was Gilbert's first attempt at a full-length play without songs. This points forward to Gilbert's "serious" style, a style further developed in plays such as *Charity* and *The Ne'er-Do-Weel.*

However, I wish to leave these strands on one side for the moment so that I may concentrate instead on a third strand that develops most naturally from Gilbert's previous experience in extravaganza: fairy comedy. In fact, the play that I wish to examine first under this heading, *The Princess* (1870), may be described with equal justice as the last and most restrained of his burlesques.

Fairy Comedies

The Princess is the earliest of the plays that Gilbert thought worthy of preservation in the four volumes of his *Original Plays*—though the version that appears there is somewhat different from the original version as published by Thomas Hailes Lacy. It appears that when he prepared the

play for *Original Plays* in 1875, he cut out many of the songs that deco-
rated the original—new lyrics matched to opera/operetta favorites, in popular burlesque style. This seems to suggest a desire to cut the play to fit a
later conception of the fairy comedy (of which the first volume of *Original
Plays* provides three other examples) and to distance it from its connection
with the earlier rhymed burlesques.

This is what Gilbert wrote of the play in his short 1883 "Autobiography":

> I had for some time determined to try the experiment of a blank verse bur-
> lesque in which a picturesque story should be told in a strain of mock-heroic
> seriousness; and through the enterprise of the late Mrs. Liston (then man-
> ageress of the Olympic) I was afforded an opportunity of doing so. The story
> of Mr. Tennyson's "Princess" supplied the subject-matter of the parody, and
> I endeavoured so to treat it as to absolve myself from a charge of wilful
> irreverence.[18]

This seems a puzzling attitude to take up: a burlesque in which a "picturesque story" is united with "mock-heroic seriousness" (then where is
the bathos on which burlesque depends?); a burlesque in which a respected
poem is parodied without "wilful irreverence" (but what good is reverence
in such an exercise?).

In the event, the bathos lies in the uniting of the blank-verse style and
"picturesque story" with trivial and deflating anachronisms. There are still
puns, as in the earlier burlesques, but Gilbert allows himself to be a little
more sophisticated in their use, and he is no longer under an obligation to
bring them in at all costs. Some of them depend on a familiarity with
Shakespeare:

> His outer man, gnarled, knotted as it was,
> Seemed to his cruel and cynical within,
> Hyperion to a Saturday Review![19]

Or if (as seems possible) this is not thought particularly brilliant, we
later find:

> I blushed and stammered so, that she exclaimed:
> "Can these be men?" (then seeing this) "Why, these—"
> *"Are men!"* she would have added, but *"are men"*
> Stuck in her throat![20]

There is none of the "elevated" tone that we find in the later fairy comedies. Indeed, the style deliberately quashes all hints at such a tone, in spite
of the blank verse. Everything is deflated:

> But stay, my liege; o'er yonder mountain's brow
> Comes a small body bearing Gama's arms;
> And, now I look more closely at it, sir,
> I see attached to it King Gama's legs;
> From which I gather this corollary—
> That that small body must be Gama's own![21]

The imagery commonly contains modern Victorian references, as when Gama says that Ida's college girls are "safety-matches, sir, / And they light only on the knowledge box."[22]

In view of this general tone of systematic deflation, it is not surprising that Ida's experiment of women's education is scoffed at in terms that do not sit easily today. As in the later rewritten version for Sullivan, *Princess Ida* (1884), there are passages that seem to imply that Ida's women have moved out of their natural sphere and left behind their natural role (by implication, the domestic, wifely role). The students are more interested in their robes than in their academic studies; the lady surgeon faints at the sight of blood; Ida's trained troops are scared that their muskets might "in the heat and turmoil of the fight, / . . . go off."[23]

The three plays that are generally understood to constitute Gilbert's sequence of fairy comedies, *The Palace of Truth* (1870), *Pygmalion and Galatea* (1871), and *The Wicked World* (1873), were all written for the Haymarket Theatre, which had been particularly associated with Planché's extravaganzas in the 1840s, and they all starred J. B. Buckstone, for whom Planché had written such topical pieces as *Mr. Buckstone's Voyage Round the Globe (in Leicester Square)* (1854). Gilbert mentions in "Autobiography" that he could "remember the time (about thirty-eight years since, I think) when [the Haymarket Theatre] was still lighted by wax candles."[24] This means that he must have seen plays at the Haymarket around the year 1845, in which year Planché provided the theater with three plays, including *The Golden Fleece*. In short, Gilbert undoubtedly knew Planché's works well, and at first hand; and it seems, at the least, very probable that he was consciously building on that tradition in these fairy comedies. Thus we have *The Palace of Truth*, based on a French source (Mme Genlis's *Le Palais de la Vérité*), just as Planché based many of his extravaganzas on French sources; and we also have *Pygmalion and Galatea*, which elaborated on classical myth, just as Planché had often done. Only with *The Wicked World* did Gilbert take a subject original to himself.

In these three plays the burlesque tone of *The Princess* is set aside: there are no deliberate anachronisms, there are no puns, and, while impossible events occur, the action is entirely consistent within the conventions created by the play's world. These sound like advantages, but the result is that many of the liveliest features of *The Princess* have been bleached out of its successors. The characters do not speak in the rhythms of Victorian London: blank verse and historical authenticity ensure that. The language is instead formal, stilted, and bland. Ninety percent of the vitality of Gilbert's style has been carefully removed in the interest of creating a refined, civilized, elegant effect in imitation of Planché.

William Archer, writing in 1882, felt obliged to devote considerable space to discussion of Gilbert's blank-verse plays in his brief assessment of Gilbert's overall output; that is at least a testament to the plays' high critical standing in their own day. *The Princess* and the three mature fairy comedies were successful financially as well as critically, and Stedman notes that "By the 1890s it [*Pygmalion and Galatea*] had been played everywhere from Calcutta to St Petersburg,"[25] and it continued to have a life in performance well into the twentieth century.

But Archer's assessment of these plays is far from laudatory. Speaking of Gilbert's six blank-verse plays, he says:

> Supposing each play to contain on an average 1500 lines—a modest computation—we find that Mr. Gilbert has written at least 9000 lines of blank-verse. Of these 9000 I venture to assert that there is not one which has the smallest metrical beauty. As a rule they are correctly enough measured off into ten syllables, but there is not one whose cadence lingers in the memory.[26]

A little later he says, "Mr. Gilbert is neither a poet nor a master of its mysteries, and in binding himself down to cut his thoughts into lengths of five feet, he has merely made their expression needlessly verbose."[27] These are harsh judgements, but it is difficult to assert that they are unjust. Archer asks, "why choose this hampering medium of expression?"[28] The answer, which he does not find, or at any rate does not express, is surely that blank verse was the form of "literary" drama; by using it in these mythological/supernatural pieces, Gilbert was asserting his right to be respected in a profession that was still, on the whole, not much respected. There was still a division in the mind of the educated Victorian between the unactable "closet dramas" of the poets (Browning, Swinburne, etc.) and the "actable" drama that was felt to have no perceptible literary merit whatsoever.[29] To create a series of blank-verse plays that were at the same time "actable" and actually enjoyable from the audience's point of view was a tremendous step forward for Gilbert's reputation. For that reason, from a purely historical perspective, the fairy comedies are important to an understanding of Gilbert's career. It is true that they do not seem very exciting or brilliant today, but we must not disregard them on that count.

It would be a mistake to say that Gilbert wrote them to make himself "reputable," in the base way in which, it has sometimes been said, he wrote his more purely comic/farcical pieces to make himself rich. There is no reason to doubt that Gilbert was earnestly attempting to create serious works of art in these plays: they do have a kind of artistic integrity to them.

Each of the three Haymarket plays has an abstract thesis that the action of the play attempts to prove. The remote settings may be seen as an attempt to sweep away from the action all the irrelevancies of Victorian life that might otherwise muddy the waters and make the logic of the argument more difficult to follow. Thus in *The Palace of Truth* we have a group of characters who visit an enchanted palace where everyone must speak the truth. The thesis is not just that *"Man is a hypocrite, and invariably affects to be better and wiser than he really is,"*[30] as Gilbert was later to assert in *The Mountebanks* (1892), for the Palace of Truth reveals the hidden virtues of the surly and the shy. But it is asserted that Man is a natural liar, and that if he were suddenly to lose this capacity for lying, society would collapse. As Bernard Mandeville observed, "he that . . . offers to speak the Truth of his Heart, and what he feels within, is the most contemptible Creature upon Earth, tho' he committed no other Fault."[31]

By making his characters courtiers from a far-off land, Gilbert is able to divorce them from the local characteristics of his own society and to present them as distilled essences of certain character types: the cynic, the coquette, the dandy, and so on. Of course, he brings the assumptions of his own day to the task, and so Victorian society intrudes in spite of itself; but the illusion of remoteness is still important, if only so that the audience may enjoy the play without the uncomfortable feeling that it is itself being held up for examination.

The same process takes place in *The Wicked World*, which I now propose to examine in some detail. The thesis is explicitly stated in the prologue (as spoken by Buckstone):

> The Author begs you'll kind attention pay
> While I explain the object of his play.
> You have been taught, no doubt, by those professing
> To understand the thing, that Love's a blessing:
> Well, *he* intends to teach you the reverse—
> That Love is not a blessing, but a curse![32]

A scene from *The Wicked World*: the unfortunate effects of mortal love in Fairy Land. (The Raymond Mander and Joe Mitchenson Theatre Collection.)

But the actor distances himself from the attitudes of "the Author" and in the end casts doubt on the thesis that he says Gilbert is propounding. The prologue ends on a note of doubt:

> But prithee be not led too far away,
> By the hack author of a mere stage-play:
> It's easy to affect this cynic tone,
> But, let me ask you, had the world ne'er known
> Such Love as you, and I, and he, must mean—
> Pray where would you, or I, or he, have been?[33]

These last words make it as clear as it could be made on the stage of the time that Gilbert is talking about sexual love. The central idea of the play is not so much a thesis as a dilemma: is sexual love a blessing or a curse? The scene is Fairy Land, populated by nonsexual beings who look down on the mortal world with all its vices and wonder what it is that makes life worthwhile for Man. Their Fairy Queen, Selene, explains that it is

> The gift of Love! Not as we use the word,
> To signify mere tranquil brotherhood;
> But in some sense that is unknown to us.
> Their love bears like relation to our own,
> That the fierce beauty of the noonday sun
> Bears to the calm of a soft summer's eve.
> It nerves the wearied mortal with hot life,
> And bathes his soul in hazy happiness.
> The richest man is poor who hath it not,
> And he who hath it laughs at poverty.
> It hath no conqueror.[34]

And so on. However, Lutin, a male fairy who has at least visited the "wicked world" below them, has an entirely different perspective on the matter:

> Why Love's the germ
> Of every sin that stalks upon the earth:
> The brawler fights for love—the drunkard drinks
> To toast the girl who loves him, or to drown
> Remembrance of the girl who loves him not! . . .
> Be not deceived—this love is but the seed;
> The branching tree that springs from it is Hate![35]

The fairies make the scientific experiment of bringing three mortal men into Fairy Land, ostensibly to turn the men away from their wicked lives and bring home to them the benefits of a pure existence, but really, as we understand, from curiosity to learn about this mortal love of theirs. Of course the Fairies' tranquillity is destroyed, and the community is riven with desire and jealousy. Only when the mortals are returned to earth is the spell broken and order restored. When, in the final scene, a message is brought that the Fairy King has decided to confer on them the gift "that we may love as mortals love!,"[36] Selene replies *"eagerly"*:

> No, no—not that. . . .
> It is a deadly snare—beware of it!
> Such love is for mankind, and not for us;
> It is the very essence of the earth,
> A mortal emblem, bringing in its train
> The direst passions of its antitype. . . .
> Let us glide through our immortality
> Upon the placid lake of sister-love,
> Nor tempt the angry billows of a sea,
> Which, though it carry us to unknown lands,
> Is so beset with rocks and hidden shoals,
> That we may perish ere our vessel reach
> The unsafe haven of its distant shore.[37]

Gilbert's intention in this play seems clear enough. He imagines a world without "mortal love," to which he then introduces this alien element. The idea is to show the emotions and attitudes that are dependent upon mortal love and to place them in a setting that will lay bare the logic of the argument he is setting forth. Gilbert's Fairy Land is here being used as a kind of petri dish, a sterile environment in which the thing to be examined may develop in isolation and without the confusing influence of other elements such as might disrupt the clarity of the experiment.

However, by choosing this remote setting and these nonhuman characters, Gilbert risks alienating his audience. After all, what possible point of contact is there between the pure, righteous fairies of his imagining and the respectable, but mortal, playgoers who visited the Haymarket in 1873?

One possible answer springs to mind almost immediately. Let us suppose for a moment that what Gilbert is really talking about is that most famous of Victorian traits, the suppression of sex. The fairies are what the Victorians aspired to be in their most respectable moments: pure, virtuous, nonsexual. Since the population of Fairy Land is mostly female, we are talking in particular about the "angel in the house," the nonsexual ideal of womanhood. But this ideal cannot be sustained: there will inevitably arrive from below intimations of "mortal love" that will wreak havoc if not prepared for. We might be tempted to see the central part of the play as a lesson against attempting to sunder the two halves of human nature.

The play's conclusion—banishment of the mortals, restoration of order—does not appear, to the modern eye, a satisfactory conclusion to such an argument; it appears to support the stereotypical "Victorian" revulsion toward sex. But there are definite ambiguities in Selene's final rejection of "mortal love." Though she chooses to prefer the calm tranquillity of her former existence, we are left feeling that this is a decision that will be thought desirable only among immortal beings. Gilbert comes down pretty clearly on the side of "hot life"; the decision of the fairies must therefore be understood in an ironic spirit. As in the prologue, the "dominant" idea of proving that "Love is not a blessing, but a curse"[38] is undercut with doubt.

The whole play depends on an inversion: the desires of fairies are not the same as the desires of mortals, and the only way the mortal audience of *The Wicked World* can extract a useful message from the play is by bearing this difference of desires very carefully in mind. This being so, a proper understanding of what is going on in the play depends on establishing from the start an ironic distance between fairies and audience: we must always be able to stand back a little from the views they express and examine them dispassionately.

Thus the prologue clearly states their "one little fault. . .— / *An overweening sense of righteousness*";[39] and in the body of the play they display a prurient curiosity about the sins of the "wicked world" that casts doubt on their easy assumption of superiority. The ease with which they fall into attitudes of jealousy and spite once the mortals come among them suggests that their absence of sin arose from absence of temptation rather than from strength of mind. Indeed, Selene makes precisely this point in the final scene of the play:

> . . . is there so wide a gulf between
> The humbled wretch who, being tempted, falls,
> And that good man who rears an honoured head
> Because temptation hath not come to him?[40]

This is an idea that runs through Gilbert's work from start to finish, as Stedman has observed.[41]

The play is very well constructed at the level of ideas, though the central part of the play, in which the fairies fall in love with the mortals, does seem rather crudely done. The blank verse has an unfortunate deadening effect on the whole, and Gilbert seems much more satisfied with some of his "poetic" phrases than we might feel he has any right to be, but that is an inevitable side effect of the more serious tone he was trying to cultivate in these plays. I might add that the blank verse also blunts the force of the ideas it is trying to express.

In short, what we have here is a less acute case of the problem we found in the verse extravaganzas: Gilbert's imagination and inventiveness struggling for expression through the limitations of form. The theme, structure, and ideas of the play clearly show Gilbert's increasing sophistication, and the use of irony and inversion to give weight to opposing ideas looks forward to the Savoy operas, as we shall see, but the style of the play's execution does not match the concept. That Gilbert himself felt he had not got everything out of *The Wicked World* is suggested by the fact that, as late as 1909, he produced a rewritten libretto version of it, entitled *Fallen Fairies.*

Something needs to be said of *Broken Hearts* (1875), though it is a serious, not to say lachrymose, "fairy play," rather than a fairy comedy. It deals, like *The Princess* and *The Wicked World*, with a community of women, who in this case have retreated to the Island of Broken Hearts to escape men and their dangerous love. Instead, the women redirect their love to inanimate objects—Lady Hilda loves a fountain, Lady Vavir a sundial. The only man on the island is Mousta, their hunchbacked servant. However, at the start of the play Prince Florian arrives on the island, with a magic veil that makes the wearer invisible. He uses the veil to play a trick on the women, pretending to be the voice of, in turn, the fountain and the sundial. Florian repents when he sees the intensity of the women's love of these things, but the delicate Lady Vavir goes into a decline, dying at the end of act 3 and so leaving Florian and Hilda together.

The magical and fantastic elements in the play are difficult to swallow, especially since there is very little relieving humor. The verse is not very startling, though there is a flash of Gilbertian unconventionality at the end of Lady Hilda's description of Florian:

> He was a prince—a brave, God-fearing knight—
> The very pink and bloom of Chivalry,
> Proud as a war-horse—fair as the dawn of day—
> Staunch as a Woman—tender as a Man![42]

The central theme, the destructive power of love, is a variation of that of *The Wicked World:* again the intrusion of man into loveless tranquillity creates havoc, though here the consequences are much more serious. However, it is insisted that love need not always destroy. Both Hilda and Vavir love Florian, but only Vavir dies. The inanimate love totems of the two women are clearly symbolic: Hilda's fountain is a life-giving thing, while Vavir's sundial is a symbol of time, and so, obliquely, of transience and death. Hilda is revived by love, not killed by it.

There is a similar symbolic contrast between the two men, Florian and the Caliban-like Mousta. Florian is, despite his original thoughtless conduct, a chivalrous man, the embodiment of romantic love, while Mousta, embittered and made desperate by his ugliness, will stoop to any trick to gain love. He is ridiculed and reviled by all the other characters whenever he tries to suggest that he, too, might need to be loved; the scenes with him are the most powerful and disturbing in the play. We are never quite sure if we are supposed to be moved to pity or disgust by him, but he alone transcends the pasteboard characterization of the other figures in the drama.

Mousta seems a clear representation of the dark, desperate side of male sexuality. Florian is much more "civilized," but he is rather a conceited fop, of a type we have already met in *The Princess* and *The Wicked World* and will meet again in *The Yeomen of the Guard.* These characters take it for granted that they must be the hero of the story they are in, and, because they assume it, it becomes true. Florian's easy conceit contrasts grimly with Mousta's angry self-loathing.

Vavir and Hilda are a much less colorful contrast, but the worrying equation of love and death that is clear in Vavir is thankfully denied in Hilda. Is love a blessing or a curse? Gilbert has still not found an answer, though the ending of the play focuses exclusively on Vavir's death. *Broken Hearts* was one of Gilbert's favorite works, but one must conclude that its concerns are too intensely personal for the good of the play as a whole.

The fairy comedies earned Gilbert a high reputation in their own time, but they were not the ideal mode of expression for his ideas. The blank verse imposed on his characters a wearisome blandness of expression, out of which quickness of wit and sharpness of expression have been deliberately drained. However, at the same time as he was writing these plays, Gilbert was also beginning to write in a style that had much more vitality and in which the beginnings of the mature "Savoy style" are clearly visible. The fairy comedies are lifeless monuments, but in Gilbert's early librettos for German Reed we have pieces that are still, more than a century later, flushed with a very real zest and vitality.

THE GERMAN REED LIBRETTOS

The Gallery of Illustration was a small theater on Regent Street, where Thomas German Reed and a small company of actors (including his wife Priscilla) produced small-scale comic entertainments. The name "Gallery of Illustration" was a transparent subterfuge to ward off the moral stigma of being, in reality, a theater, though by the time Gilbert started writing for it the middle classes had largely come to accept theaters as respectable places once more, and the subterfuge was no longer necessary. Still, the genteel name indicates the kind of audience the Gallery courted, and, therefore, the kind of entertainment expected of it.

From 1869 to 1875, Gilbert wrote for this company six short musical pieces, most in one act (the exception being *A Sensation Novel*) and none requiring more than six actors. The emphasis in these pieces was on intimacy over spectacle; the limitations imposed by budget and setting forced Gilbert to pay more attention to such matters as characterization, invention, and wit. As Stedman observes, "On a stage *sans* trapdoors and pantomime machinery, his magic depended on sparkling wit rather than on the sudden proliferation of gold leaf."[43] They differed from Gilbert's earlier burlesques in that spectacle could not be invoked to draw attention away from flaws in construction. The writer was of much greater importance in the scheme of things and shouldered proportionately more responsibility.

In the first two of these librettos—*No Cards* and *Ages Ago* (both 1869)—Gilbert was still feeling his way toward a style. *No Cards* is essentially a farce of disguises on the lines of his earlier one-acter *Highly Improbable* (1867) but with the addition of songs. It is competently written, and there are occasional flashes of satire, but by and large it sticks to the modest ambition of providing a pleasant hour's entertainment. Most of the songs have a slightly tacked-on feel, and indeed one of them is a cut-down version of Gilbert's Bab Ballad "The Precocious Baby." And while there is an appreciable advance in the sophistication of the lyrics of the next piece, *Ages Ago,* again the piece's purpose, first and last, is clearly to entertain. The tone of *Ages Ago* is surprisingly mellow for Gilbert, and perhaps this contributed to its popularity—it was the most successful of the Gallery's pieces.

Both librettos are constructed around the traditional romantic-comedy plot of the heroine and the impecunious suitor—and in each case this is played without irony. *Ages Ago* is more complex in that this stock plot is merely a framing mechanism to the central action, in which the portraits in a gallery come to life and work through the logic of their situation (very entertainingly), but in both pieces plot is paramount, and Gilbert's inventiveness has to find corners of habitation wherever it will allow. In *No Cards* the farce of disguises that is one of the main elements allows Gilbert some scope in this direction, and he is able to commit one or two good satirical digs; but in *Ages Ago* almost everything is subordinate to construction. The tone is more romantic than satirical—and, indeed, has a genuine warmth that is very rare in Gilbert's works. We seem to have surprised in him a real nostalgia for past ages that is elsewhere kept firmly in check.

But both these pieces are essentially explorations of the territory, and in neither do we feel that Gilbert had found his ideal form—though each is, in its own way, a good and entertaining piece of craftsmanship. He tried musical farce and musicalized romantic comedy, but in neither did he feel entirely at home. (However, in *Ages Ago* he explored a faculty for taking a situation through to its logical conclusion that would be extremely useful to him in his later career.) In *Our Island Home* (1870) he began to settle into a personal style, trying techniques that he would later develop to excellent effect and palpably enjoying his own comic invention.

Our Island Home is essentially an improvisation around the central idea of a group of characters stranded on a desert island. The first piece of inventiveness lies in the fact that the characters are distorted versions of the actors playing them: the characters are called Mr. and Mrs. German Reed, Miss Holland, and so on, and they are on the desert island as a result of plaguing the steamship with too many renditions of *Ages Ago* while on an Asiatic tour with that piece. The passengers and crew have pitched them onto the first desert island they came to, and here they are.

Though the characters bear the names of their actors, they have personalities radically different from them. The mild-mannered Arthur Cecil becomes a melodramatic villain and the amiable Priscilla Reed an unreasonable harridan. These characters enact a plot based around ownership of the various parts of the island; then, when this reaches its natural conclusion, the whole thing is wrapped up with an irrelevant but marvelous display of invention in which a new character, Captain Bang, the Pirate King of the southern seas, is introduced. The fact that the few pages in which Bang appears form the basis of *The Pirates of Penzance* (1879) is an indication of the throwaway invention of the scene.

More important is the fact that it is in this play that Gilbert begins to realize the potential in parodying the conventions of melodrama. He had put hints of this into his rhymed burlesques, and his parody reviews for the comic magazine *Fun* were also an important place of development for this aspect of his style, but it is only now, in *Our Island Home,* that it comes into full flower in a stage piece.

Thus, for example, we have the villainous behavior of "that black-hearted monster, Arthur Cecil,"[44] who has a hold over the other characters based on the uncanny mesmeric power of his eye:

> *Miss Holland.* . . . *(Aside)* Ha! that eye!
> (*He gazes sternly at her, and she quails.*)
> *Cecil. (Aside).* My favourite orb has done its duty well.
> *Miss Holland.* Mysterious man, what is the secret of the influence that attaches to that extraordinary eye? Its wild lustre dazzles me. (*As if fascinated.*) Oh, thou mysterious orb.
> *Cecil. (Aside).* She little thinks that it is a glass one.[45]

This melodramatic device, made ridiculous enough in the above passage, is reduced to absolute fatuity below:

> *Cecil.* . . . I must again resort to my invaluable eye.
> (*Melodramatic stare as before.*)
> *Mrs. Reed.* Ha! ha! I anticipated it. We are prepared.
> (*Mr. and Mrs. Reed and Miss Holland put on green spectacles and return his stare without shrinking.*)
> *Cecil.* Ha! Baffled![46]

Gilbert had experienced quite enough of this sort of nonsense, treated seriously, as theater critic in the 1860s, and was able to make the most of it now. Most jokes have a point—particularly Gilbert's jokes—and the point here is that such things bear no conceivable relationship to real life and are therefore ridiculous. This attitude obviously implies support for a style of drama that bears a more direct relationship to real life. Gilbert was, as we shall see, not suited to the writing of such drama: when he tried to write plays that reflected reality they turned both insipid and cliché-ridden. It has sometimes been pointed out that his beliefs were negative rather than positive: for instance, G. K. Chesterton noted that "Gilbert was fighting against a hundred follies and illogicalities; but he was not fighting for anything."[47] He could not see a way forward to a less melodramatic style, and he distrusted that which emerged in the 1890s.[48] So this element of parody perfectly suited his capabilities.

One useful way of thinking about Gilbert's development as a writer can be seen in an image Joe Orton used about his own writing: "I always say to myself that the theatre is the Temple of Dionysus, and not Apollo. You do the Dionysus thing on your typewriter, and then you allow a little Apollo in, just a little to shape and guide it along certain lines you may want to go along. But you can't allow Apollo in completely."[49] Orton expresses himself rather gnomically, but I take it that Dionysus here represents creativity and Apollo order. There must be an overall structure to any work of art, but far more important is the unpredictable, Dionysian element of "inspiration," of the unrepeatable creativity that occurs when a writer is in the process of writing. Apollo, the force of order, is important only to keep Dionysus within reasonable bounds and prevent the whole work of art from degenerating into chaos.

In the earlier plays, we can see Gilbert struggling with the demands of structure; it is only with some difficulty that we can detect his distinctive style struggling to emerge. The verse extravaganzas imprisoned his invention within too many constrictive bonds. The early German Reed pieces allowed for more freedom of invention but were still held back by the conventions of romantic comedy. But in *Our Island Home* Gilbert begins to break free from such things: there is no "love interest," the dramatic conventions are ridiculed, and unity of plot is flouted. Dionysus is in the ascendant.

Perhaps there is slightly too little of Apollo's shaping hand evident in *Our Island Home*—Gilbert was certainly no enthusiast for free-form invention, and his later plays show no tendency to continue in this direction. Indeed, the fairy comedies, which he was writing in the same period, are very much Apollonian rather than Dionysian in nature. They are designed specifically to elaborate an argument; the dialogue is written in a bland, "classical" style in which anachronism and all the lively elements of Victorian speech have no place.

However, by allowing in *Our Island Home* such scope for improvisatory invention, Gilbert was able to mix together parody, exaggeration, invention, and a sheer love of words in a way he had not been able to in his previous plays. In the early years of his career as a dramatist, he was, naturally, mainly concerned with learning the basics of his craft and delivering the most accomplished article he could provide; he was learning the Apollonian skills of construction. But now he had learned these basics and was able to give his attention to the development of a personal style—the creative, Dionysian element. And this is where his writings begin to get interesting, for, after all, the theater is the Temple of Dionysus, not Apollo.

Still, the two elements must be properly balanced against each other, and I have suggested that the balance was not quite right in *Our Island Home*. However, I believe he got it almost completely right in *A Sensation Novel* (1871).

The full title is *A Sensation Novel in Three Volumes:* for the first and only time at the Gallery of Illustration Gilbert was allowed to write a piece in more than one act. The "three volumes" are in fact three short acts, each requiring a different set.

The central idea is startlingly original. We are first introduced to an Author of Sensation Novels, who has made a pact with the Demon of Romance that allows him to write fifty three-volume novels a year. In a short scene between these two characters, we learn that the stock characters the Demon allows the author to use have an existence independent of the novel and indeed have "wishes, schemes and plans"[50] entirely opposed to those the Author has given them within the plot of the novel. In the two intervals between the novel's volumes, and just before the last chapter, these characters are given a short space of release from the fictitious desires allotted them by the Author. The main body of the play is taken up with these three meetings, in which the characters mock the absurdity of the plot they must work through, rail against the "happy ending" none of them truly desires, and finally force the Author to create an ending that will give them what they *really* want.

Like *Our Island Home, A Sensation Novel* contains clear "metatheatrical" elements. Both pieces draw attention to their own theatricality; there is an interesting parallel between *A Sensation Novel* and Pirandello's *Six Characters in Search of an Author* (1921), in that both involve an intrusion of fictional characters on the "real" world. In both cases these characters break free from the Author who created them. And, oddly enough, in both cases the characters mock artistic conventions because they are not realistic. Thus, in *Six Characters in Search of an Author,* when actors try to recreate a scene the characters have already shown them, this is what happens:

> *Leading Actor. . . . . .* May I take off your hat?
> *The Leading Actor says this line in such a way and adds to it such a gesture that the Stepdaughter, even with her hand over her mouth trying to stop herself laughing, can't prevent a noisy burst of laughter.*[51]

Compare this to the sensation characters of Gilbert's play, re-enacting a romantic scene they have just had to play out for real in the preceding volume:

> *Herbert (reads).* "They were alone—with the moon. They heard the throbbings of each other's hearts, which beat like rival watches, wound up in each other! He drew her gently towards him, and imprinted a solitary kiss on her soft—

Alice (taking the MS. from him). "On her soft little hand!" Oh you
goose!
    All. Ha! Ha! Ha![52]

There is, it must be admitted, much greater psychological subtlety in Pirandello's play than in Gilbert's, but then Gilbert never claimed psychological subtlety as one of his virtues. He dealt in types, distillations of
current characteristics. However, in another respect Gilbert's play appears
rather more subtle in approach, because of Pirandello's distressing tendency to make his creations pontificate crudely on the relationship between Art and Life. In Gilbert's work, the existence of such larger issues is
for the most part implied but not explicitly stated. Pirandello uses the central "metatheatrical" idea to propound a thesis, whereas Gilbert uses it to
entertain: Apollo and Dionysus again. Indeed, comparison of these two
plays reminds me of Chesterton's dictum that "what is hailed as a new
style or a new school in literature often consists of doing as a novelty what
a Victorian did long ago as a joke."[53]

It should be mentioned here that self-reflexive techniques were an accepted theatrical joke in Victorian popular theater. Several farces by the
early/mid-Victorian farceur John Maddison Morton play around with the
conventions, such as *Slasher and Crasher!,* which opens with the characters *"standing in a line, facing the Audience, as in the tag of a Piece":*[54]
Blowhard is just drawing to the conclusion of his speech by appealing for
the audience's approval in the traditional manner when the "happy ending"
is disrupted and the farce begins. This kind of "metatheatricality," which
I fear has more to do with high spirits than a kind of premature post-
modernism, is an incidental feature in many such farces.

Susan Bassnett-McGuire says, in her study of Pirandello, that

> Pirandello's attack on the naturalist conventions of bourgeois theatre was not
> unique by any means, and his work should be seen in the context of a series
> of radical experiments in theatre practice. From the late nineteenth century
> onwards various alternatives to the conventions of the fourth wall were in
> evidence in theatres throughout Europe.[55]

The central warning against making Pirandello seem more innovative than
he was is sound, but the terms in which the point is made demonstrates
how far apart Pirandello and such predecessors as Morton and Gilbert
were. Pieces such as *Slasher and Crasher!* and *A Sensation Novel* do not
pretend to be anything other than exercises in pure entertainment. To call
them radical experiments or attacks on the conventions of bourgeois

theater is to talk in a language completely inappropriate to the subject and to risk missing the point.

The whole point about early Victorian theater is that it was *not* bourgeois. It provided entertainment for the urban masses, and up to the 1860s one of the main problems the theater had to face was that it was not "respectable": the educated middle classes largely felt that theaters were not appropriate places for them to go. Morton's farces, with their bombast, farcical violence, and lower-middle-class characters, had a healthy vulgarity that was tailor-made for the healthy vulgar. Gilbert, writing for a new middle class audience, used self-reflexive techniques in a much more sophisticated fashion, more as a bourgeois attack on the conventions of the older, more working-class theater.

What is going on in *A Sensation Novel* is essentially an extension of the techniques of the earlier generation of comic theater, now reemployed by Gilbert in the face of the slow trend toward naturalism. However, these self-reflexive techniques were usually, as I understand it, used in very small doses; I should be very surprised to find an earlier example of their use at anything like the level of *A Sensation Novel.*

In Gilbert they are generally used in order to criticize the theatrical conventions: many of his plays and librettos are supposed to be understood as reflections not of reality but of other plays. Thus in *Dulcamara* we have seen that one of the main butts of the burlesque was burlesque itself. This kind of parody runs through almost all his comic plays after *Our Island Home.*

The premise of *A Sensation Novel*—the idea of sensation characters having an existence outside their novel, allowing them to criticize their conduct *inside* the novel—is simply an extremely ingenious way of signaling to the audience the parodistic intent of the piece; though in Gilbert's hands it becomes more than just a tool of criticism—it is an idea to be enjoyed in its own right.

Much is made of sensation fiction's shortcomings as a mirror of reality: as the novel's "hero," Herbert, observes cynically, "Marry and live happily ever after! And this is a novel that pretends to give a picture of life as it is."[56] Sensation fiction provided lurid accounts of high life, with an accompanying assurance that this was how things were, but of course they were as tightly bound by foolish conventions as are the "grittily realistic" television dramas of today.

Thus Gripper, the detective, no sooner appears than explains that his function is to avoid catching criminals. When reprimanded by the others for being late, he replies:

Well, I'm afraid I am; but then I am a sensation detective, and sensation detectives always *are* late. The reason's obvious enough. If the detective of a sensation novel were not always just too late, the novel would come to an end long before its time. If I bring to justice all the villains of the novel in the course of the first volume, what's to prevent the virtuous governess marrying the good young curate at once, and if she does that there's an end of everything.[57]

This is a technique Gilbert had often used in his parody reviews: making a character state a plot function that is usually decently hidden from public view. For instance, from his review of *Jezebel:*

> *Madame D'Art.*—. . . I poisoned him, and he pretended to die in the first act. I thought he was dead, but I find he lives, and has married you.
> *Gretchen (simply).*—But, dear me, ma'am, you have been on the stage a considerable time, and your experience ought to have told you that MR. HENRY NEVILLE never dies in the first act of a three act drama.[58]

The hero of *A Sensation Novel* is shown to be really in love with the villainess, "the lovely fiend of fiction, / With the yellow, yellow hair";[59] the heroine is in love with the villain Sir Ruthven Glenaloon. Therefore everything that brings them closer to the conventional "happy ending" planned for them by the Author simply makes them more angry and unhappy.

The libretto's premise frees Gilbert from all pretense of reflecting reality, and as a result this is very probably Gilbert's most wildly inventive dramatic work. For instance, Gripper (played by the rotund and bass-voiced Corney Grain) turns out to be Sir Ruthven's granddaughter, exchanged at birth, and is described in the "novel" in these terms: "his figure was slight, indeed, almost girlish, and his voice had a touching accent in it that was invaluable to him in his assumption of female characters."[60] But the most extravagant moment of all is reserved for the "third volume," in which a passage from the "novel" is read out, describing Sir Ruthven's suicide:

> "Now, said Sir Ruthven, when he had ascertained by passing his thumb over the edge of the hatchet that it was sufficiently sharp for the work before it.— Now, said he, to end a life that has long been too burthensome to bear. . . . He locked the door, and going up to a cheval glass, took one long look at the magnificent but diabolical face, which had worked so much mischief in its time. As he looked he saw one solitary tear trickle from his left eye and course its way down his detestable cheek. It is the first said he, and it shall be the last. And so saying he swung the ponderous axe three times round his

head and towards the middle of the third swing the blade shot like lightning through the thickest part of the bad man's neck. The head bounded into the air and fell heavily on the floor. The lips still moved spasmodically. With a frightful effort, they managed to hiss out the dreadful words 'a very neat blow' when the jaw fell, and the vital spark departed never to return."[61]

It is this that finally prompts the other characters to rebel against the Author; they demand that Sir Ruthven be restored to life, and when the Author objects, "But I've chopped his head off; I can't stick it on again," Alice assures him, "Science can do anything."[62] By this time Gilbert has severed all links with reality: we are in a world where absolutely anything may happen.

Throughout, Gilbert exhibits an almost palpable relish at his own wit and invention; he has here created for himself an ideal framework for the "Dionysian" creative element that was most congenial to him—the extension into absurdity of accepted conventions. And despite the extravagance of the execution, the very tight overall structure is followed without any sense of strain. There is the occasional sign of haste in the writing, but despite such small flaws this is, I believe, the first of Gilbert's dramatic pieces in which the best elements of his style come together to create something that transcends its own time.

Little need be said of the last two German Reed pieces, *Happy Arcadia* (1872) and *Eyes and No Eyes* (1875). The former is an accomplished piece of work that, as Stedman notes, takes as its central idea the ridicule of "man's fallacious definition of the good life, in which he praises innocuity while prefering excitement, and exalts simple rustic delights while enjoying artificial city pleasures."[63] The four central characters are each given a magical talisman, and each wishes that he/she was one of the other characters, upon which they immediately change bodies. Since Gilbert sees "imperfection, dissatisfaction, and inconsistency as inherent in human nature,"[64] to quote Stedman again, they are of course even unhappier with their new bodies than their old.

People, being human beings, are no happier in "happy Arcadia" than elsewhere, and it is probably in this idea that we get closest to the central idea behind Gilbert's social satire. Archer said that Gilbert's cynicism, as expressed in such plays as *Engaged,* "is so unrelieved, that we recognize it as a mere trick or mannerism, and not the result of genuine insight. The jester who railed at every one from king to scullion, offended no one."[65] But this is to miss the point, which, I take it, is that all human beings are equally ridiculous. The human condition is absurd: we are deluded, conceited individuals blithely distorting reason, morality, and reality to our own selfish ends (much as Mandeville suggested in *The Fable of the Bees*). Is it really impossible for such an idea to be "the result of genuine insight"?

Happy Arcadia shows the Gilbertian style establishing itself: it displays great relish in language and a wonderful free flow of wit, built around an excellent central idea that is part parody of the senseless conventions of the idealized Arcadian life. But once Gilbert had found for himself a congenial style, it was simply a matter of refining the techniques, and little needs to be said in commentary.

Eyes and No Eyes stands apart from its predecessors, simply because of the three-year hiatus that separates it from the earlier sequence. By this time the Gallery of Illustration had moved to St. George's Hall, and Cecil had left; the atmosphere was changing. What is more, Gilbert himself had had three years in which to develop his style in theaters with more resources to command, and the piece he provided them with here, though polished, is relatively unambitious. It is a variation on "The Emperor's New Clothes"; though amusing, it has little of the invention of which Gilbert was now thoroughly capable. He was clearly keeping that part of his abilities for works on the larger scale.

Gilbert had now outgrown the Gallery of Illustration, though it had been an invaluable nursery for his talents. In the early 1870s he began to develop this newly discovered style in other theaters apart from the Gallery, and we shall of course deal with those later. But for the moment we must turn back the clock to 1869, to look briefly at the third line of Gilbert's development.

SERIOUS PROSE DRAMAS

We have seen how, in the first phase of Gilbert's career, he wrote rhymed extravaganzas with musical interludes; we have also seen how, after he had come to the end of what he could do in that form, he developed the skills he had used in extravaganza in two different directions: refining the formal element into blank-verse "fairy comedy" and developing the idea of comedy with music into the German Reed librettos. One of the things that bind these three strands together is the fact that none is an avowedly realistic form of drama. By the use of rhymed couplets, blank verse, or songs a clear signal is sent out to the audience that what is happening on stage should not be taken as a simple reflection of reality: it might be a parody of some other dramatic/operatic work, perhaps involving a satirical exaggeration of human foibles, or, as in the case of the fairy comedies, it might be a classically simple treatment of some serious theme, the local characteristics of Victorian society having been removed.

However, Gilbert was also attempting at this time to write dramas that would reflect reality in a much simpler way or would at least do so as nearly as the dramatic conventions would allow. These plays are commonly dismissed as melodramas (for instance, Isaac Goldberg calls *On Guard* a "cheap melodrama"),[66] but the word is unfair to them. Generally speaking these plays do not conform to the strict rules and types of melodrama, and are more original in their ideas than the crude populism of true melodrama permits. The word is used because, set alongside the "naturalism" of Ibsen or even Pinero, the dialogue appears stiff and the construction convention-bound. Gilbert learned his craft a little too early to learn, or see the virtue in, a freer style of drama. Yet these plays are experimental, too, in their way, and, though his achievements in this direction are comparatively minor, they merit at least a brief glance.

The plays I should place in this category range from his first, *Uncle Baby* (1863), to his last, *The Hooligan* (1911). I must here concentrate on a handful from his earliest period.

Not much space need be spent discussing *Uncle Baby*. It is a slight one-acter with an overinvolved plot, the most interesting character being Uncle John, the "Uncle Baby" of the title, who sponges on his young relatives and spends their money on gambling and drink. Of course he reforms in the play's last few minutes. There is a similarity with the much more accomplished *An Old Score,* in that both center around strained family relationships. While the family in *Uncle Baby* suffers from John's dissipations, the Calthorpes of *An Old Score* are riven apart by the dishonesty and hypocrisy of the family's wealthy head, Colonel Calthorpe. He throws his son, Harold, out of his house on learning of Harold's debts and love for the children's governess, Mary Waters, and we are left in no doubt how unreasonable and hard-hearted the Colonel is being in doing so. In the last act, the Colonel's one great act of philanthropy is shown up to be a sham, and he is revealed to us (though not to the world) as a forger.

The world of *An Old Score* is not the cozy world of domestic melodrama. There is none of the idealizing of family life that such plays usually featured. Harold Calthorpe, who is the nearest thing to a young hero, is a scapegrace who, though good at heart, struggles throughout the play with his bohemian habits. His ladylove, Mary Waters, mentions almost incidentally the more brutal side to family life:

> *Mary.* . . . I don't know much about fathers. I lost mine when I was ten years old. He was an artist—
> *Harold.* An artist?
> *Mary.* Yes; he drew valentines.
> *Harold.* Poor little Mary; you must often think with regret of the happy days when your father and mother were alive and you all lived together!
> *Mary.* No, I don't. *My* papa used to drink, and then he beat me. But he drew such beautiful valentines, and he wrote the poetry under them, too— beautiful little poems about eternal constancy—woman's love—and the happiness of married life.
> *Harold.* Inspired, I suppose, by your mamma?
> *Mary.* Oh! no; mamma had run away from him years before. . . .[67]

There is a touch of the familiar Gilbert here, in Harold's conventional clichés set brutally against Mary's offhand realities. The jaundiced attitudes to family life in some of these early plays may possibly be a reflection of his parents' strained relationship: William Gilbert Sr. finally left his wife in 1876 amidst considerable acrimony, which must surely have been building up over many years. "Marry and live happily ever after! And this is a novel that pretends to give a picture of life as it is."[68]

John Hollingshead was the manager of the Gaiety Theatre, at which *An Old Score* was produced. In his autobiography, *My Lifetime,* he briefly discusses this play—particularly why it failed. He says, "It was too like real life, and too unconventional. . . . The dialogue was not playhouse pap. It was a little too brutally straightforward."[69] Gilbert's "serious" plays never broke completely free of the conventions, and *An Old Score* often falls back on them, but all the same there is probably much truth in Hollingshead's assessment. Still, this is not necessarily a compliment to the play: the artistic ideal is surely not only to present to the public an original vision of life, but also to do so in a way that wins the public over. For of what use is a message that its intended audience refuses to hear?

The play's failure may have been partly due to its not having had the right tone for the theater, as the Gaiety was known for its burlesques (Hollingshead famously spoke of keeping alight the sacred lamp of burlesque). Pieces such as *Robert the Devil* were appropriate for the Gaiety, but *An Old Score* was not. Hollingshead himself acknowledged that the play may have "offended the domestic sentiment of the broad public."[70]

It is interesting to notice how Gilbert struggled to find theaters appropriate to his style. He wrote an extravaganza for the Gaiety but then made the mistake of trying his first "serious" play at the same place. He developed an intelligently witty style at the Gallery of Illustration, with its self-consciously respectable name; at the Haymarket, a previous home of Planché's extravaganzas, he wrote his three main fairy comedies. His natural audience was the middle class, which was, fortunately, now almost reconciled to theaters as places at which one might be seen without disgrace, but he had to serve his apprenticeship in the vulgar depths of burlesque before being trusted to entertain the people for whom his humor was best suited. I have already suggested, however, that we can see throughout Gilbert's career conflicting impulses toward "respectability" and "vulgarity." The production of *An Old Score* at the Gaiety may be seen as a symbol of this confusion.

The play has many points of interest and states an idea that will reappear in some later plays. Harold Calthorpe is shown to be, despite his dissipations, essentially good, and the respectable Colonel Calthorpe is a hypocrite and a cheat. There is a clear distrust of the rigid moralism of the heavy Victorian father, which we shall see again in *Charity* (1874). Gilbert was concerned not so much with individual transgressions as with the overall tenor of a character's outlook: one may live a life of public righteousness and yet be essentially corrupt, just as one may have done foolish things but be a much better person. This idea was central to Gilbert's thought, and it received its clearest expression in these comparatively serious plays, where the complicating factors of irony and inversion do not intrude.

Randall's Thumb and *On Guard* are disappointingly tame in comparison, though neither is without virtues. *On Guard* in particular has several interesting characters and some witty dialogue but is let down by a trivial plot. Gilbert seems to have been trying to fit some of the attitudes he had expressed in *An Old Score* into a more conventional plot framework. It was only with *Charity* that plot began to catch up with manner once more.

Its central character, Mrs. Van Brugh, is revolutionary for the time. It emerges in the course of the play that she was never formally married to the man she had lived with as her husband: for Mr. Van Brugh's real wife had run away from him and was still legally married to him when he first met the woman now presented to us as Mrs. Van Brugh. She has, for some years, been atoning for her sin by doing charitable work among the destitute, including "fallen women" such as Ruth Tredgett.

Against her is pitted the pharasaical Mr. Smailey, a pillar of moral righteousness who seeks to expose Mrs. Van Brugh's horrid secret, and who it turns out had been the corrupting force on Ruth Tredgett. As Mrs. Van Brugh observes: "Earth teaches us that there is one sin for which there is no pardon—when the sinner is a woman!"[71] Smailey and his son Fred are developed in Gilbert's ironical manner as hypocrites who, in every word they speak, unconsciously reveal their true selves. For instance, Mr. Smailey is given the habit of saying, "I have no desire to press hardly on any fellow-creature"[72]—a statement which sounds hollower and hollower as the play progresses.

Fred Smailey believes his father to be as virtuous as he pretends and is forced to become just as industrious a hypocrite in order to keep up the family reputation: thus a very surprising touch from the play's closing scene. Mr. Smailey has been exposed as the villain he is, and his life is in ruins. At this moment Gilbert unexpectedly drops the ironic guard that has kept us at arm's length from these two throughout, and we see a glimpse of real feeling:

> *Mr. Smailey.* I care not what may follow. Whatever punishment may be in store for me, will be as nothing compared to the bitter shame of my degradation in the eyes of my poor boy, whom I have loved. He will desert me now! . . .
> *Fred.* Father, I swear that where you are, there will I be to the end. . . . Whatever you may have been—whatever I may have been—I am your son, and I love you; and I will be with you—to the end![73]

This is thoroughly inartistic, of course: having set them in an ironical frame, Gilbert ought to have kept them there right to the end; and yet it is absolutely right that, having pleaded for forgiveness for people like Mrs. Van Brugh, Gilbert should extend a morsel of sympathy toward even the Smaileys.

As always in those of Gilbert's plays written in a "serious" vein, there is a problem of style. At its best, the dialogue is stylized but saved by its wit and polish; at its worst, it is sentimental, windy, and melodramatic. The best qualities of Gilbert's style are seen when he is developing an idea with an ironic twist—a grim irony, perhaps, as in *The Hooligan,* or a sentimental irony, as in *Sweethearts*—or one extravagant irony among many, as in any number of his best comic works. When there is no such ironic twist to enliven a dramatic situation, he tends to fall back on banalities. This weakness is kept reasonably at bay in the first three acts of *Charity,* but unfortunately it overwhelms the fourth, last act.

Hesketh Pearson, in his biography of Gilbert, wrote of the play in somewhat contemptuous terms:

> [Mrs. Van Brugh's] "sin" is discussed by herself and others in language that would be excessive if it had brought about the decimation of the world's population by the wrath of God. To exhibit the difference between the mid-Victorian and the modern mental attitudes to sex, this play should provide

the historian's text-book. It was condemned as immoral at the time, a verdict with which, for different reasons, the present age will agree. . . .[74]

That first sentence is a ridiculous exaggeration, but it is certainly true that Gilbert seems to agree with everyone in the play—from Mr. Smailey to Mrs. Van Brugh—that for a couple to live as husband and wife without having gone through the form of marriage is a serious sin. The play takes this as a "given," but, bearing in mind the role of the Lord Chamberlain's department as a dramatic censor and the playgoing public's firm views on stage morality, it could hardly do otherwise.

In such an atmosphere, it is remarkable enough that Gilbert should have dealt with the subject at all. More interesting is the play's *central* message (for this is, without doubt, a play with a message): that forgiveness is just as integral to Christian morality as the ten commandments. In this respect, *Charity* is emphatically *not* an immoral play but as right in its instincts as any enlightened modern might wish. Of course all this is separate from the question of whether it is a *good* play.

Ought We to Visit Her?, premiered just two weeks after *Charity,* should be bracketed alongside it; it, too, concerns a woman who battles for social acceptance against the hypocritical code of "respectable" society. *Ought We to Visit Her?* is a dramatization of a novel by Annie Edwardes, and one should beware of attributing to Gilbert ideas that are properly Edwardes's. But at the same time Gilbert would scarcely have chosen to dramatize the novel if he had not found it sympathetic to his own ideas.

It concerns Jane Theobald, who used to be a dancer in a theater but has married the rich and respectable Francis Theobald: she now finds it impossible to gain social acceptance because of her disgraceful past. The play insists throughout that theater life is actually much more honest and worthy of respect than the hypocritical, idle life of the privileged set. This is symbolized in an exchange in which her husband tells her that "when we set up as Brahmins. . . . you'll have to stiffen up a bit—you mustn't loll then," and she replies: "till the time you raised me above my station, sir, I was trained to move my limbs well; and although I'm in the position of a lady now, I can't remember always to be awkward."[75]

This is the main moral point of the play: to contrast the healthy honesty of the theatrical world against the hothouse corruption of "society." Stedman notes that Gilbert goes further with this idea than Edwardes herself.[76] The sexual double standard is glanced at but is much less important here than in *Charity*. But in both plays the target is the self-righteous "Brahmins" of respectable society. Gilbert's antiestablishment tendencies were probably more in evidence now than at any other time of his career. In the previous year, 1873, he had deliberately attacked the government and the Lord Chamberlain's Office in *The Happy Land* and *The Realm of Joy;* in 1874 he was to attack British institutions from another angle in *Topsey-turveydom.* Later in his career his attitudes toward the establishment were to be more ambiguous.

The only other of Gilbert's "serious" plays that needs to be mentioned here is *Sweethearts,* a play in two brief acts. The plot is extremely simple. In the first act Harry Spreadbrow visits Jenny Northcott to tell her that he has been unexpectedly called to India, and that they are meeting for the last time. He is fervently romantic, she cold and rebuffing. Realizing that his suit is hopeless, he leaves; then Jenny's self-possession deserts her and she breaks down in tears. Act 2 takes place thirty years later. Jenny is still unmarried, and Spreadbrow returns to her house to revisit old haunts. He remembers vaguely that they had some sort of romantic attachment— which she, of course, remembers in every detail. The roles are now reversed: he matter-of-fact, she fervently romantic. The play ends, perhaps slightly unconvincingly, with the romance promising to continue where it left off.

Unusually for Gilbert, character takes precedence over plot—the only events are small incidents that reveal the characters of the two central figures. It has often been said, truly, that this was Gilbert's tribute to his mentor, Tom Robertson.[77] The illumination of character by the use of small incidents and natural-seeming dialogue is more Robertson's territory than Gilbert's—though Gilbert's use of them here is very effective.

Even in this slight and rather charming piece we can see an aspect of what his first critics called his cynicism. Harry Spreadbrow's professions of love are shown to have been sincere but shallow—as he cheerfully confesses in the second act: "I told you that I adored you, didn't I? . . . Ha, ha! my dear Jane, before I'd been a week on board I was saying the same thing to a middle-aged governess whose name has entirely escaped me."[78] This is not a usual attitude in Victorian drama—not even in Robertson, whose ideas were somewhat conventional except where stage technique was concerned.

It is in these "serious" plays that Gilbert most clearly expresses his personal view of life. His is a world where the rich and the titled are not necessarily virtuous or even good-natured: Colonel Calthorpe (later Lord Ovington) of *An Old Score* is a crooked businessman; Mr. Smailey of *Charity* is a self-righteous hypocrite; Lady Rose Golightly of *Ought We to Visit Her?* is, it is hinted pretty plainly, a "fast woman," though accepted in *all* the best circles. Honesty, simplicity, and a decent sympathy for those less fortunate than ourselves are held up as the most important virtues. People, being human, may not be able to live up to some abstract ideal of virtuous behaviour, but such shortcomings, if properly repented, should be forgiven. It is a person's overall *attitude* to life that is important.

In these plays, the idea of "happy ever after" has no real place: the characters are not the flawless beings to whom alone such an idea is appropriate. Harold Calthorpe, the "hero" of *An Old Score,* is rather a bohemian character, overfond of drink and gambling; Jessie Blake, the "heroine" of *On Guard,* is an incorrigible flirt (though in a perfectly innocent way, of course); and then we have the terrible sin of Mrs. Van Brugh of *Charity.* Clearly perfect futures cannot be expected of people with such imperfect pasts: the best that can be hoped for is "Utopia, Limited."

Aspects of these ideas also appear in Gilbert's comic plays: I have already twice quoted the line from *A Sensation Novel,* deriding the idea of "happy ever after"; much later in Gilbert's career, he will make the Mikado mention, almost as an aside, that "virtue is triumphant only in theatrical performances."[79] Gilbert had a view of life that, though not abnormally jaundiced, did not fit in with the Pollyanna conventions of the theater of the day. This is probably one of the main reasons most of those plays in which he attempted to mirror life in a straightforward manner were among his more notable commercial failures. Such ideas were bearable in novels but when put on stage became disgracefully cynical.

Gilbert was to continue to write plays in this serious style throughout the rest of his career—*The Ne'er-Do-Weel, The Fortune-Hunter, The Hooligan*—but for the most part he turned to the much lighter style of writing that he had started to develop in the German Reed pieces and was to reach its full fruition in the Savoy operas. In these pieces he was able to express much the same views of life that we have seen in his "serious" plays, but they were so disguised by irony and inversion that they became acceptable to the playgoing public. This was at last the distinctive Gilbertian voice he had, consciously or not, been seeking, and it was to bring him his greatest triumphs.

2

THE CRAFT OF THE PLAYWRIGHT

GILBERT WROTE IN A LETTER ON 1 JULY 1907 ABOUT HAVING BEEN
knighted the previous day:

> I found myself politely described in the official list as Mr. William Gilbert,
> *playwright,* suggesting that my work was analogical to that of a wheelwright,
> or a millwright, or a wainwright, or a shipwright, as regards the mechanical
> character of the process by which our respective results are achieved. There
> is an excellent word "dramatist" which seems to fit the situation, but it is not
> applied until we are dead, and then we become dramatists as oxen, sheep,
> and pigs are transfigured into beef, mutton and pork after their demise. You
> never hear of a novel-wright or a picture-wright, or a poem-wright; and why
> a playwright?[1]

Clearly he was objecting here to being described, by implication, as a
craftsman rather than as an artist. However, when he discussed playwriting, in his article "A Stage Play" (1873) or in an interview with William
Archer (1901), to take two handy examples, it was always as a craft, not an
art. That is to say he talked not of the expression of a personal worldview
or any of the usual concerns of literary figures today but instead of structure, balance, fulfilling the requirements of the company for which he was
writing, and so on. Everything goes to suggest that he was, first and foremost, a "playwright" by his own definition: a craftsman whose primary
duty is to provide a product that fits the given specifications. He may em-
bellish the result with "artistic" elements that are distinctively his own, just
as a cabinetmaker may amuse himself with a little ornamentation at the appropriate spots, but art is always subordinate to craft.

Archer's interview shows Gilbert defending the old style of "well-
made" play, as against the "New Drama" style of play in which the old
conventions are not so important. Yet Gilbert had been, in the 1860s and
1870s, as critical of the old conventions as Archer. In some of his techniques he was an innovator, and in some respects he pointed the way

toward the establishment of an atmosphere in which the New Drama could develop. Indeed, Archer suggested as much when he told Gilbert: "I shall always feel that, as regards serious drama, you were in advance of your time. . . . Whether you admit the dramatic revival or not, you were one of the prime movers in it. You restored the literary self-respect of the English stage."[2]

There is no doubt that Gilbert was a much more conservative-minded man in 1901 than he had been in the 1870s; his reluctance to accept Archer's compliment does not imply its falsity. Several of his plays from the 1870s suggest a movement toward the ideas of the New Drama that in 1901 he spent so much time telling Archer he disliked. Certainly such articles as "A Hornpipe in Fetters" (1879)—an article I shall discuss further in chapter 5—do not suggest great contentment with what then was the state of the drama. Gilbert's plays are, by and large, governed by the old rules of stagecraft, but there are daring modifications—of which the critics of the time were very aware. We must not allow the Gilbert of the 1900s to bamboozle us into thinking the Gilbert of the 1870s had been equally deferential to the conventions of the theater.

So in this chapter I intend to pause a little in my chronological survey and examine certain aspects of Gilbert's craft, taking as my starting point Gilbert's own writings on the subject and the writings of others who have tried to make sense of him. With their help we may come to a clearer understanding of the mechanisms at work in the plays.

A SENSE OF BALANCE

Gilbert's article "A Stage Play" describes how a dramatist would write a play, by following the fictitious "Horace Facile" from the commissioning of a play from him through to its production. Facile is clearly a portrait of Gilbert himself, or at least of one aspect of him. He is the embodiment of the playwright as craftsman, writing to order.

A manager has commissioned from Facile "a three-act comedy drama . . . with parts for Jones and Brown and Robinson,"[3] upon which "a 'general idea' must be fixed upon, and in selecting it, Facile is guided, to a considerable extent, by the resources of the company he is to write for. . . . the nature of the 'general idea' will depend upon the powers or peculiarities of the actor or actress who is principally entitled to consideration."[4] Facile is bound by the practical restraints of the commission, and we may gather that most established dramatists of this period acted under similar restraints, writing for an established cast—unlike their modern counterparts, who have much greater freedom in this respect. The actors for whom he is writing exert an influence not only in terms of what their acting strengths are but also when it comes to such questions as whether "They want an 'entrance,' that they may receive special and individual 'receptions.'"[5]

However, even within these restraints, Facile has enough artistic freedom to write according to his own inclinations. The "general idea" and the manner of its development may still be constructed according to his own ideas; here craft shades into art.

The play Gilbert shows Facile writing, *The Pulpit and the Stage,* is deliberately ridiculous, centering around a theatrical Harlequin who has taken holy orders, but the "general idea" behind it is the serious issue of "the unnecessary antagonism existing between the Theatre and the Church."[6] Gilbert shows how good dramatic conflicts and "situations" can be constructed around this theme: the Harlequin being in love with the Bishop's daughter; the Bishop being "a bitter enemy to the stage,"[7] though he "happens to be the freeholder of the very theatre in which the Harlequin is engaged";[8] and so on.

"The next thing Facile does is to arrange striking situations for the end of each act."[9] That is, each act is constructed so as to lead up to a good "picture." Here, Facile is unashamedly a traditional craftsman. The three acts of his comedy divide neatly into Exposition, Development, and Resolution. The conventions of the "well-made play" are clearly displayed here. Gilbert always adhered to the general principles laid down by Eugène Scribe (1791–1861), though he often turned them to innovative ends, and he was still defending them in 1901, in his conversation with Archer:

> The modern playwright is rather apt to huddle up his action anyhow in his last act. He works up to his great effect in his third act (if it is a four-act play) and leaves his fourth act a sheer anti-climax, sometimes introducing a thinly-disguised *deus ex machinâ* to cut the knot. There is nothing easier than to write a good first act, and even the heightening of the complication in the second act is not very difficult. The dramatist's real problem is, and always must be, the solution in the last act. Now, in my time, a skilled playwright would usually begin by constructing his last act, and having that clear before him,—just as you set up a target before shooting at it. Doesn't that strike you as a rational proceeding?[10]

This is absolutely in keeping with the ideas of Scribe, who, as Patrick J. Smith notes in *The Tenth Muse,* "first calculated the effect, then built backward to construct the cause."[11] When Archer objected that in real life such neat conclusions do not occur, Gilbert replied:

> True; but in real life no curtain descends to tell you that the story is at an end. In point of fact, in real life the story never does end. Certainly it never ends with a marriage. But in constructing a play I hold that you are not justified in interesting your audiences in the adventures of a group of personages, unless you are prepared to furnish those audiences with some information as to what becomes of that group.[12]

There is something a little unconvincing in that last sentence: there is no real reason why an audience should feel cheated by not being assured of the future lives of the characters. But the main point that a work of art must inevitably be unrealistic in some sense is still absolutely true. The difference of opinion between Gilbert and Archer was really to do with what artistic distortions are acceptable and which elements in a play ought to approximate reality. These are questions that will have different answers in every generation.[13]

It is important to realize, however, that what Scribe meant by a *piece bien faite* had less to do with construction than with creating an exciting sequence of events. As John Russell Taylor said of Scribe:

> Construction, the nice balancing of part by part, is for literature; but theatre is something different, a matter of immediate experience. . . . [Scribe] is interested only in what an audience will or will not accept in the heat of the moment.[14]

Gilbert was much more concerned with "the nice balancing of part by part," and to this extent he used as his model not Scribe but someone such as Victorien Sardou (1831–1908), a later refiner of Scribe's ideas.

"Facile then sets to work to write the dialogue. He first tries his hand upon bits of dialogue that arise from suggestive situations. . . . After he has settled half-a-dozen little scenes of this description, he feels that it is time to arrange how the piece is to begin."[15] This aspect of Facile's writing method—which was also Gilbert's—is rather startling. The play is not written sequentially from start to finish, which is the simplest way of creating an organic whole, but constructed piecemeal, like a machine. Obviously, this reduces to a minimum the scope for improvised creativity. Each individual scene may be brilliantly written, but there is likely to be a cost when it comes to the relationship between these individual parts. Even with the most meticulously worked-out plot the internal logic may suffer from such a method of writing. For instance, in *Engaged* (1877) we find a character called The McQuibbigaskie suddenly alluded to in act 3, without explanation; though we gradually infer that he is the owner of the cottage around which the plot hinges, the matter is not properly explained. It seems reasonable to assume that this was the result of Gilbert's having written the scenes of the play out of sequence.

Gilbert's method of writing his later librettos for Sullivan may be seen as a refinement of that described in "A Stage Play." In a piece in *The New-York Tribune* on 9 August 1885 he explained his methods in some detail: how, for instance, he would draft the plot perhaps a dozen times before being satisfied with it; how the "libretto in its first form is simply the scenario reduced to dialogue of the baldest and simplest nature";[16] how he would then write the lyrics before elaborating the dialogue. By this stage in his career, Gilbert was able to allow himself more time to create a libretto—certainly much more than the two months that the manager in "A Stage Play" thinks ample time to allow Horace Facile—and his methods reflected this. He took more care to ensure that every detail of plot, dialogue, and lyric was absolutely right: and so the libretto was slowly built up, like a machine—framework first, and with the details added bit by bit later.

It is interesting to see how little attention "A Stage Play" and the 1885 interview give to the imaginative aspects of writing. The creation of a viable plot is reduced to a mechanical process, and Gilbert's comments seem to imply that the actual writing of a play is nothing more than a matter of overcoming the practical and logistical difficulties of making something that will fit the requirements of the actors. To judge from "A Stage Play," playwriting is a craft pure and simple: art has nothing to do with it.

But of course we should beware of concluding that Gilbert was simply a dramatic craftsman. He took too many risks for us to be satisfied with such an idea; he had too many flights of imagination—particularly of comic imagination. We may suppose that if Gilbert did not describe the imaginative side of writing this was because imaginative processes are difficult, perhaps impossible, to describe.

However, Gilbert's attention to stagecraft is undoubtedly an important part of the virtue of his plays. He wrote in the last year of his life that the profession of the dramatist "demands shrewdness of observation, a nimble brain, a faculty for expressing oneself concisely, a sense of balance in the construction of plots and in the construction of sentences."[17] It is this sense of balance that lies behind his preoccupation with structure.

We have already seen how Gilbert was caught between two apparently opposing desires: to write in the popular style and to earn the approbation of serious critics. This meant combining the accepted tricks of stagecraft with literary polish—a combination it was generally thought impossible to achieve. This opposition lies at the heart of "Actors, Authors and Audiences," a skit Gilbert seems to have written in the mid-1870s. In it, a dramatic author is put on trial for having written a dull play, *Lead,* the main defect of which is its excessively literary feel. The production is described as having been handicapped by the actors' introduction of grossly inappropriate "business" in the attempt to make the play conform to their own ideas of what a play should be.

The Author defends himself at length, and says, among other things:

> It is easy to write an original play that will succeed. Every play which contains a house on fire, a sinking steamer, a railway accident, and a dance in a casino will (if it is liberally placed on the stage) succeed in spite of itself. In point of fact, nothing could wreck such a piece but carefully written dialogue, and a strict attention to probability.[18]

Gilbert's distaste for this kind of unashamedly sensational play is clear—and the Author seems to be his mouthpiece here. And yet the Judge seems also to be speaking for Gilbert when he says later:

> literary merit is only one of many elements—and by no means an indispensable one—that go to make a successful stage-play. It is but one of the constituents of the dramatic pudding. Stage-craft is the water that binds these constituents into an attractive mass; without it the fabric will not hold together.[19]

The problem of how to combine these two elements dogged many of Gilbert's early plays. For instance, John Hollingshead said of *An Old Score:*

> Its literary merits were very great, and it could be read with pleasure. . . . I liked the play—in manuscript, but manuscript is not the stage; the closet is not the theatre.[20]

Similarly, we are told in "Actors, Authors and Audiences":

> Those who had had an opportunity of reading his [the Author's] play had admitted that it was not deficient in thoughtful dialogue and in a certain subtle humour. . . . [But he] had no right to call upon an audience to buy a copy of his play and study it carefully before committing themselves to an opinion upon it.[21]

The fairy comedies were a more successful experiment in combining literary style with the accepted rules of stagecraft. When the third of these, *The Wicked World,* was premiered, the *Times* critic wrote:

> Before his *Palace of Truth* the combination of poetry with supernatural agency for the purposes of genuine comedy would have seemed a monstrosity. . . . Mr. Gilbert has not only invented a new species of drama, but he has made it popular. The audience on Saturday night perfectly knew what sort of play they were about to see, and they were not only curious, but prepared to be highly gratified. . . . Of all Mr. Gilbert's plays, *The Wicked World* is unquestionably the most poetical, and most strongly marks the contempt of the author for the traditional prejudices of the stage.[22]

That last phrase refers to Gilbert's disregard of the accepted conventions of how love is to be treated on the stage—in particular to the way in which *The Wicked World*'s happy ending is brought out by the banishment of "mortal love." The fairy comedies are daring in their defiance of some of the stage conventions—but of course other conventions remain: for instance a ring, a love token, becomes a counter in the plot development of *The Wicked World*—a very "well-made" idea.

The main problem with the fairy comedies from the modern point of view is that they are overstructured. There is no sense of freedom in their overneat plots, or in their dignified, but blank, verse. They lack the characteristic of his best comic work, which I can only call vulgar zest—an element not necessary to Scribean stagecraft or compatible with "literariness" as Gilbert seems to have understood it.

The fairy comedies show Gilbert's "sense of balance" taken to excess. There is too much craft and not enough creativity. But in his best work it is an asset, not a liability: it keeps the wildness under control without stifling it. It is only one part of Gilbert's "method," but a very important one.

PROSE STYLE

We have seen that Gilbert thought a dramatist needed to have "a faculty for expressing oneself concisely, a sense of balance . . . in the construction of sentences."[23] A further indication of where Gilbert's priorities lay in the matter of prose style can be gathered from the following passage from a letter to the Reverend George Bainton, quoted in Bainton's *The Art of Authorship* (1890):

> I have always endeavoured . . . to express my meaning in the most simple
> and direct fashion, frequently writing a single sentence over and over again,
> with the view to ascertain in how few words my full meaning could be ade-
> quately expressed. . . . The English of the late Tudor and early Stuart periods
> may, I think, be studied with the utmost advantage; for simplicity, directness,
> and perspicuity there is, in my opinion, no existing work to be compared
> with the historical books of the Bible.[24]

"Simplicity, directness, and perspicuity": this is the essence of the
matter. Yet his prose has been condemned for having the opposite vice of
willful complexity. "The pomposity of his language at times swells his
plays to bursting point. . . . Gilbert never lost his fondness for inflated
rhetoric."[25] So said Isaac Goldberg. And Max Beerbohm, reviewing Gilbert's *The Fairy's Dilemma* (1904), wrote: "Mr. Gilbert's prose is, and
always has been, peculiarly dull and heavy. . . . Mr. Gilbert's one notion of
humorous prose is to use as many long words and as many formal constructions as possible—a most tedious trick, much practised by other mid-
Victorian writers."[26]

It must be admitted that there is some very pompous stuff in *The Fairy's
Dilemma*—such as, to take a random example:

> But if you will allow me to make a suggestion, Clarissa, it seems to me that
> the hat and mantle you are wearing are scarcely in accordance with the
> modest and unobtrusive nature of the process to which we are about to
> submit ourselves.[27]

But it would be unfair to take this very late work as being typical of
Gilbert: broadly speaking, his style deteriorated after 1890. In this last
period we often find him composing vast, intricate sentences that he seems
to have forgotten are supposed to be spoken rather than read. The patience
of the audience and the breath control of the actors are alike placed under
severe trial.

One need ask for no clearer example of this than the first spoken words
of *Utopia, Limited* (1893):

> *Calynx.* Good news! Great news! His Majesty's eldest daughter,
> Princess Zara, who left our shores five years since to go to England—the
> greatest, the most powerful, the wisest country in the world—has taken a
> high degree at Girton, and is on her way home again, having achieved a
> complete mastery over all the elements that have tended to raise that
> glorious country to her present pre-eminent position among civilized
> nations![28]

It would be difficult to show that this passage flouted Gilbert's ideal of conciseness, in that there is certainly a good deal of information packed into these few lines, but the ludicrous complexity of the construction stands in the way of its being intelligibly spoken in the theater.

However, if we go back to the 1870s, when Gilbert's dramatic productivity was at its height, we see a rather different picture. Here is the opening monologue from *Tom Cobb* (1875):

> *Tom.* I haven't a penny—I haven't the ghost of a prospect of a penny. In debt everywhere, and now I'm told that judgment's been signed against me for £250 by the cruellest Jew in Christendom! Upon my soul, it's enough to make a fellow shy things about, I swear it is! But everything always *did* go wrong with me, even before I was born, for I was always expected to be a girl, and turned out something quite different, and no fault of mine, I'm sure! (*Producing pistol.*) Oh, if I was only quite, quite sure I knew how to load it, I'd blow my brains out this minute! I would, upon my word and honour![29]

Here we have short, vivid sentences, colloquially expressed, that make us immediately familiar with Tom's desperate situation. This example is enough, in itself, to dispose of Beerbohm's statement about pompous constructions being "Mr. Gilbert's one notion of humorous prose."

It is, of course, true that Gilbert's characters exhibit a kind of clipped exactness of speech that we rarely find in real life. One would never mistake his dialogue for a faithful reproduction of ordinary conversation. But that is not the essential point: the only relevant thing is whether the Gilbertian style of dialogue is artistically right. By this I mean: does it achieve everything it sets out to achieve?; is it consonant with all other aspects of Gilbert's art?; is it, indeed, an essential part of his overall vision?

Naturally, I wish to argue that the answer to all these questions is "yes." In Gilbert's most characteristic ironical comedies, the relationship between stage action and the reality of the outside world is oblique, not direct; there is a pervasive air of parody, which is supported by the language. Gilbert constantly questions and ridicules the conventions of melodrama, including its rhetoric; I have already mentioned this in relation to the German Reed pieces. At the same time there is an evident relish simply in the sound of words, particularly in odd combinations. Examples of this could be multiplied indefinitely, but I shall content myself with the case of Mrs Effingham calling Tom "Deliberate and systematic viper!"[30] in Tom Cobb.

Bernard Mandeville wrote in *The Fable of the Bees, Part II* (1729): "All favourite Expressions in *French* are such, as either sooth or tickle; and nothing is more admired in *English,* than what pierces or strikes."[31] This characteristic of piercing and striking is absolutely fundamental to Gilbert's style: almost always we feel that he has deliberately chosen words with a certain sharp-edged quality to them. This attacking quality can be seen everywhere in Gilbert: to take a convenient example, in the phrase "ghost of a prospect of a penny"[32] from the monologue, already quoted, that opens *Tom Cobb.* Or again, from the same play: "fettered by stern destiny to the office stool of an obscure attorney";[33] or ". . . how nobly you would lead your troops into action, caracolling at their head on a proud Arabian barb";[34] or "I was moved to pity by yer plausible tale and yer broken boots."[35] There is a clear preference for short, clipped syllables packed with hard consonants; and this barbed language fits in perfectly with the barbed ideas that it expresses.

Gilbert's dialogue is concise but full of verbal flourishes: brilliant phrases meticulously placed. His characters speak in perfect sentences arranged in a strict logical sequence. These characters are, so to speak, ideal versions of themselves, people miraculously granted the gift of tongues. The inhabitants of Gilbert's "Palace of Truth" may reveal more about themselves than they want, but at least they are never lost for words.

However, the point is that Gilbert's ideal of "simplicity, directness, and perspicuity" takes us away from naturalistic dialogue, with its pauses, evasions, half-finished thoughts, and phatic utterances, and toward a much more "packed" style of dialogue in which it is more important to convey the *meaning* the speaker is trying to express than to reproduce the form of words the speaker would, in reality, use to communicate it. Despite Gilbert's commitment to surface naturalism in the staging of his plays, the plays themselves are much more concerned with revealing the underlying reality as Gilbert understood it, the reality that the rules of society ensured was normally kept decently hidden.

In the Gilbertian comedies, style and substance match each other perfectly. However, the issue is less clear-cut when we come to such prose plays as *Charity,* in which the intention is to reflect reality in a much more straightforward way. Gilbert's love of conciseness and the good phrase is here a liability, since it expresses itself in melodramatic rhetoric:

> *Mrs. Van Brugh.* We will never part again, Ruth. Under the guidance of our loving friend, we will sail to the new land, where, humbly as becomes penitents, cheerfully as becomes those who have hope, earnestly as becomes those who speak out of the fulness of their experience, we will teach lessons of loving-kindness, patience, faith, forbearance, hope, and charity.[36]

This kind of full-frontal preachiness is very much of its day and does not have much appeal in these modern times: we much prefer the twisted ironies of the comic pieces. It is usually felt that "messages" like this should not be spelled out in this way; it is much better simply to let the stage action speak for itself. But the style seems positively restrained beside some of the more lachrymose passages in Dickens, and really the main problem is that there has been a shift in taste. It must also be emphasized that this serious style of Gilbert's is the natural counterpart to his comic style and not in any way a negation of it. The same techniques are being applied to different effect, that is all.

THE DEEPER LEVEL OF MEANING

I have already highlighted Gilbert's emphasis on using drama as a way of exploring ideas. This was a very unusual concept at the time. For the most part the dramatists of the day were concerned only with the working up of good theatrical effects: if an interesting theme appears in a play, it gives the impression of having done so by accident, and it usually disappears again soon enough to make way for the well-made conventionalities. Michael R. Booth notes that "Victorian playwrights did not as a rule think out their ideas clearly and develop them carefully."[37] He adds that even Tom Robertson, despite such play titles as *Society, Caste,* and *Progress,* which promised the exploration of important themes, always allowed the serious underpinning to be muddied or forgotten in a welter of traditional plot devices. In *Birth* (1870), "potential significance of theme is frittered away after the first act in trivial love complications and irrelevant melodramatic incidents."[38] Archer, in an introduction to a reprint of Gilbert's article "A Stage Play," expresses his surprise that Gilbert should have "the assumption that a play should have a 'general idea', a theme, or, as we should say, a problem. . . . His contemporaries, as a rule, thought of nothing but the telling of a perfectly trivial story, comic or sentimental, with no more social or spiritual relevance than may be found in the legend of Mother Hubbard."[39]

Gilbert was regarded in his own time as a revolutionary in the matter of structure: for instance, a bewildered critic wrote of Gilbert's farce *Foggerty's Fairy* (1881): "In departing from the ordinary standards of dramatic literature Mr Gilbert appears to have ventured upon a strange ocean, where his barque has been drifted hither and thither without any settled idea as to what port he could make for."[40] The modern reader of the play will probably find this comment baffling: though the play does contain a note of wild invention, it is kept within bounds by a strong, coherent plot. In the end, it looks as if the critic were confused by the play's originality, for in that era a play's purpose was held to be to entertain, not to propagate new ideas. Strange oceans were to be avoided.

In this respect Gilbert was indeed a revolutionary. He did not fear to break the conventions of the theater: to confirm this, one need only point to the political satire of *The Happy Land.* This iconoclastic spirit was often fueled by nothing more noble than high spirits, but he also broke the stage conventions in order to make a serious point. For instance, by blurring the roles of hero and villain in such pieces as *Engaged* and *Ruddigore,* he reminds his audience of the falsity of the usual stage assumptions.

Gilbert took a very grave risk in *An Old Score* (1869) by misdirecting audience sympathies. In the first scene Harold Calthorpe says of James Casby that "he owes every penny he possesses . . . to my unfortunate governor, and . . . he repays the debt with a sulky close-fisted indifference."[41] Casby is thus set up from the start as an ungrateful villain, and it is only in the last act that the reason for his "ingratitude" is set forth and he earns a full measure of audience sympathy. Whether this was a deliberate ploy on Gilbert's part or simply a miscalculation, it seems probable that it contributed to the play's failure.

Gilbert sometimes used his plays as a means to convey quite complex moral ideas (complex, that is, for a play of that time): a good instance of this is *Charity.* Here we find Gilbert debating, in essence, the old religious question of whether it is faith or works that make for the true Christian. He comes down on the side of works without allowing the other side much chance to put its case, but the details of the plot imply that Gilbert is attempting to make a rather sophisticated distinction. The means by which this is achieved suggest that Gilbert has followed his own advice in "A Stage Play."

Mrs. Van Brugh, representative of the Works side of the equation, runs an almshouse that accepts not only God-fearing Anglicans but also Roman Catholics, Jews, and (worst of all) Dissenters. In short, her gospel is one of charity and toleration. Against her is pitted Mr. Smailey, whose one idea of Christianity is conformity with the norm. Convinced that the only true Christian behavior is absolute rectitude combined with an absolute disdain of all those who fall short of this ideal, he has become a vicious, intolerant hypocrite.

Both characters have sins in their past: Smailey seduced and ruined a young woman, and Mrs. Van Brugh was never formally married to Mr.

Van Brugh. (Again Gilbert takes the severe risk of alienating the sympathies of his audience from Mrs. Van Brugh by making her guilty of technical adultery. In the drama of the time, it is unusually subtle thus to avoid
making the heroine a paragon of virtue.) The difference between them lies
in the way they react to their respective sins. Mrs. Van Brugh, conscience-
stricken, has been trying to set the balance straight with good works and
looks with particular kindness on other committers of sexual sin; Mr.
Smailey, however, desperately tries to excuse himself because of his youth
("I was barely forty then")[42] and looks upon other sinners with revulsion.
Mrs. Van Brugh, tolerant of the failings of others, does not find it so easy
to forgive herself; while Mr. Smailey, with his harsh morality, applies the
gospel of forgiveness *only* to himself. This is not only neat but also psy-
chologically true.

It must be admitted that Gilbert's characters are, by and large, not complex beings. Their behavior is governed by a small number of guiding
characteristics, and they tend to be, if not stereotypes, then at least types.
They are typical examples of certain tendencies in humanity whose behavior is presented to the audience for its amusement and edification. As in the
vast majority of drama of this time, character is subservient to plot; and
it is not appropriate to analyze Gilbert's works in a way that supposes
otherwise.

It is at this level of plot and the meanings that lie behind it that Gilbert's
plays can be best appreciated from a literary-critical point of view. If we
are to understand Gilbert's plays, it is vital to realize that they were deliberately planned to have thematic unity and to explore serious ideas in a rig-
orous, though often absurd, manner. These things do not happen by
chance: when, for instance, we look at the parody of melodrama that lies at
the heart of *Ruddigore* (1887) and notice that almost all of it hinges on
questions of morality, we can only conclude that there is something deeper
than coincidence at work. Gilbert wrote for a purpose: not merely to entertain (though indeed that is purpose enough) but also to explore ideas, to
question them, and perhaps even to answer the questions.

The inversions that became such an integral part of Gilbert's style
are closely involved in this. They rid the plays of the distressing smell
of propaganda; they lull the audience into a false sense of security. By
making Gilbert's manipulation of ideas absurd, extravagant, and wildly
entertaining, they make the serious essence acceptable to a public hostile
to serious ideas in the theater. In the famous words of the jester Jack Point
in The *Yeomen of the Guard:* ". . . he who'd make his fellow-creatures
wise / Should always gild the philosophic pill!"[43] Gilbert's humor almost

always has a purpose: there is actually very little pure nonsense in his
works. Inside the majority of his jokes there is a philosophic pill.

Given the importance of this intellectual underpinning, it may be appropriate to say a few words about George Bernard Shaw's criticisms of
Gilbert, which center on precisely this point. In an article from 8 July 1891
he wrote:

> Mr Gilbert, at his best, was a much cleverer man than most of the play-
> wrights of his day: he could always see beneath the surface of things; and
> if he could only have seen through them, he might have made his mark as a
> serious dramatist. . . . The theme of The Pirates of Penzance is essentially the
> same as that of Ibsen's Wild Duck; but we all understood that the joke of the
> pirate being "the slave of duty" lay in the utter absurdity and topsyturviness
> of such a proposition, whereas when we read The Wild Duck we see that the
> exhibition of the same sort of slave there as a mischievous fool is no joke at
> all, but a grimly serious attack on our notion that we need stick at nothing in
> the cause of duty.[44]

There is much food for thought, and also much justice in this. But it is
interesting to note that Shaw, of all people, should think that an idea
expressed in terms of "absurdity and topsyturviness" could have no serious purpose behind it. He seems to be saying that a joke, by its very
nature, means nothing, and that an argument against an idea such as Duty
can be properly expressed only as a "grimly serious attack." It is probably
superfluous to note that this idea is denied by the practical evidence of
many of Shaw's own plays.

The charge that Gilbert's satire depended on the "general assumption of
the validity of the very things he ridiculed" is an approximation of what I
believe to have been true: we can see in many of Gilbert's plays a certain
attitude of ambiguity toward the satirized object, as I shall argue in greater
depth in chapter 5. This does not amount to an assumption of the validity
of the things ridiculed, however—more, I might suggest, a sneaking suspi-
cion of validity lurking behind all the trenchant ridicule that assumes their
falsity.

Does such an attitude mean that Gilbert necessarily missed his mark as
a serious dramatist? It is difficult to see why this should be so. It only
means that he had missed his mark as a polemicist, which is a very different thing. Ambiguities and contradictions, if well handled, enrich a play:
indeed, a knack for seeing the validity of contradictory opinions may be
thought an essential quality in someone hoping to create drama in the
proper sense of the word. Of course, one could have this quality and still

be a very bad dramatist, but well handled it is surely a primary element in the craft.

Shaw's view of Gilbert seems to have been based on a misapprehension. Shaw wrote to Archer on 30 December 1916: "Observe that Gilbert, who did really hold the mirror up to nature, was led to believe that his mirror was a distorting one because it did not reflect theatrical characters, and so missed his chance of importance as a serious dramatist."[45] That insistence, again, that Gilbert missed out on being "important"! Yet there is no real reason to suppose that Gilbert did not have a personal vision of life distinct from the theatrical conventions: indeed, we can see from *An Old Score* (and others) that he did. Such plays as this, in which Gilbert showed us his vision of the world "right way up," are invaluable as indications of his positive beliefs—flawed though they may be as works of art.

Charity, similarly, shows that his idea of morally correct behavior diverged from the unexamined orthodoxy. True, the idea that it is better to give others practical help than to be a mere self-righteous churchgoer is in accordance with a Dickensian strain of thought current at the time, but the terms in which this is argued are far from conventional stage morality.

Shaw wrote on another occasion (23rd April 1894):

> Gilbert is simply a paradoxically humorous cynic. He accepts the conventional ideals implicitly, but observes that people do not really live up to them. This he regards as a failure on their part at which he mocks bitterly. . . . It is a perfectly barren position: nothing comes of it but cynicism, pessimism, & irony. . . . As Gilbert sees, they [conventional ideals] dont work; but what Gilbert does not see is that there is something else that does work, and that in that something else there is a completely satisfactory asylum for the affections.[46]

Shaw was here writing to Archer in the attempt to prove that his play *Arms and the Man* was not, as Archer had argued, an example of the "Gilbertian" style of comedy. Consequently Shaw is overemphatic in his insistence that Gilbert is inferior to himself, and we should not be surprised to be told that the mysterious "asylum for the affections" referred to above can be discovered by close attention to *Arms and the Man.* Essentially, Shaw convicts Gilbert of nothing more serious than not being a Shavian. The note of bitterness in Shaw's tone can be ascribed to the fact that their styles are otherwise so near allied. Such other Victorian playwrights as Morton and Robertson are treated by Shaw with indulgent affection despite the conventionality of their philosophies of life, but Gilbert is dangerously close to being a rival and has forfeited such indulgence.

Yet elsewhere Shaw sounds a note of grudging admiration and comes close to admitting that Gilbert was, after all, a genuine artist with a voice uniquely his own—as here, in an article from 27 April 1892: "The Gilbertian opera . . . was an altogether peculiar product, extravagant and sometimes vulgar, . . . but still with an intellectual foundation—with a certain criticism of life in it."[47] This reminds me of Archer's assessment of Gilbert: "in all his work we feel that there is an 'awakened' intellect, a thinking brain behind it."[48] The surprised tone of this comment tells us as much as we need to know about the general standard of English drama at the time Archer was writing (1882).

I hope I do not seem to be spending too much time proving the existence of the "intellectual foundation" Shaw refers to, but Gilbert's reputation is so firmly associated with mere "good, clean fun" (which is of no intellectual interest whatsoever) that I feel I must establish the idea firmly, even at the risk of laboring my point.

3
1870–1877—The World Turned Right Side Up

Gɪʟʙᴇʀᴛ's ᴍᴀᴛᴜʀᴇ sᴛʏʟᴇ ᴅɪᴅ ɴᴏᴛ sᴘʀɪɴɢ ꜰᴜʟʟʏ ꜰʟᴇᴅɢᴇᴅ ꜰʀᴏᴍ ᴛʜᴇ egg. He experimented with likely seeming genres, finding his strengths and weaknesses by testing them. It was only when he began to write short librettos for the German Reeds at the Gallery of Illustration that the distinctive Gilbertian voice began to be heard with any consistency. There is, indeed, much truth in the old joke that the Gilbert of the Savoy operas was cradled among the Reeds.

In these librettos, as in the extravaganzas, dialogue alternated with songs; but they improved on the earlier pieces by containing dialogue in prose, rather than in rhymed couplets. Thus Gilbert gave himself the freedom to express his ideas simply, without the contortions of rhythm and rhyme interceding between audience and meaning. In prose dialogue, Gilbert's wit—bizarre ideas expressed in a compound of fastidious phraseology and philistine slang—blossomed.

However, by interspersing such dialogue with songs he signaled to the audience that this was not a direct reflection of life but an oblique commentary on it. In his librettos, impossible events are commonplace; various self-reflexive techniques are used, including parody; the dialogue is unnaturally compact and does not have even the partial naturalism of such a play as *Randall's Thumb*. The libretto form allowed Gilbert to do things that in any other form would be impossible, or at any rate much riskier.

Inversion (of which irony is a part) was always Gilbert's main weapon, the technique which best stimulated his imagination. It plays an important part even in his "serious" plays: for instance, in *An Old Score*, in which the accepted character "types" are constantly subverted. It appears, kept under strict control, in the fairy comedies—in *The Palace of Truth*, to take an obvious example. But it was only in his comic librettos that Gilbert felt free to pile inversion on inversion, irony on irony.

Everything pointed Gilbert toward the comic libretto as his natural form. It allowed him to say the serious things he wanted to say, without offending; it gave him full scope to use all the techniques of inversion that most attracted him. The talent for comic verse he had already demonstrated in his Bab Ballads also pulled him in this direction. From this point on, the shape of his career seems almost inevitable, the development of the Savoy operas a natural culmination of previous tendencies.

Roughly speaking, Gilbert was beginning to outgrow the Gallery of Illustration by the time of *Happy Arcadia,* and so he began to write other librettos for other theaters with more extensive resources. At the end of 1871 he wrote the libretto for *Thespis,* which was set to music by a gentleman named Arthur Sullivan, but it would not be until 1875 that collaboration was resumed—at which point Gilbert's fate was, practically speaking, sealed.

In this chapter I shall trace the development of Gilbert's style in this area, culminating in an analysis of *Engaged* (1877), which, though not a libretto, uses many of the techniques that are best associated with his librettos. This is a convenient cutoff point, because Gilbert's next theater piece after *Engaged* was *The Sorcerer,* which I have chosen to regard as the starting point of the main Gilbert-Sullivan collaboration.

However, before I go on to dissect a few examples, I feel it might be useful to clarify the purpose behind Gilbert's use of irony, inversion, and everything else that in Gilbert's case is usually identified by the word "Topsyturvydom."

There is a common misconception that Gilbert's Topsyturvydom is an escapist realm. Hesketh Pearson, in his biography of Gilbert, found an "explanation" of this in the strained relations between his parents:

> The absence of human feeling in most of his plays, the false exaggeration of the sentiment wherever it occurs, his inability to portray real people, his constant resort to the fancies of fairyland, his frequent pictures of a topsyturvy universe; all these, taken together, suggest an internal discomfort, a desire to see things as they are not, born of his early contact with an unpleasant actuality.[1]

But there is surely no great "desire to see things as they are not" in such plays as *An Old Score* and *Charity*. The reviewers' constant insistence on Gilbert's "cynicism" does not appear to bear out any desire on his part to edit out the more unpleasant side of life. The criticisms that *Engaged* garnered in 1877 suggest that he was doing precisely the opposite to an extent uncommon in other dramatists of that age:

[Gilbert] strips off the outward covering concealing our imperfections, and makes us stand shivering. The failings we are aware of, the thoughts we scarcely dare utter are proclaimed to the world and diagnosed by this merciless surgeon.[2]

Critics responded to *Engaged* with extravagant praise and extravagant condemnation, and we need not accept their own estimation of its qualities, but such extreme reactions do suggest that the critics were used to the theaters presenting them with something rather more anodyne.

No, Topsyturvydom is not an escapist concept; it is, on the contrary, a way of making uncomfortable truths acceptable to a public that was unwilling to listen to anything except escapism. For this reason, I think of Gilbert's Topsyturvydom as "The World Turned Right Side Up." There is actually very little pure nonsense in any of Gilbert's plays, however unreal the setting may appear to be, however impossible the plot. There is almost always a very firm relationship with the realities as experienced by Gilbert and his fellow Londoners.

Gilbert was not alone in using this idea of illuminating our own society by portraying a bizarre alien society: there was a distinct tendency for writers to invent "otherworlds" at this time. One need only think of Lewis Carroll's *Alice's Adventures in Wonderland* (1865), Samuel Butler's *Erewhon* (1872), or Edwin A. Abbott's *Flatland* (1884). It might be interesting to make a separate study of such works and to theorize about the causes of this tendency: whether the authors wished to "escape" from the realities of their own society, or, alternatively, to *explain* those realities by oblique methods—or, indeed, a little of both. That last possibility might, indeed, apply to Gilbert, for, in spite of the constantly emphasized satirical intent behind his fantasy lands, he also palpably relished the fantasy for its own sake.

In this chapter, I intend to examine the development of Gilbert's comic style from the high point of his achievement at the Gallery of Illustration to the moment when the collaboration with Sullivan took over his career. Inversion is the central idea throughout this strand, employed in a variety of ways—some of them developments from techniques used in the other strands we have already examined:

1. Parody, used in a way that emphasizes the complete divorce of theatrical conventions from reality: this is used haphazardly in the rhymed extravaganzas, and developed in such pieces as *A Sensation Novel*

2. Use of a remote setting, with an implied pretense that what takes place there has no relationship to life in England: there is an element of this in the fairy comedies, such as *The Palace of Truth,* and the idea is explored with more point in such pieces as *Topseyturveydom* (1874)

3. Extrapolation of an accepted idea to its logical, absurd conclusion, so that it becomes clear that people's stated beliefs are something apart from the beliefs they demonstrate in their actions: this idea comes into its own only later in Gilbert's career, in such pieces as *The Pirates of Penzance* and *Patience*

4. Use of the supernatural as a means by which the barrier between a desire and its fulfilment can be broken down: used in *Happy Arcadia* and many of Gilbert's later pieces

5. Contrasting characters' surface adherence to the polite conventionalities with their actual determination to look after number one: used in *An Old Score*, for instance, to portray Colonel Calthorpe, and applied to all characters in such later pieces as *Engaged*

6. Simple inversion of an accepted idea, so that the idea can be discredited by showing the inversion to be the truth: as in *Topseyturveydom,* again.

Clearly some of these ideas overlap, and they all have the same overall purpose: to demonstrate that the "official" values of Victorian society are not carried out in people's actions. There is an implication throughout much of Gilbert's comic work that the ideals his society stated as truisms were in fact the reverse of the truth. Since the conventions are a lie, one need only invert them in order to reveal the truth. This idea runs alongside the idea of inversion as a distancing technique and is not contradicted by it.

FROM *The Gentleman in Black* TO *Princess Toto*

The Gentleman in Black (1870) spreads itself over two acts and is more ambitious than any of Gilbert's previous librettos—in cast size and the introduction of a chorus, as well as in the matter of length. The chorus is much more passive than in the best of his librettos, however, being the usual Chorus of Villagers; and the setting is the usual German village of operetta land. However, we do see an aspect of the familiar Gilbert in the logical working out of the absurd premise of what happens when two people exchange souls. Also, an interesting idea appears in the interaction between these two characters—a cruel Baron and a simple peasant lad,

Hans. The Baron is clever, unscrupulous, ugly, and strangely attractive to women; Hans is stupid, virtuous, and universally ridiculed. But characteristics that are attractive in a nobleman become simply repulsive in a peasant lad, and the Baron in Hans's body is universally reviled. Hans in the Baron's body is humane and well-liked. However, the Baron's cleverness gives him the advantage: he tricks Hans into swapping their social positions again with a ridiculous story of their having been exchanged at birth. Hans is easily duped, and a happy ending is brought about only by an arbitrary piece of logic involving a change in the calendar. Setting aside this plainly artificial ending, the plot's natural conclusion is surely the triumph of the evil Baron. Virtue is indeed triumphant only in theatrical performances. Gilbert's slightly jaundiced attitudes are barely held in check by the dramatic conventions.

Thespis (1871) is a step forward in at least one respect, in that the chorus is now a part of the plot. The Gods of Olympus are disturbed by the arrival of a group of picnicking actors, the Thespians, and it is this chorus invasion that sets up the initial conflict. Otherwise, the piece is written with a clear aim of entertaining and nothing else: the central idea, of actors taking over the roles of the gods and creating chaos on earth, is developed as a series of comic episodes and shows signs of considerable haste. There is no doubt that this libretto would be as little-known today as *The Gentleman in Black* if it were not for the accident that it was the first collaboration between Gilbert and Sullivan. Even as it is, it is not very well-known, because most of the music has been lost.

However, one aspect to *Thespis* deserves comment. There is an obvious comparison to be made between it and Offenbach's *Orphée aux Enfers* (1858), which had a libretto by Hector-Jonathan Crémieux and Ludovic Halévy: here, too, the classical gods are ridiculed, and their decision to holiday in the Underworld is imitated in *Thespis* when the gods decide to swap places with the actors. Clearly, *Thespis* is a direct response to *Orphée aux Enfers* and to Offenbach's operettas in general, perhaps with a nationalistic implication that the English could beat the French at their own game.

In this light, Gilbert's choice of central character looks highly significant. The idea for *Orphée aux Enfers* had been Offenbach's own,[3] and the work of his librettists was secondary to his own ideas and music. By appropriating from such classical masters as Gluck the legend of the most famous classical musician, Offenbach was able to set out, clearly and memorably, his own ideas about music as an instrument of pleasure. He implies that operetta is primarily the musician's realm.

But Gilbert's libretto places Thespis, "the Father of the Drama,"[4] at the center instead, suggesting that it is the dramatist, not the musician, who should be the central figure in operetta. Of course Gilbert's choice of theme may have been a mere coincidence, but the choice is, at any rate, entirely consistent with his practice as librettist. His attitude was always that the librettist came first: his was the vision, and it was to be interpreted according to his ideas. The composer was merely an assistant in realizing that vision. This was, and is, such an unusual attitude that it must be emphasized from the start.

Significantly, earlier that year (1871) Gilbert had translated the Meilhac/Halévy libretto of Offenbach's *Les Brigands* for Boosey & Co. So we now find him assimilating ideas from the Offenbach operettas, particularly about how to incorporate incidental satire into a work without damaging its accessibility. In 1873–74 he went through a minicareer as translator: *The Realm of Joy* and *Committed for Trial* being based on plays by Meilhac and Halévy, *The Wedding March* and *The Blue-Legged Lady* on plays by Labiche and Marc-Michel. After this period Gilbert's comic pieces became more sophisticated in their use of different comic techniques, though it would be difficult to prove a direct connection with his earlier translating work. There is a clear similarity between Gilbert's comic style and that of the French farceurs, and it seems reasonable to suppose that he was able to learn something from them: indeed, an anonymous lady who mixed in the literary and theatrical circles of the 1890s has noted that "Gilbert admitted freely his own debt to Labiche."[5] At the crudest level of influence, elements from *Les Brigands* re-emerge in *Princess Toto* (1876), *The Pirates of Penzance* (1879), *The Mountebanks* (1892), and *The Grand Duke* (1896).

However, as George McElroy has noted, Gilbert's approach to comedy is essentially opposed to that of Meilhac and Halévy: "where a Savoy opera presents a meticulously 'realistic' setting and peoples it with out-of-this-world characters, an Offenbachiade commonly has a fantastic setting . . . inhabited by characters very much of this world—the world of the Parisian Boulevardes."[6] The French precedent may have given Gilbert some useful ideas, but he then proceeded to apply them to his own ends.

The Happy Land (1873) deserves comment on several counts. Most obviously, it was probably the most direct political satire the English stage had seen in living memory. In defiance of the Lord Chamberlain's rules, it succeeded in portraying Gladstone and two of his ministers on stage, and satirizing their policies and their personal mannerisms, without any real pretense at disguise. It was banned after three days, and it returned to the stage in somewhat emasculated form, but it has been suggested that even this later version succeeded in bypassing the Lord Chamberlain's ruling on personal satire.[7]

Gilbert wrote the piece under the pseudonym of "F. Tomline" and in collaboration with Gilbert à Beckett. The precise extent of à Beckett's involvement is unknown, but it is certain that Gilbert drew up the plot, and it is probable that he did the lion's share of the actual writing as well.[8] The weakest lines, from the modern perspective, are the topical political jokes, which seem crude even when they are understandable, but there are other passages that show Gilbert working in his best vein, by "explaining" specific absurdities in the political system with insane logic:

> *Mr. A.* [i.e., Ayrton] My dear, it[']s one of the beautiful principles of our system of government never to appoint anybody to any post to which he is at all fitted. Our government offices are so many elementary schools for the instruction of ministers. To take a minister who knows his duties, and to send him to an elementary school to learn them, is an obvious waste of educational power. Nature has pointed you out as eminently qualified for First Lord of the Admiralty, *because* you don't know anything about ships. You take office—you learn all about ships—and when you *know* all about ships, the Opposition comes in, out you go, and somebody else, who doesn't know anything about ships, comes in and takes your place. That's how we educate our ministers.[9]

There can be little doubt that this passage was written by Gilbert.

The Happy Land is an act of deliberate provocation against both the government and the Lord Chamberlain's Office. It shows Gilbert in his most iconoclastic mood, daring the wrath of the censor: should we wish to prove Gilbert a radical satirist, we need look no further than this. But at the same time we must bear in mind that he hid behind a pseudonym and that it was Gladstone's reforming government that he was attacking, on the grounds of its being heedless of the national honor. Anyone seeking a symbol of heroic defiance is doomed to failure. There was always an ambivalence between his scorn for the establishment and his desire to become part of it, and that is clearly shown in the case of *The Happy Land*.

The play was, remarkably, a burlesque of Gilbert's own fairy comedy *The Wicked World*; where in the original play it is Love that is brought to Fairy Land, in the burlesque it is Popular Government—though in each case the result is chaos. The plot that is treated seriously and elegantly in *The Wicked World* is parodied, trivialized, and ridiculed in *The Happy Land*—all with, at the very least, Gilbert's sanction. Just under two months separate the premieres of the two plays: surely this must indicate some

A scene from *The Happy Land*: rejoicings as Gladstonian government is introduced to Fairyland. (The Raymond Mander
and Joe Mitchenson Theatre Collection.)

ambivalence in Gilbert's attitudes toward the fairy comedies that had done so much to earn him a serious reputation as a dramatist. Perhaps in *The Happy Land* he does not quite show himself a fearless defier of authority, but he does seem suddenly desperate to avoid the respectability to which he had been dooming himself. There is something of this same mood of rebellion in *The Realm of Joy,* a translation of a Meilhac and Halévy farce into which he put references to *The Happy Land* and the brouhaha that surrounded it: the Lord Chamberlain, for instance, is referred to throughout as "The Lord High Disinfectant."[10]

Topseyturveydom (1874)[11] seems, at one level, like a deliberate attempt to show that Gilbert was not a political partisan in choosing targets for his satire. First performed less than two months after a general election had returned Disraeli at the head of a Conservative government, it depicts a new Conservative MP, Mr. Satis, who is idiotically satisfied with all aspects of British life. He believes his country has now entered a state of absolute perfection: "A Member who wants to do good is actually reduced to making fishery laws and protecting sea gulls."[12] As another character sardonically observes, "no one would have thought of legislating for sea gulls until the men and women of these islands had had everything possible done for them."[13]

An envoy from Topseyturveydom arrives and invites Satis to tour that far-off land: Satis agrees, and the rest of the play takes place in Topseyturveydom itself. It should be obvious, bearing in mind the play's satirical opening, that this main part of the play is not likely to be pure nonsensical fantasy: in fact, a good number of satirical points are made by contrasting Satis's rosy view of his country with the frank avowals of the Topseyturveyites. For instance, Satis says, "I should particularly like to be present at the deliberations of the collective wisdom of a country that is so unlike our own. . . . I should like to be present at a sitting of the House."[14] The King of Topseyturveydom says that "we only admit the most learned and intellectual men in the kingdom into our House" ("This place is not so topsy turvy after all," says Satis),[15] and it is only after a little more of this that the King realizes they have been talking at cross-purposes:

> Oh, I beg your pardon. You asked to see the collective wisdom of the country. I thought you meant the workhouse. Our Parliament is composed principally of wealthy donkeys who are elected partly because they are wealthy and partly because they are donkeys.[16]

From start to finish Satis fails to make any connection between what he has seen and the state of affairs in his own country—this despite having been warned: "Extremes meet and the difference [from Britain] may not be so great as you imagine."[17]

There is, unfortunately, an uncertainty of purpose in Gilbert's treatment of the theme: in other parts of the play Topseyturveydom is simply used as a vehicle for Gilbert's love of taking absurd premises to their logical conclusions—as in the material concerning the way Topseyturveyites live their lives *backward,* from the grave to the cradle. This material has its charm but does not really fit in with the more satirical sections, and the play does not quite make a satisfactory artistic whole. We are forcibly reminded that Gilbert was still to some extent feeling his way toward a congenial style, though by this time he was very near attaining it. The dry, ironic tone, the calm acceptance of impossibilities, the complete faith in the power of logic, the satirical points wrapped up in a series of inversions, the use of song to drive home the satire, and the use of the frankly arbitrary "happy ending": all these things are firmly in place. The problem is simply one of ensuring that these elements are all made to serve a single, unified end.

However, if this blend of fantasy and satire detracts from the artistic unity of the whole, this flaw is also present in Butler's *Erewhon* (1872), which also presents a vision of a land that is both an inversion and a reflection of England. The distinction between these two opposing purposes is, in both instances, sometimes blurred, leaving the reader/spectator slightly confused about the work's intent.

The pieces I have been discussing in this section are all librettos, in the sense that they contain sections to be sung. But music is of varying importance in them, some (such as *Topseyturveydom*) being merely plays with music. The songs give point to the dialogue, but that seems to be the extent of their role. The importance of the music in such a piece as *Thespis* is greater, and the plot is carried forward, or its details fleshed out, in some of the more elaborate musical sections. But all these pieces show that Gilbert was still trying to work out the precise role of song in his librettos. In *Thespis* we have song used so that Mercury can tell us about his character ("Oh, I'm the celestial drudge");[18] song used to tell a story with a moral of passing relevance to the plot ("I once knew a chap who discharged a function");[19] the traditional love duet ("Here far away from all the world");[20] chorus music to introduce and to establish an atmosphere ("Climbing over rocky mountain");[21] song to press home a plot point made in the dialogue ("So that's arranged");[22] and song that itself drives the plot forward ("We can't stand this").[23] All these, except the last, involve a stepping back from the plot as developed in the dialogue in order to establish a broader point, to create a fresh atmosphere, or to express something that cannot be said in dialogue. Music comments on the events that have taken place in the spoken scenes.

This idea needs to be established so that we may understand what is happening in the one-acter *Trial by Jury* (1875). This is unique in Gilbert's dramatic works in that it is written to be sung from start to finish. It is not broken up with straight dialogue in the operetta style. Therefore, it exists *entirely* at the level of commentary. We should not be surprised to find that it contains very little plot: it consists almost entirely of a burlesque deconstruction of legal procedures. Angelina sues Edwin for breach of promise of marriage; the functionaries of the court arrive and explain their attitudes with unusual frankness; and in the end the Judge solves the dispute by offering to marry Angelina himself. In terms of plot, that is all that happens. Almost the entire interest of the piece lies in its incidental revelations and the way it views common situations from odd angles. Aside from the ending, nothing essentially improbable happens. The characters do not speak but sing, and so they reveal their true attitudes, which are usually, and prudently, hidden from view.

Obviously this is simply an example of one of the most familiar of the Gilbertian elements, the "Palace of Truth" idea in which, as William Archer noted, "people naively reveal their inmost thoughts, unconscious of their egotism, vanity, baseness, or cruelty."[24] It had been a feature of some of his earlier comic librettos—*Topseyturveydom,* for instance—but it fits into the style of *Trial by Jury* particularly naturally because it is commonly expected that characters singing in opera/operetta will communicate at a deeper level of truth than they would in mere speech. Song indicates to the audience that we have entered the Palace of Truth.

Something of this idea survives in the later Gilbert and Sullivan operas, particularly in the patter baritone's songs, successors to "When I, good friends" in *Trial by Jury.* As Isaac Goldberg notes, "In the autobiographical songs they are under some compulsion to speak the inner truth."[25] Thus the Judge explains in detail the path of corruption that led him to his present high station. This is simply the most obvious example of an idea that runs throughout *Trial by Jury.*

But the music also has another effect on the words—an effect that we shall find repeated in Gilbert's later collaborations with Sullivan. The libretto holds judicial procedures up to mockery by exposing the corruption and unchecked biases that riddle the supposedly "impartial" courts of law. The style is frivolous, but the criticisms are not, and the meaning Gilbert is trying to put across is never in any doubt. And yet neither its original audiences nor later generations have ever thought it appropriate to think of the piece in those terms (A. H. Godwin, for instance, characterizes the piece by its "wealth of good spirit and whimsical fancy")[26]— and they are, it seems to me, right to take this view. The good humor of Sullivan's music takes the bite out of Gilbert's words; and perhaps the form of the piece, by emphasizing the unreality of what is taking place, makes it the more difficult to accept as a serious criticism of existing conditions.

There is an allied question here, as to whether Gilbert *intended* it to be taken as a satire with a serious purpose or whether it was intended simply as a wild burlesque without deeper meaning. This question is almost impossible to answer with certainty, though the fact that the original productions ended as follows suggests an emphasis on the unreality of proceedings:

> (JUDGE *and* PLAINTIFF *dance back on to the Bench—the* BRIDES-MAIDS *take the eight garlands of roses from behind the Judge's desk [where one end of them is fastened] and draw them across floor of Court, so that they radiate from the desk. Two plaster Cupids in bar wigs descend from flies. Red fire.)*[27]

The most academically acceptable purposes of satire are *pour épater les bourgeois* (not, it seems to me, a very noble aim) and to give vent to the Swiftian *saeva indignatio*. It is rather embarrassing, after these impressive foreign phrases, to have to suggest for it the much more vulgar aim of entertaining, yet even that aim should not be despised. By entertaining, Gilbert ensured for his work the widest possible public, and his ideas became common currency, even if they were not taken seriously at the conscious level. By laughing at a joke you show that you accept its premise.

An anonymous article published in 1921 contains a highly interesting passage:

> [Gilbert] did more to cut away the props of the old world, to prepare the minds of the unthinking mass for change, than any who deliberately preached against the established order. If Gilbert had been a professed revolutionary, he would have had as little influence as Bernard Shaw. . . . Because people laughed with him, they fancied he was one of themselves and let him undermine their faith in much that they held sacred.[28]

If *An Old Score* and *Charity* failed, then their ideas could still be expounded in other, more frivolous forms, perhaps just as effectively. But it must, of course, be emphasized that Gilbert's positive beliefs were very different from those of Shaw—as the nameless writer I have quoted says,

"Gilbert had no conscious leanings toward a new order."[29] Gilbert would have been horrified to find himself praised as a more effective propagator of Shavian ideals than Shaw himself.

Again and again we run into this sense that Gilbert was unsure about whether he wanted to be seen as part of the Establishment. *The Wicked World* or *The Happy Land?* The facts do not support the idea of Gilbert as a kind of Fifth Columnist, deliberately destroying the British Empire from within—though a case might be put that his works may have played a part in doing exactly that. However, the next work I intend to look at, *Princess Toto* (1876), might be seen as an allegory of his own uncertainties on this very issue.

This three-act libretto is set in a vague fairy-tale world—as a program note to the 1881 revival says:

SCENE: Nowhere   TIME: Never[30]

Princess Toto is a highly romantic young woman, her head "filled with foolish ideas about gypsies, robbers, actors, pirates, paving commissioners, Red Indians, and outlandish people of that sort."[31] Also, she has "no memory whatever; forgets things that are not ten minutes old."[32] It is this that enables her to forget she has married Prince Doro almost as soon as the ceremony is over and to run away with another Prince, disguised as a brigand chief, at the end of act 1. She is, in fact, a kind of distilled essence of irresponsibility. The events of the opera are mainly concerned with the efforts of her father, King Portico, to get her back. The King is characterized by an absurd devotion to etiquette and the accepted forms of respectability: his chief fear is that of "appear[ing] ridiculous in the eyes of the surrounding nations."[33] A clearer figure of stiff-necked Victorian responsibility could not be imagined.

Before the King can get his daughter back, he has to humiliate himself by disguising himself as a Red Indian. But in the end she does return and is made to face her responsibilities, her last speech making her sound almost like a parody of the Victorian little wife: "now that I have a husband to look after me, I won't give you any more trouble, as he will be always at hand to pull me up whenever I attempt to act on the spur of the moment."[34]

Toto, the force of irresponsibility, is brought to heel at last—as might be expected—but responsibility, too, must be forced to grovel a little. Toto is an absurd character, and her complete lack of memory makes her a figure of fun, but her love of the romantic finds a responding chord in Gilbert.

King Portico, with his constant fear of being made to look ridiculous, sounds rather like the Gilbert of "ordinary" life, but elements of Toto express themselves in Gilbert's wilder works—including *Princess Toto* itself, which, despite its orthodox conclusion, has a mad plot that sometimes seems in danger of running out of control. (This sense of wildness may have been influenced by Meilhac and Halévy.)

The lyrics are varied and polished, a refinement of what had gone before, but it will take a few more years, working with Sullivan rather than (as here) Frederic Clay, for him to reach the pinnacle of his achievement in the libretto form.

Tom Cobb AND *Engaged*

It may come as something of a shock to realize how rarely Gilbert employed his characteristic "Gilbertian" style in straight plays. His first original play in this style was *Tom Cobb* (1875); its sole successors were *Engaged* (1877), *Foggerty's Fairy* (1881), and *The Fairy's Dilemma* (1904). For the most part, he used the style only in his librettos.

I have already touched on one possible reason why this might be so. A drama punctuated by song is clearly not tied down to the conventions of "realism" as straight drama is. Music allows for a degree of commentary on the action that would be less easy to accept in a play: a commentary that is, in Gilbert's case, for the most part ironic. Though many of his earlier plays, such as *An Old Score*, used various forms of irony, the tone was always kept within the bounds of the "realistic," as Victorian dramatists understood it. The ironic style that Gilbert had been developing in his earlier librettos set aside even this limited definition of realism, cut away from surface fidelity to life, and allowed his characters to express what Gilbert understood to be the underlying truth of things. Up to this point, Gilbert seems to have made the assumption that such a style could work *only* in the libretto framework.

It may be that Gilbert's experiences translating *The Wedding March* (1873) and *Committed for Trial* (1874) suggested otherwise. These full-length farces needed to be rendered into English in Gilbert's extravagant comic style simply in order to match the extravagances of the plots, and that is how he rendered them. Farces *were* a popular staple of English drama, but for the most part these were brief, one-act affairs, in which a distinct comic vision of life could scarcely be elaborated. After a handful of experiments in the 1860s, Gilbert gave up on the one-act farce, finding the vein uncongenial to his aims. But in 1873 he was perhaps reminded of the French tradition of longer farce, in which people such as Labiche were able to use the cover of frivolity to criticize the stupidities of their society.[35] *The Wedding March* was a great success—Gilbert later said that he had "received considerably more than two thousand pounds in return for the two days' labour . . . spent upon it."[36] If English audiences could accept such a style from a French adaptation, then surely they could also accept a home-grown product on the same lines.

So in 1875 we have *Tom Cobb*, a farce in three short acts. The plot is ridiculous but follows the good farcical rule of putting the hero through the extremes of hardship. Tom Cobb starts the play pursued by creditors. He then fakes his death and lies low for a while. When, starving and penniless, he attempts to come back to life, he finds he cannot do so and is forced to take on the false identity of Major-General Arthur Fitzpatrick. This, in turn, propels him into an unwanted imposture, complicated by fears that he is being sought to answer a charge of forgery. Only at the last moment is he released from his torments by being told he has been left a fortune in a will.

It is interesting to compare *Tom Cobb* with one of Gilbert's French models, *Un Chapeau de Paille d'Italie*—the Labiche/Marc-Michel farce from which Gilbert took *The Wedding March*. The hero, Fadinard, is about to be married, but for various reasons must combine this with a desperate, headlong search for an Italian straw hat. The plot is resolved with the discovery of exactly such a hat among his wedding presents.

Fadinard's desperation comes from his search for something: when it is found, he can settle down to a life of peace and happiness. But the motivating force behind Tom Cobb's desperation is the desire to run away from his difficulties. He wishes to evade his debts, so he pretends to die. All his later problems spring from his adoption of this panic plan. (There is a similar pattern in Gilbert's later farce *Foggerty's Fairy.*) This implies that Tom Cobb (and Gilbert?) sees happiness in negative terms—as the absence of debts, hunger, prosecutions for forgery, and so on; while to Fadinard happiness lies in the achievement of a positive goal—even if it is such a ridiculous goal as that of finding a hat. It is true that Tom Cobb ends his play with wealth and a beautiful bride, but he has pursued neither: they appear in a kind of material counterbalance to the disappearance of the threats that he thought pursued him. All this seems to fit in with the idea of Gilbert as a man of critical, rather than constructive, temperament.

The play is written in Gilbert's best style—witty, inventive, extravagant, and yet controlled. In *Tom Cobb*, *Princess Toto* and *Engaged* the Dionysian elements of Gilbert's style are allowed full scope for expression, with just enough of the Apollonian element of construction to keep everything under control.

Tom Cobb seems to have been a "success" on its opening night, if the *Times* review is to be believed (Monday, 26 April 1875); though in the end it achieved a run of only fifty-three performances.[37] Apparently it did not provoke anything like the kind of controversy that greeted *Engaged* two years later, though the *Times* review credits it with a similar satirical purpose:

> . . . the author never allows his fancy to tempt him from his purpose, which is that of steady, unflinching satire. He loves to make his audience roar by flinging at them a palpable absurdity, to stimulate their admiration by a succession of sparkling lines, but his main object is to lash "humbug" in its divers manifestations. He never becomes frivolous; the feeling expressed by Juvenal's declaration, *"Difficit est satiram non scribere,"* lies at the foundation of his work.[38]

This satirical purpose was almost universally recognized in *Engaged*, though not universally applauded. Michael R. Booth has made an excellent compilation of some of the reviews it garnered, from which I should like to quote the most extreme of the critical reactions. It comes from *Figaro* (10 October 1877):

> To tell the story of "Engaged" is more than can be expected of anyone who assisted at its first representation. One does not care to relate the details of a rough passage across the Channel, if one is not proof against sea-sickness. The recapitulation of the symptoms of nausea is neither pleasant to the sufferer, nor edifying to his audience. Let our readers conceive a play in three acts, during which every character only opens his or her mouth to ridicule, in the coarsest manner, every feeling that is generally held in respect by any decent man or woman. . . . speeches in which the language ordinarily employed by true feeling is used for the purpose of deriding every virtue which any honest man reverences, even if he does not possess, are tediously reiterated by actresses whom one would wish to associate only with what is pure and modest. . . . To answer that "all this is a burlesque" seems to us but a poor defence; the characters are dressed in the ordinary costume of the present day; the language, as we have said, is precisely that which would be employed in serious drama; there are few if any of those amusing exaggerations which, in true burlesque, dispel, almost before it has time to form, any idea that the speaker is really in earnest. We do not believe that, except among the most repulsive comedies of the seventeenth century, or in the very lowest specimens of French farce, can there be found anything to equal in its heartlessness Mr. Gilbert's latest original work.[39]

It is probably superfluous to say that the writer of the above was not approaching the play in the proper spirit: indeed, his general attitudes to satire and burlesque show a complete lack of sympathy and understanding for what Gilbert was trying to do. The reviewer can only accept burlesque that, by the use of "amusing exaggerations" and outlandish costumes, proclaims that it has no connection to the world in which he lives. But for Gilbert that is exactly why traditional burlesque was wrong, and that is why he attached to the text of *Engaged* the following note:

> It is absolutely essential to the success of this piece that it should be played with the most perfect earnestness and gravity throughout. There should be no exaggeration in costume, make-up, or demeanour; and the characters, one and all, should appear to believe, throughout, in the perfect sincerity of their words and actions. Directly the actors show that they are conscious of the absurdity of their utterances the piece begins to drag.[40]

He wrote a similar note to the text of *The Wedding March.*

Taking a hint from the *Figaro* reviewer, we can see that this insistence that pieces such as *Engaged* should be acted with an absolute appearance of seriousness is allied to a desire to drive home the satirical points behind the burlesque tone. To that extent *Engaged* was undoubtedly a success: the fact that it was attacked with such vitriol shows clearly enough that the point had struck home. It was not a failure in commercial terms, running for 110 performances and being revived several times in Gilbert's lifetime.

The play is a deliberate provocation from start to finish. It begins with a scene designed to "wrong-foot" the audience into thinking it a comedy of the sentimental rural sort (such as Gilbert's own *Dan'l Druce, Blacksmith*)—a love scene between a Lowland Peasant Lad and his Lassie. But after a couple of minutes strange notes appear in the dialogue:

> *Angus (wiping his eyes).* Dinna heed the water in my ee—it will come when I'm ower glad. Yes, I'm a fairly prosperous man. What wi' farmin' a bit land, and gillieing odd times, and a bit o' poachin' now and again; and what wi' my illicit whusky still—and throwin' trains off the line, that the poor distracted passengers may come to my cot, I've mair ways than one of making an honest living—and I'll work them a'nicht and day for my bonnie Meg![41]

Playing this kind of trick on an audience can backfire by setting up false expectations that are then frustrated, leaving the audience bewildered. This, and similar games with the dramatic conventions, may have contributed to the strong feelings the play aroused. Cheviot Hill, the apparent hero, is a miserly philanderer; Belvawney, who has the mesmeric eye of a stock villain, is actually a much more likable character; the baby-talking Minnie Symperson has a much shrewder financial eye than she pretends; and everyone, from top to bottom, uses the noble language of melodrama to justify entirely selfish acts. The play's last speech, spoken by Cheviot, sounds in isolation like the last speech of an ordinary, sentimental comedy, but it sounds entirely different—much more ironic, much bitterer—when placed in the context of a play during which Cheviot has addressed almost exactly these same words to a long series of different women:

> *Cheviot (embracing her).* My own! my own! Tender blossom of my budding hopes! Star of my life! Essence of happiness! Tree upon which the fruit of my heart is growing! My Past, my Present, my To Come![42]

This play does not escape the stage conventions of the day but by distorting them, parodying them, and twisting them to Gilbert's own ends, suggests a view of the world that was extremely unusual for the time, one the conventions ought to make impossible to express. For instance, it adheres to the surface convention of the happy ending while at the same time making the falsity of such a thing abundantly clear.

Everyone in the play acts from absolutely selfish motives; this, and the complex web of irony in which it is enmeshed, makes it extremely difficult to disentangle the positive meaning behind it, but the following soliloquy by Symperson seems to express something like Gilbert's attitude:

> What a terrible thing is this incessant craving after money! Upon my word, some people seem to think that they're sent into the world for no other purpose but to acquire wealth; and, by Jove, they'll sacrifice their nearest and dearest relations to get it.[43]

True, these words are spoken by a man who has just been trying to get his daughter to marry the detestable Cheviot Hill in order to secure for himself an income of a thousand pounds a year, but this need not affect the validity of what he is saying.

The attitude to Victorian society is essentially the same as in *An Old Score*, but the techniques used are much more sophisticated. In the earlier play Gilbert had contrasted the self-serving Colonel Calthorpe with his good-hearted son Harold; here we are not given the other side of the moral coin but are expected to provide it for ourselves. There are clear dangers with this approach: the play could be interpreted as a demonstration that all people are selfish and that it is useless to pretend otherwise.

But it is all one with Gilbert's comic theories, as expressed for instance in this reworking of Hamlet's speech to the actors, in *Rosencrantz* and *Guildenstern* (1874):

> I pray you, let there be no huge red noses, nor extravagant monstrous wigs, nor coarse men garbed as women, in this comi-tragedy; for such things are as much as to say, "I am a comick fellow—I pray you laugh at me, and hold what I say to be cleverly ridiculous." Such labelling of humour is an impertinence to your audience, for it seemeth to imply that they are unable to recognize a joke unless it be pointed out to them. I pray you avoid it.[44]

Gilbert's ironic comedy demands an active, intelligent reaction from its audience, as the "amusing exaggerations" of burlesque do not. Gilbert's comment two years later in his article "A Hornpipe in Fetters" (1879) sounds like a final comment on *Engaged:*

> It has recently been discovered by many dramatic critics that satire and cynicism are misplaced in comedy, and that the propriety of repartee is to be estimated by the standard of conversation in a refined drawing-room. It is fortunate for Sheridan that this ukase had not been pronounced when he wrote *The School for Scandal.*[45]

CONCLUSION

The story I have been telling so far is the story of how Gilbert managed to find a personal style. Starting in the genre of rhymed extravaganza, he quickly realized that this was not the most congenial field for him—though the elements of parody, fantasy, and song were, of course, integral to the mature style. His blank-verse fairy comedies had much more artistic integrity but gave too little opportunity for the wild humor that was essential to the best use of his creativity. His serious prose dramas were baldly critical of the hypocrisies of his time; their unconventionality made them unpopular with the public, and though he continued to write in this vein, it was never the dominant style. It was only when he started writing short comic librettos for the Gallery of Illustration that he found a congenial, and popular, vehicle for his talents.

Slowly he developed this comic style, gathering a wide range of comic and ironic techniques that allowed him to entertain and to convey serious ideas at the same time. This kind of integrity of underlying purpose was extremely rare in the theater of that era: anything that approached preachiness was frowned upon. In using drama as a vehicle for ideas, Gilbert was fighting against a universally accepted assumption that frivolity and truisms were the only acceptable ingredients of drama.

In seeking a congenial style, Gilbert was not only trying to find accommodation with the assumptions of his age, he was also trying to balance the warring instincts in his own mind—toward respectability on the one hand and toward disrespectful vulgarity on the other. He was never able to resolve this conflict properly, and this sometimes led to his appearing to bite the hand that fed him. For instance, when he accepted a knighthood in 1907, he was very careful to dismiss it as "a tin-pot, twopenny-halfpenny sort of distinction"[46] and "a sort of commuted old-age pension."[47]

Though he always set great store by his blank-verse plays, there is something strained and empty about them; it is only in the ebullient, ingenious, wildly inventive comic plays—the librettos and the farces—that we find a truly natural style emerging. Orton's image of Dionysus as the presiding god of Drama is the best way I can think of the matter. It is the ungovernable creative element that breathes life into the structures created under the influence of Apollo; it is the reason why people read for pleasure. It is literature's most important element—but also the part of literature that criticism cannot define.

This Dionysian spirit, as it appeared in Gilbert, could only flourish in certain forms: in the comic libretto, as Gilbert early found, and, as he began to realize several years later, in a certain kind of farce, more familiar in France than in England. His style came to something very near maturity in the early 1870s, and from that point it was merely a matter of refining the elements and keeping the wildness under control.

We have reached the point in Gilbert's career when he has at last succeeded in creating a personal, distinctive voice: he now trembles on the brink of that decisive moment when, in conjunction with Sullivan and Richard D'Oyly Carte, he is to seal his fate by devoting his life to the creation of what is to become known as Savoy opera.

4
Gilbert's "Stage Management"

Plays are designed to be acted, not read, and it is not surprising that Gilbert did not feel his job had ended with the final polishing of the playscript. Most of his plays were, after all, more than simply an entertaining sequence of dramatic "situations": they were expressions of various aspects of Gilbert's view of the world. It was essential for him to remain in control of his play as it was prepared for stage production, so as to ensure that the result conformed as closely as possible to his original vision. Gilbert's article "Actors, Authors and Audiences" has some bitter things to say about actors who introduce inappropriate comic "business" and irrelevant "breakdown" dances into their parts—and it seems clear that this was based at least partly on Gilbert's own experience. By "stage-managing" (or, as we should say, "directing") his own plays and keeping a controlling eye on all other aspects of production, he was able to prevent the worst excesses of misinterpretation. He wrote in his article "An Appeal to the Press" (1878):

> When a novel is published, the only person who comes between the author and the public is the publisher; and if the novel does not convey an accurate, unmistakable idea of its author's intention, it is his own fault, and he is fairly saddled with all responsibility. But before a play is presented to the public the intellectual assistance of thirty or forty people is placed under contribution, and every one of these has it in his power to affect the result in some appreciable degree.[1]

These thirty or forty people—actors, scenic artist, leader of the orchestra, prompter, property man, limelight man, costumier, and so on—may each have a separate conception of the play they are associated with, and there clearly needs to be a controlling vision for them all to follow if chaos is not to break out. Stage management was still a developing art in the 1870s: the duties of this post were confined to the supervision of practical matters of stage movement and setting, except in a few exceptional

87

cases. The idea of author as stage manager was not new with Gilbert—others, such as James Robinson Planché, Dion Boucicault, and Tom Robertson, were there before him—but it was still a rarity in Gilbert's time; and the use of this role to realize the author's very idiosyncratic view of the world was rarer still. To return to Gilbert's 1873 article "A Stage Play":

> Facile knows something of stage management, and invariably stage-manages his own pieces—an exceptional thing in England, but the common custom in France. . . . [He] takes particular good care that whatever his wishes are, they shall be carried out to the letter, unless good cause is shown to the contrary. He has his own way: and if the piece is a success, he feels that he has contributed more than the mere words that are spoken.[2]

The autocratic note in this is obvious, and writers on Gilbert's stage management have not been slow to pick up on similar comments made by him elsewhere, but the sentence that follows it should also be noted: "At the same time, if Facile is not a self-sufficient donkey, he is only too glad to avail himself of valuable suggestions offered by persons who have ten times his experience in the details of stage management."[3]

Gilbert's debt to Robertson in the area of stage management is always emphasized, but in "A Stage Play" we find Gilbert turning to the French theater for his precedent. Later on in the article he argues, through Facile, that plays should be rehearsed much more thoroughly than they are in England:

> In first class French theatres this system is adopted. Parts are distributed, learnt perfectly, and then rehearsed for six weeks or two months, sometimes for three or four months. Scene rehearsals and dress rehearsals occupy the last week of preparations.[4]

Gilbert was familiar with the French theater from his visits to Paris, and we have already seen its influence on his style of writing. Much of what was sophisticated in Gilbert's ideas about the theater can be traced to a French influence, though he seems to have had a genuine distaste for the "immorality" of the French stage, and he was at pains to write in a distinctively English style.

In a letter dated 11 December 1889, Gilbert told Cairus James, who was playing Ko-Ko in a touring company: "The principle of subordination must be maintained in a theatre as in a regiment."[5] Reading accounts of Gilbert's rehearsal techniques, one sometimes feels that he is carrying the analogy too far. He would work out all the stage movements on a model theater before the first rehearsal was called; he would drill his actors in every movement and every gesture, in every inflexion of every speech, and even, as Henry Lytton said, "When everything else was perfect, I have known Gilbert to spend many long hours making his company practise facial expressions, tiny movements of the hands and of the feet."[6] These are the techniques he employed when he was at the height of his influence at the Savoy Theatre, and it may be argued that such a large company, principals and chorus trapped on a small stage, needs to be meticulously drilled in order to create a pleasing result, but it seems that these were merely the perfection of techniques Gilbert had already been using previously.

It is difficult to avoid the idea that Gilbert was trying to create from the D'Oyly Carte company a troupe of marionettes that could mimic the effects he wanted. That is an unsympathetic way of putting it, and it is of course an exaggeration: there is ample evidence to show that he would often collaborate with the actors to create "business" and would sometimes even incorporate actors' ad-libs into the authorized text. The autocratic methods may be defended as necessary in a theatrical world in which actors were often reluctant to yield to the ideas of others in professional matters, just as the methods may be attacked as the expression of a domineering personality. But the essential point is that Gilbert's methods had one end in view: the presentation on stage of the play in a form as near as possible to his own conception of it. Jane W. Stedman says, embedding a quotation from Gilbert in her sentence: "For Gilbert, no manager had a right 'to interpose between me and the realization of my ideas.'"[7] This is as clear a demonstration of my point as anyone could wish. All that remains to be discussed is the nature of these ideas and the effects Gilbert thought would best realize them.

Gilbert wrote to Percy Fitzgerald: "I have no notion . . . what Gilbertian humour may be. It seems to me that all humour, properly so called, is based upon a grave and quasi-respectful treatment of the ridiculous and absurd."[8] Despite Gilbert's protestations, this is in fact an excellent definition of his comic style. It is the essence of the mock-heroic style, also called High Burlesque. Gilbert's note to *Engaged,* which I have already quoted in full, emphasizes that the play "should be played with the most perfect earnestness and gravity throughout."[9] This idea was not original to him: Planché and Robertson, for instance, had said similar things before him. But in Gilbert's hands it was more than simply good comic practice, it was the basis of a philosophy of comic theater.

Robertson was Gilbert's mentor in stage management and, in Gilbert's assessment, a pioneer in the field:

> Why, he invented stage-management. It was an unknown art before his time [the 1860s]. Formerly, in a conversation scene for instance, you simply brought down two or three chairs from the flat and placed them in a row in the middle of the stage, and the people sat down and talked, and when the conversation was ended the chairs were replaced. Robertson showed how to give life and variety and nature to the scene, by breaking it up with all sorts of little incidents and delicate by-play. I have been at many of his rehearsals and learnt a great deal from them.[10]

It was from Robertson that Gilbert got his enthusiasm for real-seeming sets and costumes and his ideas of realism in acting. This last was mainly defined by the fact of its not being bound by the rigid conventions of the melodramatic style. Robertson replaced bombast with small talk, and this change in substance was matched with a change in acting style. The stock gestures of melodrama were, if not eliminated, then at least whittled down, and in their place appeared small, understated gestures copied from reality. Robertson was not the first to do such things, but it was he who popularized them, and even if he did not originate them he did at any rate advocate them when they were unusual and daring things to do.

Gilbert, like Robertson, insisted that sets and costumes should reproduce the details of real life. Examples of this could easily be multiplied, but I need only mention the original set of *H.M.S. Pinafore,* based on Gilbert's sketches of the *Victory,* and the pains taken to ensure that the sailors' dress and demeanor were as "authentic" as possible. But whereas in Robertson this concern to reflect the outward trappings of the world was allied to the new note of naturalism in dialogue, both elements combining to create a convincing world of middle-class understatement and discreet sentimentality, in Gilbert the same means were used for entirely different ends.

That statement needs qualifying: Gilbert wrote in a variety of styles, from the jaundiced "realism" of *An Old Score* (1869) to the overt fantasy of *The Wicked World* (1873), with *Sweethearts* (1874), that exercise in the Robertsonian style, somewhere in between. For the moment I wish to concentrate on those pieces written in the "Gilbertian" comic style: the most typical of the Savoy operas, alongside which we may also put the German Reed librettos, the satirical and extravagant early librettos, and the two farces.

In these pieces Gilbert is clearly not aiming to show us a simple reflection of reality. The dialogue is, as we have noted, compact and highly articulate, but it has nothing to do with the real patterns of speech—not even to a limited, Robertsonian, extent. People sing. ("*Margaret*. . . . they are all mad—quite mad! / *Rose*. What makes you think that? / *Margaret*. Hush! They sing choruses in public. That's mad enough, I think!")[11] And the things that happen in these pieces are always bizarre, often grotesque and wildly improbable, sometimes impossible. No, these pieces are not "naturalistic" in that sense. So why does Gilbert bring to them the conventions of naturalism?

The answer can be seen in the statement of Gilbert's I have already quoted: "It seems to me that all humour, properly so called, is based upon a grave and quasi-respectful treatment of the ridiculous and absurd." The humor lies in the contrast between absurd content and "quasi-respectful" treatment—thus Gilbert's insistence that an actor should never let the audience know that he knows what he is saying is funny. George Grossmith recounted how Gilbert would tell an actor: "I don't want you to tell the audience you're the funny man. They'll find it out, if you are, quickly enough."[12]

This is simply a practical issue of how to get the best out of a comic piece. But it seems at least possible that there might be something deeper in the method than this. By surrounding the bizarre events of the piece with an aura of realism, Gilbert may be hinting to the audience that these things are not as unreal as one might think. It is interesting to read this in Michael R. Booth's introduction to a volume of Robertson's plays:

> This audience [at the Prince of Wales's] did not seek to have its comfortable middle-class values challenged, nor was it sceptical and looking for the faith of honest doubt; that sort of comic territory was uniquely the property of Gilbert, not Robertson. What it got from Robertson was reassurance, the comic exploitation but not the discrediting of an unshakeable class position, and the fulfilment of class dreams related to money, ambition, and love; there is much fantasy in Robertson.[13]

So it was Robertson, not Gilbert, who was the fantasist, in spite of Robertson's careful reproduction of ordinary life, and in spite of Gilbert's wild reversals. Robertson was essentially telling his audience what it wanted to hear and so could say these things fairly directly, but Gilbert had much less palatable things to say and had to disguise them. But the scrupulous accuracy of Gilbert's sets and costumes, and the lack of exaggeration in the acting, may be interpreted as a deliberate indication that the fantasy was a disguise. After *An Old Score,* Gilbert was generally a little careful about saying unpleasant things in too straightforward a manner.

The contrast between content and delivery might be expressed another way. Gilbert's enthusiasm for the theater dated back to the 1840s, the era of Planché and Morton, of fantastic burlesque, "screaming farce," and full-blooded melodrama. His plays reflect this era in their style of dialogue. His best comic plays usually parody some aspect of the old style of melodrama, so we may see the contrast as being between the old style of play and the new. Gilbert parodied the inflated rhetoric of melodrama with evident relish and in doing so exhibited a good deal of affection for the thing he was ridiculing, as many writers on Gilbert and Sullivan have noticed. He created much humor from the contrast between the two, but there was an interesting ambiguity in his attitude. Gilbert sincerely believed in the Robertsonian techniques, but these were of comparatively recent growth in his mind, and their hold on him seems superficial. In the actual scripts of his plays, he returned again and again to the old theatrical types, though adding his own twists to the characterization. In the matter of theatrical innovation, Gilbert's brain was well rooted in the 1870s, but his heart belonged firmly to the 1840s.

Gilbert did not confine these techniques of stage management to his comic pieces: he used them in his serious plays also. This suggests that Gilbert held, first and foremost, the Robertsonian idea that the stage should try to reproduce the outward forms of real life; it also suggests that Gilbert's discovery of the comic possibilities of uniting this to an absurd script was secondary to it.

William Cox-Ife quotes Percy Marmont, who acted in a revival of *The Palace of Truth* directed by Gilbert, as saying: "Of course . . . Gilbert insisted that the lines be spoken exactly as he wanted, but, at the same time, we learned to think as we spoke."[14] This is an interesting point that is very rarely mentioned. The usual impression is that Gilbert was concerned only with the external gestures and inflections of acting, as implied in François Cellier's statement that Gilbert "had a deep-rooted creed that . . . acting, being mimetic, was as much a matter of instruction as elementary mathematics."[15] But Cox-Ife also hints that Gilbert used a more psychological approach as well. He quotes a note from Gilbert's first draft of *The Wicked World,* a suggestion about the state of mind of one of the characters during a speech:

> The arguments used by Selene are urged with the most perfect modesty, though with a certain demure slyness and semi-consciousness that her arguments are to a certain extent specious and artificial.[16]

This aspect of Gilbert's methods was probably a fundamental part of his coaching of experienced and trusted actors, the "mimetic" approach being reserved for those who had yet to be molded into Gilbert's preferred shapes.

Any praise in Hesketh Pearson's assessments of Gilbert's work away from Sullivan is usually qualified at best, and the compliment in the following passage is backhanded, but it does contain an important point about Gilbert as stage manager.

> For the first time at a leading London theatre audiences were treated to performances that were as faultless as human ingenuity could make them. . . . He paid as much attention to the costumes, scenery, properties and lighting as to the grouping and interaction of the characters, and so complete was the illusion attained that his verse seemed poetic, his prose facile, his sentiments pleasing, his dramatis personae natural. The magnitude of his achievement can perhaps only be appreciated by those who have read his plays. But his influence on stagecraft was so great that he may be called the father of modern play-production.[17]

Pearson makes the plays seem worse than they are, and there is probably also some exaggeration in his assessment of Gilbert's importance as stage manager: Pearson's first priority was to make a clear-cut and reasonably amusing contrast between the two. But all the same there is much truth in what he tells us. The fairy comedies are dull things in the reading, and the success they achieved in the 1870s probably did owe much to the production values Gilbert imposed upon them.

It may seem something of an irrelevance to devote a whole chapter to Gilbert's ideas of stage management. It is an extra-literary influence: surely it is not essential to the study of the plays themselves. But the matter is not as simple as that. A play comes into full existence only in the theater, in performance, and the script is merely a convenient notation for it: in Stanley Wells's words, "to read a play is an artificial experience, akin to reading the score of an orchestral composition without hearing the sounds that it symbolises."[18] Gilbert wrote the scripts of his plays with very clear ideas about how they should be performed, and in most cases he made sure that they were performed in a way that conformed to his vision as closely as possible. Practical considerations mean that when I say I am discussing Gilbert's plays, I mean that I am discussing their printed embodiment, though this may fall far short of the original productions in which Gilbert's artistic vision reached their full flowering. But it is clearly vital that at least the broad aims of these productions should be mentioned. Pearson is entirely right to say that the way Gilbert produced his fairy comedies must have improved immeasurably on the mere flat print of their scripts, but should this be taken as an insult to Gilbert's abilities as a playwright? Some of the best poets of the Victorian era produced some of its worst plays: these were "closet dramas" that worked as things to be read rather than produced in the theater. But Gilbert was a man of the theater, and despite their literary pretensions the fairy comedies were primarily designed as plays to be seen, not read. It may be our loss that we can now experience them only as bald lines of dialogue unnaturally trapped in a book.

5

1877–1882—THE LAND WHERE
CONTRADICTIONS MEET

GILBERT'S PROFESSIONAL CAREER WAS NOT TRANSFORMED AS SOON AS HE began to collaborate with Sullivan: it took six or seven years for this aspect of his work to overshadow all others. Their first opera, *Thespis* (1871), had been a reasonable financial success but no more so than many of Gilbert's other dramatic works. It had been a respectable addition to his list of works but nothing more than that.

Trial by Jury (1875), it is true, had been a much more significant success. Though only a one-act piece, it had been rapturously received by audiences and critics. But, again, it must be asked whether this success altered the nature of Gilbert's career. The fact that he produced three more plays later that year—*Tom Cobb*, *Eyes and No Eyes*, and *Broken Hearts*—suggests at least that the change was not immediately felt. The impresario Richard D'Oyly Carte had been the commissioning force behind *Trial by Jury*, and, following its success, he certainly felt that he had in Gilbert and Sullivan a combination worth supporting. He had, apparently, nursed for some time the dream of creating a company devoted to the revival of English comic opera, and in 1874 he had suggested the idea to both Gilbert and Sullivan, but, as Carte later said, "it fell through because I was short of money."[1]

However, in 1876 Carte was able to establish the Comedy Opera Company, the first artistic fruit of which was the third Gilbert and Sullivan opera, *The Sorcerer* (1877). Apparently, Carte's original idea was for other composers and librettists to contribute works for the company, but, as it turned out, Gilbert and Sullivan pieces were to be the company's sole diet (except for one-act fillers) till the 1890s.

What did this venture of Carte's mean to Gilbert in 1877? The sheer audacity of the experiment cannot have escaped him: the survival of the Comedy Opera Company, not to mention the livelihoods of the specially picked cast, depended on *The Sorcerer*'s success. In these terms, at any rate, the opera must have been important to him, but it would be a mistake to suppose that he was thinking at this time in terms of a collaboration with Sullivan that would dominate his career. *Engaged* had been premiered in the previous month; he was, as a dramatist, at the peak of his powers and at the head of his profession. He was still very concerned with straight dramatic writing. If Carte's experiment failed, he did not want to find he had put all his eggs in that particular basket.

The Sorcerer was a success by the standard of the day, running for 178 performances; it was succeeded in 1878 by *H.M.S. Pinafore*, and one gets the impression from the standard accounts that Gilbert and Sullivan understood from the start that they were to supply Carte with another opera as soon as the first came off. In a contract between Carte, Gilbert, and Sullivan signed on 8 February 1883, Carte was given the power to demand an opera from the two collaborators at six months' notice,[2] but this appears to be merely the formal embodiment of what the three had been practicing for some time.

It is well known that *H.M.S. Pinafore* was not immediately successful and that early in its run many of the directors of the Comedy Opera Company were demanding that it be taken off, so shaky were the returns as a heat wave gripped London. If Carte had bowed under this pressure, what would have happened? It is conceivable that the company would have collapsed, to be remembered only as an interesting artistic experiment, in which case Gilbert would have turned his mature dramatic skills in some other direction. But of course *H.M.S. Pinafore* succeeded to a remarkable extent (571 performances), and "Pinafore-mania" soon gripped not only Britain but also many American cities.

The game of "what-if" is interesting but barren; I do not play it here merely to engage in pointless speculation. I wish to make an important point, which is that the success of *H.M.S. Pinafore* was the turning point in Gilbert's career. Before it, Carte's venture was interesting and had important possibilities but was full of the possibility of failure. With *H.M.S. Pinafore* the company, and the team of Gilbert and Sullivan, became an international success: it suddenly became inevitable that they should follow it up with another opera. With the success of *H.M.S. Pinafore* the nature of the collaboration's future became at least conceivable. And it is also demonstrably true that after *H.M.S. Pinafore* the collaboration with Sullivan came to dominate Gilbert's career. Between *H.M.S. Pinafore* in 1878 and *The Gondoliers* in 1889, Gilbert collaborated with Sullivan on nine operas, but produced only four original plays apart from him. Gilbert had written six original plays in the two years separating *Trial by Jury* and *The Sorcerer*.

Several important questions arise from this. Bearing in mind the importance of the issues depending on the success of each opera—the livelihood of the cast, the profits to be shared by the triumvirate, and so on—were Gilbert's artistic ideals compromised? Did the nature of his pieces change during this period, and, if so, how, and for what reasons, and with what result?

I do not expect to find simple or clear-cut answers to such questions, nor do I expect to confine my investigations to the finding of such answers, but I feel that they may be useful questions to ask if I am to explore the overall nature of these operas.

There is another question I feel I must address first, which is: Why did *H.M.S. Pinafore* succeed where *The Sorcerer*, comparatively speaking, failed? Both had the same librettist and composer, largely the same cast, and even essentially the same central theme: so why the difference in the way they were received?

THE SUCCESS OF *H.M.S. Pinafore*

Many of the melodramas of the early to mid-Victorian period contained an unmistakable sympathy with the "common people" and a distrust of those with power and money. Michael R. Booth notes: "Melodrama clearly reflects class hatreds. Villains tend to be noblemen, factory owners, squires; heroes peasants, able seamen, and workmen."[3] It is saturated with the assumption that wealth brings with it evil and that poverty is invariably honest.

There is also, throughout all forms of popular Victorian theater, the assumption that money, rank, and power are as nothing when set alongside love. "Love levels all ranks," as Captain Corcoran states virtuously in *H.M.S. Pinafore*,[4] and this is the maxim that is satirically explored in both *H.M.S. Pinafore* and *The Sorcerer*. Alexis, *The Sorcerer*'s dangerously fanatical "hero," exclaims: "Oh that the world would break down the artificial barriers of rank, wealth, education, age, beauty, habits, taste, and temper, and recognize the glorious principle, that in marriage alone is to be found the panacea for every ill!"[5]

This passage makes it clear that Gilbert did not share such popular assumptions. Both operas seem to be intended, at least at one level, as complete demolitions of the idea. In *The Sorcerer* we have Alexis Pointdextre, the son of the local squire, who is so determined to impose on the village his own notions of egalitarian marriage that he distributes among everyone a strong love potion. A large number of absurd mismatches result, and affairs can be returned to a bearable complexion only by the death of the sorcerer who administered the potion. Alexis, who is at the start merely a zealot, becomes an obnoxious fanatic in the second act: he is revolted when his father, Sir Marmaduke, falls in love with the pew opener Mrs. Partlet, under the influence of the potion. Alexis insists that his betrothed, Aline, should make sure of her love for him by drinking the potion also: when she refuses on the grounds that "my love can never, never change,"[6] he spurns her.

The point Gilbert is making could hardly be clearer. He believes that the idea of social equality is unworkable. He presents Alexis as not only a fanatic but also a hypocrite; Gilbert believes that by presenting us with these ill-sorted couples he is irrefutably demonstrating the absurdity of the idea of Love the Leveller.

However, this hardly appears to be the case from a modern perspective: we find it difficult to see why it is axiomatically absurd that a baronet should marry a pew opener. Other elements in the plot cloud the picture, such as a young woman forcibly in love with a doddery old notary: the woman, Constance, avows love and revulsion for him alternately. Clearly this is a situation that has no relevance outside the confines of an impossible plot about love potions.

But the most important thing to notice about this plot is that its sympathies are unmistakably middle class. The notion of egalitarianism is laughed out of court, and the existing social structure is defended by demonstrating the anarchy of the alternative. Passages such as the following probably did not do much to endear the opera to the people of the gallery:

> *Alexis.* . . . Still I have made some converts to the principle, that men and women should be coupled in matrimony without distinction of rank. I have lectured on the subject at Mechanics' Institutes, and the mechanics were unanimous in favour of my views. I have preached in workhouses, beer-shops, and lunatic asylums, and I have been received with enthusiasm. I have addressed navvies on the advantages that would accrue to them if they married wealthy ladies of rank, and not a navvy dissented.
> *Aline.* Noble fellows! And yet there are those who hold that the uneducated classes are not open to argument! And what do the countesses say?
> *Alexis.* Why, at present, it can't be denied, the aristocracy hold aloof.
> *Aline.* The working man is the true Intelligence, after all!
> *Alexis.* He is a noble creature when he is quite sober.[7]

All support for the idea of breaking down the class divisions is presented as a matter of crude self-interest. This may be a legitimate argument to put forward, in terms of satirical caricature, but by deliberately defying a universal assumption of popular drama, by ridiculing it, and by seeming to ridicule his working-class audience, Gilbert was alienating that audience and shutting himself off from their support.

Gilbert was one of the generation of dramatists making the dangerous attempt to elevate the drama—suiting it to middle-class taste while at the same time keeping the support of the "lower orders." Naturally, he did not always succeed in getting the formula just right, and *The Sorcerer* may be considered one of these partial failures. It was a delicate balance that had to be struck, as Gilbert himself acknowledged:

> A man who sets to work to cater for the entertainment of theatrical audiences is in the position of a refreshment contractor who has engaged to supply a meal of one dish at which all classes of the community are to sit down. What should that dish be? It must not be *suprême de caille* or it will be regarded as insipid by the butcher-boy in the gallery. It must not be baked sheep's head or it will disgust the epicure in the stalls. It must, I suppose, be some dish that will fit the gastronomic mean of the audience, and I take it that that gastronomic mean will be somewhere in the neighbourhood of rump-steak and oyster sauce.[8]

The "gastronomic mean" may not have been fully achieved in *The Sorcerer*, but I take it that *H.M.S. Pinafore* succeeded in achieving it to a much greater extent. *The Sorcerer* had been well received by the critics, and a run of 178 performances was certainly not to be sniffed at, but *H.M.S. Pinafore* was an undeniably *popular* success as *The Sorcerer* was not. *H.M.S. Pinafore*'s tunes were the staple of the barrel organs, its catchphrases the pestilence of two continents. After a shaky start in London its success became so great that for a short time London boasted two rival productions simultaneously. Its success in the United States is legendary: the lack of international copyright law meant that dozens of American "pirate" productions were able to flourish without the opera's authors being able to do anything about it—except, in time, to take their "official" version to New York themselves. And the question must be repeated: Why did it take hold so certainly over those two countries?

"Love levels all ranks": we remain on familiar territory here. *The Sorcerer* had been set in the traditional rural idyll of English ballad opera, a setting that, though familiar, was perhaps vaguely felt to be a little insipid. But in *H.M.S. Pinafore* Gilbert managed to tap in to the much more

The plot of *H.M.S. Pinafore* reaches its climax. (The Raymond Mander and Joe Mitchenson Theatre Collection.)

vigorous tradition of nautical melodrama. He was intimately familiar with the conventions of the genre and was able to manipulate them to his own ends, but he was unable to prevent the conventions from, to some extent, manipulating him.

The opera's plot is very simple in essence. Ralph Rackstraw, a humble topman on board *H.M.S. Pinafore*, is in love with Josephine Corcoran, the daughter of the ship's captain. However, Captain Corcoran wants his daughter to marry Sir Joseph Porter, the First Lord of the Admiralty. Ralph persuades Josephine to elope with him, but the lovers are caught by both the Captain and Sir Joseph before they can leave the ship. Ralph is imprisoned, and all seems hopeless; but it is suddenly revealed that Ralph and Captain Corcoran were exchanged as babies, so that, in Sir Joseph's words, "Ralph is really the Captain, and the Captain is Ralph."[9] Sir Joseph refuses to marry Josephine, who is now the daughter of a topman, but Captain Rackstraw (as Ralph now calls himself) remains eager to marry her, and all ends happily.

It must be said, first of all, that this is not a typical nautical-melodrama plot, at least as described by Booth: more usually the dashing young sailor would have been in love with a woman of his own class and the woman threatened with the attentions of a high-ranked villain (for instance, see Douglas Jerrold's *Black-Ey'd Susan*). But the plot of *H.M.S. Pinafore* is, nonetheless, of a highly traditional type, the love of a common man for a woman of high social station being one of the commonplace elements in the well-made play. (The baby-swapping revelations of the last minutes come from the same stable.)

There is a recognizable line of descent from Gilbert's parody-reviews in *Fun:* the story is, in itself, a mere succession of conventions and clichés, but Gilbert handles the story in such a way as to highlight the assumptions behind the conventions and to demonstrate their absurdity. The treatment of class issues is much more sophisticated than in *The Sorcerer:* in *H.M.S. Pinafore* he takes the commonplaces of the old melodramas and of the well-made play, and he fashions from them a strictly logical debate on the subject of equality, while in *The Sorcerer* he had confined himself to a directed attack against the character of a single, invented humbug.

At the beginning of *H.M.S. Pinafore* we are presented with a happy, united crew watched over by a benevolent Captain. The social order is firmly maintained, and though the common sailor Ralph is in love with Josephine, and she with him, they seem resigned to suffering in silence. The only thing that disturbs this stability is the visit of Sir Joseph Porter, who insists that "a British sailor is any man's equal, excepting mine"[10] and distributes among the crew a song "designed to encourage independence of thought and action in the lower branches of the service."[11] The song ("A British tar is a soaring soul, / As free as a mountain bird!")[12] hits the crew like revolutionary propaganda: "Sir Joseph has explained our true position to us,"[13] as Ralph exclaims.[14]

Sir Joseph's ideas may have been completely unfamiliar to the crew, but to anyone with even a passing acquaintance with the theater of the day, they would have seemed old friends. The melodramatic figure of the British tar thrived on such sentiments. He was a combination of heroic bravery and apparently unlimited freedom of action: he might profess loyalty to his captain, but his personal sense of right was always the final arbiter (as in *Black-Ey'd Susan*). Booth quotes a line from Andrew Campbell's melodrama *Rule Britannia* (1836): "we've taught our enemies never to be sure of victory when they have to deal with Jack Tars whose song is 'Rule Britannia' and whose watch-word is Nelson."[15] The song "A British Tar is a Soaring Soul" is only a slight exaggeration of such flag-waving boastfulness. However, Gilbert makes one important change from the melodramatic attitude: while in most such pieces the aggression of the bold sailor was directed against foreign tyrants, Sir Joseph's songs and catchwords are framed so that they apply more to the tyranny of the tar's own superiors.

(Charles Hayter, discussing "A British Tar is a Soaring Soul," argues precisely the opposite, that the tyrants and dictators it refers to are by implication foreigners and that this suggests a shift from the class resentment visible in earlier melodrama.[16] But I believe this is to misunderstand the nature of the beast. In the early Victorian nautical melodramas simple patriotism was the predominant note, and the British Navy was considered axiomatically invincible. Therefore it was not thought politic to criticize the structure of the navy or to demonize its higher ranks. Though Captain Crosstree in *Black-Ey'd Susan* is the villain, he is clearly marked as an exception to the virtuous rule. What is more, Gilbert's sailors *do* take the tyrants and dictators to mean their superiors within the navy.)

And so, as Captain Corcoran later observes in bewilderment, "my kindly crew rebel":[17] taking Sir Joseph's axioms to heart, Ralph and Josephine decide to elope. The only dissentient voice is that of the sailor Dick Deadeye, the crew's "truth-teller," universally hated because of his deformity and his unfortunate name. It is Dick who observes, "When people have to obey other people's orders, equality's out of the question,"[18] to which all the other sailors reply, "Horrible! horrible!," recoiling at the hideous notion.

Their attitude is best expressed in their chorus:

> Shall we submit? Are we but slaves?
> Love comes alike to high and low—
> Britannia's sailors rule the waves,
> And shall they stoop to insult? No![19]

Only one thing more needs to be said concerning Gilbert's use of melodramatic conventions to support Ralph's claim to be treated as an equal. When he is caught trying to elope with Josephine, he brings out his trump card, the ultimate defense for all his actions:

> I, humble, poor, and lowly born,
> The meanest in the port division—
> The butt of epauletted scorn—
> The mark of quarter-deck derision—
> Have dared to raise my wormy eyes
> Above the dust to which you'd mould me,
> In manhood's glorious pride to rise.
> I am an Englishman—behold me![20]

He is a British tar, and therefore a soaring soul, and any man's equal excepting Sir Joseph's; but he is also an Englishman, and that justifies all.

All these arguments are presented to us in a skeptical spirit and given that extra twist that makes them absurd: for instance, the Boatswain argues that Ralph can claim his nationality as a virtue because "in spite of all temptations / To belong to other nations, / He remains an Englishman!"[21] And it is made clear that Sir Joseph's catchwords are to be dismissed because they come from Sir Joseph.

Significantly, in both *The Sorcerer* and *H.M.S. Pinafore* the source of the egalitarian sentiments that create the main difficulties of the plot is a member of the ruling class, rather than a disgruntled "common man." Gilbert's working people are generally content with their lot until disturbed by the beliefs of misguided superiors. Sir Joseph is, like Disraeli, a self-made man who worships his creator. He has proved to himself that there is no barrier to advancement if you set your mind to it and never go to sea; he has come to the conclusion that all men are equal but makes an exception in his own case. In short, he proves throughout that his opinion is not to be trusted. Like Alexis, he is a prig, a snob, and a hypocrite.

It seems clear that Gilbert's own position in the debate is Dick Deadeye's: "When people have to obey other people's orders, equality's out of the question."[22] Certainly the opposing view, set out by Sir Joseph and taken up by Ralph, is consistently held up to ridicule. And yet Ralph is the hero of the opera: his intention of marrying Josephine may be foolish and destructive to the fabric of social order, but there is never any doubt that he and Josephine will end up paired at the final curtain. The logic of Gilbert's argument would have resulted in the opera ending with Ralph's arrest: at this point the way is set for the restoration of order on the ship. But though Gilbert is ridiculing the conventions, the conventions are also to some extent controlling what he is allowed to do. He must perform a swift and convincing volte-face in order to satisfy the taste of the town.

The ending of the opera is deliberately absurd: if the Captain and Ralph were really exchanged as babies, then Josephine must logically be a generation younger than Ralph, and Ralph must be somewhat older than the dashing young fellow he always is in performance. It is an obvious artifice that glories in its own improbability, and as such it tells the audience not to believe it.

At the same time, however, the resolution of the plot also ties up the theme of equality that has gone through the opera. Sir Joseph had told the Captain in the first act: "I cannot permit these noble fellows to be patronized because an accident of birth has placed you above them and them below you."[23] So what more appropriate than that everything should be resolved by another accident of birth? It reduces to absurdity the whole idea of a class system based on birth.

But the satire also works in the opposite direction: the Captain, now a common sailor, makes one last-ditch attempt to save the marriage of his daughter to Sir Joseph:

> *Sir Joseph.* So it seems that you were Ralph, and Ralph was you.
> *Captain.* Yes, your honour.
> *Sir Joseph.* Well, I need not tell you that after this change in your condition, a marriage with your daughter will be out of the question.
> *Captain.* Don't say that, your honour—love levels all ranks.
> *Sir Joseph.* It does to a considerable extent, but it does not level them as much as that.[24]

The point is driven home one last time: the supporters of the ideal of equality cannot bear to see the principle applied to themselves.

So what do we have? We have an opera that uses all the conventions of melodrama and ridicules them, but in the end it is difficult to see which has won out, the conventions or the ridicule. Gilbert's satire appeals to the head, and it supports the existing social order: for both these reasons it appeals to the educated middle class in the stalls. But the melodramatic techniques, still living under Gilbert's dissecting knife, appeal strongly to the emotions and champion the downtrodden people: and for both these reasons they appeal to the working-class people in the gallery. Of course this is not to say that the stalls would not have been pulled along by the emotional force of the melodrama, or that the gallery would not have thoroughly enjoyed the jokes at the expense of Sir Joseph: I am merely suggesting overall tendencies.

Rump steak and oyster sauce? It is a slightly belittling phrase, but it is certainly true that in *H.M.S. Pinafore* Gilbert discovered a way of appealing to all classes. It was not a simple or simplistic formula, nor was it one that would be easy to repeat as a deliberate policy, but it is surely clear that, by some chance, Gilbert had managed to get something extraordinarily right. And the facts of the case suggest that it was something he and Sullivan were to continue getting right for the next decade.

The Land Where Contradictions Meet

In chapter 3, I emphasized the idea that Gilbert's use of inverting techniques such as irony was largely satirical, not escapist, in intent, and that these techniques were used to express a single, simple meaning: inversion reveals the truth. I described this as "The World Turned Right Side Up."

However, I have also hinted at another idea—that of ambiguity: the idea that in various ways the plays express the contradictory and warring impulses in Gilbert's mind. I have emphasized his impulses toward the respectable and the disrespectful and suggested that he was caught between two ages, looking simultaneously forward and backward. I now want to develop this idea, using my analysis of *H.M.S. Pinafore* as a starting point. While not dismissing the idea of "The World Turned Right Side Up," I want to suggest that the full picture is more complex than this might imply, that Gilbert's attitudes to the things that he seemed to be condemning was often ambiguous—that we can often see a half-suppressed sympathy for them. This sympathy, I shall argue, makes itself evident in several ways but most obviously by the use of techniques of inversion, which allow Gilbert to present two opposing views at one and the same time.

Gilbert did not invent this idea with *H.M.S. Pinafore*, but in it the idea receives its most sophisticated treatment so far. We saw a glimpse of it in the epilogue to *The Pretty Druidess*; it was implied in the contrast between *The Wicked World* and *The Happy Land*. It was quite clearly stated in *Princess Toto*, which dates from only two years before *H.M.S. Pinafore*.

But it is only in the mature style of the main Savoy operas that the idea is fully elaborated.

For instance, to stay with the convenient example of *H.M.S. Pinafore*, Gilbert took the accepted conventions of popular drama and held them up to ridicule, but by the act of using the conventions he was tapping into the emotional force that is the mainstay of their appeal, and we seem to witness the rare sight of someone succeeding in having his cake and eating it too.

As if to acknowledge this uncertainty of meaning, Sullivan scored an alternative ending to the opera—seemingly for a revival in 1887—so that the final bars consisted of a rousing chorus of "Rule Britannia."[25] It is not definitely known whether this version was used officially throughout the revival or whether it was scored merely for use on royal occasions, but Booth notes that "Rule Britannia" was "a tune concluding many nautical melodramas."[26] Its use throughout the 1887 revival might, therefore, have been justified on artistic terms as a final nod to the conventions it was satirizing. But there is no overt satire in Sullivan's use of it: it is pure flag-waving patriotism. It sounds odd beside the derisive tone of "He Is an Englishman."

Yet even "He Is an Englishman" has its share of ambiguity—particularly set to Sullivan's stirring music. That the song is intended as satire most Gilbert-and-Sullivan writers acknowledge; yet their attitude is sometimes oddly difficult to gauge. For instance, Ian Bradley says it "belongs to a clutch of fervently nationalistic songs in the Savoy Operas,"[27] and it is not clear if he is merely entering into the spirit of the irony or whether he actually means what he says. And Hayter gives it as an example of the "sincere patriotic sentiment"[28] that he sees running through the opera.

(It may be useful to clarify Gilbert's own attitude to the song. When he wrote a prose retelling of the opera for children in 1908, he followed the words of the song with this comment: "Speaking for myself, I do not quite see that Ralph Rackstraw deserved so very much credit for remaining an Englishman, considering that no one seems ever to have proposed to him that he should be anything else, but the crew thought otherwise and I daresay they were right.")[29]

"He Is an Englishman": satire or celebration? It may seem like an easy abdication to reply, "Both," but I believe it is the only really honest reply possible. That it is primarily intended as a devastating parody of a certain kind of patriotic song is surely undeniable, but Sullivan's setting, and Gilbert's careful building up of two of the musical scenes to conclude with reprises of the song, suggest a deliberate playing up of the patriotic frisson that it also provides.

But parody of the dramatic conventions is only one of the techniques of Gilbert's writings that suggest ambiguity or contradiction. For instance, there is the matter of his use of irony: for Gilbert was, first and foremost, an ironist. His comic theory depended on his characters saying in all innocence things that laid bare their character to the audience: they revealed their iniquities by trying to conceal them. Let me take one last example from *H.M.S. Pinafore*.

The portrait of Sir Joseph Porter is painted in the most ironic colors: he condemns himself with every word he utters. And, like many another Savoy opera figure, he even goes so far as to condemn himself in song. Max Keith Sutton has this to say of Sir Joseph's song "When I Was a Lad":

> When Sir Joseph Porter stops the action of *H.M.S. Pinafore* to tell the story of his professional success, he at once characterizes himself and deepens the work's satiric themes. His shameless egotism—"I always voted at my party's call, / And I never thought of thinking for myself at all"—makes him sound like a captive of the Palace of Truth. He is so under the spell of his self-importance that he has lost all sense of his absurdity.[30]

The song is a classic piece of Gilbertian irony: Gilbert certainly intended his audience to understand that Sir Joseph does not realize he is revealing his personality so very frankly. Yet it is still possible to see the song in a very different light, as Alan Fischler demonstrates:

> Gilbert took special care to assure these audiences that his civic magistrates—and, by implication, theirs—were not lacking in self-knowledge. His chief means of doing so became the autobiographical songs which play so prominent a part in the fame of the Savoy operas. . . . each magisterial autobiographer makes a fully voluntary confession of the flaws in his temperament, gaps in his knowledge, and deficiencies of his professional background. . . . "When I was a lad" . . . cheerfully confesses that his [Sir Joseph's] promotion to "Ruler of the Queen's Navee" had nothing whatsoever to do with intellectual acuteness or knowledge of matters nautical.[31]

It is surprising that Fischler should read Gilbert's text in this way, but the fact that a serious academic writer on Gilbert should be able to interpret the song like this does suggest at least some degree of real ambiguity in the original.

After all, what is irony in essence? It is saying one thing and meaning the opposite. Such a technique, extensively applied, may legitimately be

A self-caricature by W. S. Gilbert. (The Pierpont Morgan Library, New York.)

interpreted as indicating a half-suppressed liking for the thing supposedly ironized: the surface meaning of an ironic comment need not always be dismissed out of hand.

Gilbert once drew a self-caricature to give to a child from a neighboring family and surrounded it with brief confessions such as "I loathe everybody," "I love to bully," "I hate my fellow-man," and "I am an ill-tempered pig, & I glory in it." Clearly these confessions were intended as nothing more than a playing up to the dark side of Gilbert's public image; there is a distinct implication that by drawing the caricature he was disproving the image. But, though we would be wise not to swallow this public image whole, we may suspect that Gilbert was being a little over-defensive in his response to it, and that the confessions above quoted may be considered, at one level, as statements Gilbert feared might be true but which he was only able to own up to on the understanding that they were not to be believed.

His theory of comic acting—serious manner, absurd content—can also have a confusing effect. It pushes onto the audience the full burden of recognizing the absurdity of events, and as such it fails to cover the possibility that the audience may not fully understand that something absurd is happening. For instance, Gilbert's exaggerations of the melodramatic conventions are sometimes quite subtle, and, bearing in mind the idiocies that the audiences of real melodrama were apparently willing to swallow, it would not be surprising to learn that Gilbert's parodies might sometimes have been taken quite seriously. In the end we get to the point where, in *Utopia, Limited* (1893), many competent Gilbert-and-Sullivan writers are not quite sure whether the song "A Wonderful Joy Our Eyes to Bless" is meant ironically. Leslie Baily says that this song in praise of the "bright and beautiful English girl" "is set to quite serious music—but can it really be taken seriously?,"[32] while Isaac Goldberg has to insist, "He meant these lines."[33] This is still a matter of doubt, though personally I agree with Goldberg that the song is entirely serious in intent. The important thing to note is that Gilbert here reaches a point where no one is quite sure what he means. Ambiguity can scarcely be more clearly displayed.

Gilbert's notorious fondness for topsy-turvy ideas may also be thought of as partly a way of reconciling contradictory ideas. His play *Topseyturveydom* is, awkwardly, both a satire and a fantasy. The land of Topseyturveydom is and is not England: it is familiar and alien, a confrontation and an escape. This technique implies that the pessimistic view of English political life it suggests need not be taken quite seriously. Why, of course Topseyturveydom is corrupt: it is the opposite of England. But as Crapolee warns Satis at the beginning of the play: "Extremes meet and the difference may not be so great as you suppose."[34] Nothing is certain in Gilbert's world of inversions.

Most serious academic study of Gilbert in the past has concentrated on explicating the dominant themes of his plays—as might be expected. A little close examination of the plays generally reveals a clear intention of exposing the folly of certain modes of thought: by the strict use of logic he reveals the absurdity of commonly accepted notions. Naturally those who admire Gilbert are primarily concerned with saving him from those who have insisted for the past century that the Savoy operas are rollicking entertainments and no more than that. Mary Watkins Waters has argued that Gilbert's main artistic problem was the discovery of a "satiric method" that would ridicule the errors of the age without alienating his audience;[35] Sutton has argued that, by examining and ridiculing the fantasies of the age, Gilbert proved himself a genuine and radical satirist.[36] But others have argued precisely the opposite, that Gilbert's success lay in confirming, rather than questioning, the prejudices of his middle-class audience: for instance, Regina Kirby Higgins in "Victorian Laughter: The Comic Operas of Gilbert and Sullivan" or Fischler in *Modified Rapture*. I am more inclined to think of him as a radical satirist than as a conservative soother; yet the fact that a case can be made for both sides of the matter is significant.

That there were contradictions in aspects of Gilbert's position has certainly been noticed before. Thus Hesketh Pearson observes: "In the sentimentality of *Broken Hearts* Gilbert expressed the obverse of the savagery in *The Bab Ballads,* and each reveals the seeming contradiction in his own behaviour. His violence masked weakness, his tenderness melted rancour."[37] And many have puzzled over the problem of how Gilbert, who scoffed at the melodramatic conventions so incisively in his comic pieces, could bear to use those conventions, without irony, in his serious plays.

Goldberg, in particular, emphasizes the contradictions that were reconciled in Gilbert: "A living paradox, he was, prototype of the hundreds that he invented. Consider this hale and hearty Englishman, tyrant of the backstage, martinet of rehearsals, scenic realist down to the tiniest detail, superintending these workaday jobs with a head populated by fairies."[38] A little later he says: "He sways in a limbo between the two [i.e., prose and poetry], even as he sways between satire and sentimentality, between the precepts of morality and the liberation of beauty, between melodrama and operetta."[39]

However, as far as I know there has been no systematic attempt to examine the extent to which the conscious meaning of Gilbert's plays implies an opposite meaning, or the nature of this contradiction, or the implications that arise from it. It is my intention in this chapter and in chapter 7 to make such an attempt by examining the Gilbert and Sullivan operas premiered from 1878 to 1889—those pieces that Fischler calls the "high Savoy operas."

Pirates TO *Iolanthe:* THE METHOD REFINED

Why did the "high Savoy operas" succeed? Of course Gilbert did everything in his power to make sure they did so, but it does not follow that he made a conscious effort to reproduce in these operas ambiguities similar to the ones we can see in *H.M.S. Pinafore*. It is very easy to show that these ambiguities were a real part of his outlook on the world—perhaps more so at this point than in the earlier part of his career.

His article "A Hornpipe in Fetters" (1879) makes odd reading. It is ostensibly an attack on the stultifying censorship that he believed was holding back the development of a "national drama"; and yet he also defends the restrictions that this censorship imposed on the drama—and is apparently quite sincere in doing so.

He notes that in English drama "no married man . . . may be in love with anybody but his wife, and, in like manner, no single lady may see any charm in a married man,"[40] and he outlines a typical example of the rather anodyne drama that results from these restrictions. He concludes that this "is a kind of plot that may possibly be made faintly interesting, but cannot be compared in dramatic value with plots of the unpleasant but exciting class to which *Frou Frou* and *Le Supplice d'une Femme* belong."[41] He seems equally dissatisfied with the conventions of both French and English drama—the French, because it is "unpleasant" and the English, because it is "tame." The last paragraph of this short article shows him trying to hold these two opposing ideas in a sane balance:

> I have not a word to say against the restrictions on conjugal infidelity imposed by our dramatic common law upon English writers of original pieces. It is, on the whole, a good and wholesome law, and while it exists our drama may be dull, but will not be seriously degraded. But in estimating the dramatic value of the original plays of one country as compared with the original plays of the other, it is only fair that the restrictions imposed upon English authors of original pieces should be fully and fairly considered.[42]

In the end he endorses English drama as against the French, but the tone is scarcely ringing. He seems to consider it, on balance, the less bad of the two—dull but not degraded. His denouncing of the immoral French drama does not seem ironic. Contrast this with the praise he had given the French theater in "A Stage Play" (1873). His attitude toward it now, in 1879, is much less positive, and he finds himself trapped uneasily between French licentiousness and English prudery, trying to find a way of balancing the two. The obvious solution to his difficulty would be to find a third course—to discover how to write drama that would be neither dull nor degraded. It would be very easy to show that this is, in fact, what Gilbert had managed to do in his best plays, but the significant point is that this article does not seem even to consider such a possibility.

It is, I think, legitimate to see in this article the midpoint of a larger change in Gilbert's views, from the mainly "radical" Gilbert of the early plays to the largely "Tory" Gilbert of later life. When Gilbert gave evidence on stage censorship before a joint committee of Lords and Commons in 1909, he related the case of *The Happy Land* and added, "My maturer judgment is that the interference [of the Lord Chamberlain] was absolutely justified."[43] This is a far cry from the Gilbert who had written a public letter to *The Era* in 1872 stating that "Mr Donne [the examiner of plays] has, on three occasions, taken objection to passages in my plays. . . . I have systematically declined to take the slightest notice of his instructions."[44]

We can see the tendency of Gilbert's change in opinions, and a very unsurprising tendency it is, too. He was becoming richer, more "respectable," more satisfied with his position in life. His opinions were never so simple to define, however: we can see reactionary tendencies in his early writings and almost revolutionary ones in some of his later writings. But the proportions in which these different impulses were mixed changed with the years, and at about this time, just after the success of *H.M.S. Pinafore*, the mix was more or less equally balanced between the two.

Gilbert was born in 1836, of a generation that was to grow up in the early Victorian atmosphere of moral absolutes, of that grim steadiness of purpose that Samuel Butler, born in 1835, was to stigmatize as "earnestness." This was the generation that came to maturity at the moment when the ignited bomb of Darwin's *Origin of Species* (1859) was thrown into the cultural mix; when the horrors of Crimea (1853–56) and the pessimism of Omar Khayyám (Fitzgerald translation: 1859) suggested that the early Victorian scheme of things was, in some vague way, not enough. Broadly speaking these doubts came to full bloom in English culture in the 1870s: not properly assimilated or consistently expressed but definable all the same.

We have the case of Samuel Butler, for instance, who wrote in *Erewhon* (1872) of a land whose inhabitants held beliefs that were ridiculous partly because they were so similar to English beliefs and partly because they were utterly different. Butler's *The Fair Haven* (1873) was ostensibly a defense of Christianity, written in the voice of an invented writer, a skeptic turned believer named John Pickard Owen, whereas Butler himself, a believer turned skeptic, intended it as a satire on such Christian apologetics. And *Life and Habit* (1877), a serious book on evolution, contains this startling avowal: "when I began to write upon my subject I did not seriously believe in it. I saw, as it were, a pebble upon the ground, with a sheen that pleased me. . . ."[45] Butler and Gilbert were two very different men who led very different lives, but the works of both have in them this quality of inversion, of straight-faced irony, of uncertainty of meaning. Butler, like Gilbert, seemed to be struggling with ideas that he could neither reject nor wholly accept. These two men had not been given the permission to believe in nothing, which came only with the nineties, and, caught between two ages, neither could decide which way to go. They were dissatisfied with the ground on which they stood and the path by which they had reached that spot, but they feared the abyss which they saw yawning in front of them.

This chapter is mainly concerned with Gilbert's collaborations with Sullivan, which dominated Gilbert's work during this period, but I must say a word or two here about his verse tragedy *Gretchen* (1879). This was the play into which he put most of his creative effort in 1878. He later told an interviewer: "I took immense pains over my 'Gretchen,' but it only ran a fortnight. I wrote it to please myself, and not the public."[46] Bearing in mind the intellectual uncertainties that I have suggested were assailing Gilbert at this time, we ought to be able to find in *Gretchen* at least some reflection of these concerns.

The plot is a variation on the Faust myth, adapted to Gilbert's own ends via Goethe. Faustus is, at the beginning of the play, a monk who is repenting of his vows. He had once been a soldier and had loved a woman, but she had left him for a wealthier man, and Faustus, disillusioned with women and the world, became a monk in order to escape from both. But he now realizes that he is living a hollow sham, and he craves the real life of the world though still hopelessly disillusioned with it. He seeks the example of a truly pure woman, and the Devil (here called Mephisto) shows him a vision of such a woman—Gretchen.

Faustus returns to the world to find her, and when he has done so, they find themselves irresistibly drawn to each other, and Faustus is torn between love for her and the knowledge that to go down that path would mean corrupting her. Of course they end up in each other's arms. Three months later she is apparently pregnant by him; he confesses that he has taken the monastic vow, and she, horrified, tells him to leave her and return to his bride, "thy Church."[47] In the usual manner of Victorian heroines, she falls seriously ill because of her sin; she dies at the end of the fourth act in a wave of highly sentimental forgiveness.

Gretchen is not a good play, and it contains much that is conventional, but the character of Faustus himself is very interesting. In act 1 he is presented to us as a shattered cynic (which it is very tempting to associate with Gilbert's own public image), dissatisfied with the moral absolutes of the church and also with the realities of the world. He can only see things in negative terms: he craves a symbol of real, positive goodness. When he finds such a symbol in Gretchen and tries to show his appreciation of her goodness, he succeeds only in corrupting her. Faustus is a man to whom there is no correct course: everything he does is wrong, and he can only ricochet between the church and the world in the vain search for peace. That he finally finds it when Gretchen forgives him, with the implicit promise that he will devote the rest of his life to "faith, and truth, and works of charity,"[48] is an unsatisfactory solution because there is no reason to believe that, if Faustus could not be held to that course before, he will be able to do it now. But, discounting the ending, we can see in Faustus an interestingly ambiguous figure—sympathetic but flawed and confused. Gilbert is trying to escape the moral absolutes of most Victorian drama, though it must be repeated that the play as a whole is much less satisfactory than his comic plays, in which the moral absolutes are also blurred.

In 1879, *H.M.S. Pinafore* became an unauthorized success in the United States. Gilbert, Sullivan, and Carte decided to take an official company over to the States themselves and earn a little from the opera's popularity there. And it was in the middle of this visit that at the Fifth Avenue Theatre in New York they premiered their new joint opera: *The Pirates of Penzance.*

The central theme of *The Pirates of Penzance* is that most "earnest" of ideas, sense of duty: the nominal hero, Frederic, lives his life entirely by "sense of duty's stern dictation"[49]—at the expense of personal advantage, ordinary morality, and human compassion. Thus, having been mistakenly apprenticed to a pirate as a child, he has been duty-bound to work out the term of his indentures, despite his personal abhorrence of the crimes he has had to commit in the meantime.

It is pretty clear that the idea of duty (as expounded, for instance, by Samuel Smiles) is here being held up to complete ridicule: Gilbert is showing us, by reductio ad absurdum, that sense of duty is not, by itself, a sufficient guide to conduct.

There are obvious similarities between Frederic and Alexis of *The Sorcerer:* both are zealots for an absurd ideal—an ideal that the action of the opera thoroughly discredits. But there is at least one significant difference between them, in that Frederic is prepared to suffer for his ideals but Alexis is not. When it is pointed out to him that he has been indentured as a pirate until his twenty-first birthday and that, having been born on a leap-year day, this will not happen until 1940, he accepts with stoicism the prospect of a life of crime that he detests. He also accepts the fact that he will have to wait more than sixty years before he is free to marry his loved one, Mabel. Alexis, as we have seen, objected to the egalitarian ideal being applied to his own family.

Gilbert and Sullivan were interviewed as soon as they arrived in New York, and they gave out a few hints about the new opera: "It's a sort of *reductio ad absurdum* of melodrama," Gilbert said,[50] while Sullivan said that it was the story of a modern Zampa, "of pirates and escapades of 200 years ago, which, if dressed up in our modern clothes, must seem very absurd."[51] Thus the Pirate King says of Frederic that "a keener hand at scuttling a Cunarder or cutting out a White Star never shipped a handspike."[52]

As in *H.M.S. Pinafore*, an issue of contemporary interest is investigated against the background of parody of a kind of melodrama. Yet the tone is very different: while in *H.M.S. Pinafore* Gilbert presented us, at the most conscious level, with a middle-class argument about the necessity of a stratified society, throughout *The Pirates of Penzance* a much more anti-authoritarian note is consistently sounded. Of course the Pirate King is a pure parody of the old melodramatic figure, but the parody is very affectionate: we feel that Gilbert is on his side because, whatever his faults, he is not a hypocrite. As the Pirate King says: "I don't think much of our profession, but, contrasted with respectability, it is comparatively honest."[53] And when he bursts into song, it is to sing:

> Oh, better far to live and die
> Under the brave black flag I fly,
> Than play a sanctimonious part
> With a pirate head and a pirate heart.[54]

Gilbert's "Bab" illustration for "The Policeman's Lot".

This sounds like a simple extension of a certain kind of bandit character who can be found in some early "Gothic" melodramas: for instance, Booth mentions Planché's *The Brigand* (1829), "with a Robin Hood-like bandit hero and a villain who is chief of the Roman police."[55] He calls the play "strongly rebellious and anti-authoritarian in tone," adding that "something still survived of the fervent liberalism of Goethe and Schiller and the early melodramatists of the French Revolution."[56] There are similarities, too, with the brigand chief Falsacappa in the libretto Meilhac and Halévy wrote for Offenbach's *Les Brigands*. But the point to note is that Gilbert is not here ridiculing this tradition but actually conforming to it: the Pirate King gives his own satirical spin to the idea, but he is not condemning himself by doing so.

We can begin to see now that Frederic's choice is not so simple, after all. On the one hand, a respectable life within the law; on the other, a life that, though lawless, is at least honest with itself. His "sense of duty" sends him ricocheting between the two options, but would a "common-sense" appeal to the conscience be any more reliable as a guide?

There is a sense of wildness in this opera that we do not find in *H.M.S. Pinafore*. The juxtaposition of melodramatic convention and prosaic reality is much more bizarre, the action is much more farcical—particularly in the second act. Also, the musical sequences are longer and more elaborate; we are no longer in the realms of ballad opera but are approaching a fully fledged opéra comique. The music gives body to the drama and deepens its emotional content: Sullivan forces us to identify with the characters, despite Gilbert's protests. Everyone is made at least slightly ridiculous, but there is not that sense of chilly disapproval that surrounds Alexis Pointdextre or Sir Joseph Porter. However, I do not believe this sense of emotional connection is entirely attributable to Sullivan's music.

The Chorus of Policemen is, of course, one of the piece's highlights: they are terrified by the prospect of violence, and too tenderhearted to rejoice in the arrest of criminals (for, after all, "When the coster's finished jumping on his mother . . . / He loves to lie a-basking in the sun").[57] Are they to be ridiculed for this? A drawing made by Gilbert some years later to illustrate "The Policeman's Lot" shows a policeman taking a tough-looking party into custody and weeping into his handkerchief all the while. Clearly this suggests that tenderheartedness can be taken to excess. But in performance these policemen are nothing more than endearingly human. As Hayter notes, "They also have a duty to do [just as Frederic does], but it is performed in the context of sympathy for their fellow human beings."[58] He suggests that they represent a sane and balanced attitude to life—broadly speaking, Gilbert's own view. But of course they are also farcical figures, desperately balancing their professional duties against their absolute horror of any kind of violence.

The opera's ending is built around a couple of unexpected reversals, each containing a satirical point. The Pirates and the Police fight, and the Pirates win. But the Police have one final weapon in their armory: the Sergeant, prostrate before the Pirate King, calmly tells them: "We charge you yield, in Queen Victoria's name!"—upon which the Pirates immediately sheath their swords and give themselves up to the Police because, as they explain, "with all our faults, we love our Queen."[59] The point is clearly to show how absurd it would be if this stock police phrase were actually to have an effect on anybody, and there is an obvious implication of mockery against the queen herself, or at any rate against the reverence in which she was publicly held.

The final twist occurs when the Pirates, about to be led off to their punishment, are suddenly revealed to be "noblemen, who have gone wrong!"[60]—upon which the Major-General exclaims:

No Englishman unmoved that statement hears,
Because, with all our faults, we love our House of Peers.

[*All kneel to* Pirates.

. . . I pray you pardon me, ex-Pirate King,
Peers will be peers, and youth will have its fling.
Resume your ranks and legislative duties,
And take my daughters, all of whom are beauties.[61]

The satirical point scarcely needs laboring. "The Policeman's Story," a Bab ballad published in May 1879, has the ironical refrain, "there's but one law for the peasant and the peer,"[62] and we are on similar territory here. What a difference a title makes!

If we look at the opera and try to find in it a logically consistent attitude, we shall be long looking. There are satirical points throughout, and the whole is bound together around the theme of "duty," but there is no obvious positive conclusion that comes out of it all. Everything ends happily, and the means by which this happy ending is reached, though barbed, has no bearing on the central themes. However, the direction of the satire is clear throughout: "sense of duty," respectability, the Queen, the House of Peers—all are held up to ridicule. Perhaps Gilbert cannot see a clear way forward, but even if he is looking backward, he is not pleased with what he sees.

The Sorcerer, H.M.S. Pinafore, and *The Pirates of Penzance* are bound together by their tenor heroes, each to some extent ridiculous (Ralph Rackstraw less than the others), and each placed squarely at the center of the action. But Gilbert had problems with his tenors—George Bentham, the first Alexis, was replaced halfway through the first run of *The Sorcerer,*[63] and Hugh Talbot, who played Frederic in the New York production of *Pirates,* was apparently completely incompetent in the role.[64] It is not surprising, therefore, to see that in the next two operas the tenor roles are much smaller and less significant. Generally speaking, from now on the Savoy operas revolved round the comic parts—those created by either George Grossmith or Rutland Barrington. Gilbert clearly felt that these two actors were much better fitted to shoulder such responsibility. Thus, in *Patience* (1881), the tenor plays the minor role of the Duke of Dunstable, and the main interest is shared between the two rival aesthetic poets, Bunthorne (Grossmith) and Grosvenor (Barrington).

In *Patience* as in *Tom Cobb,* Gilbert holds the posturings of aesthetes up to ridicule. His attitudes seem unashamedly Philistine throughout. The "fleshly poet" Bunthorne candidly admits, when alone:

> . . . my mediaevalism's affectation,
> Born of a morbid love of admiration![65]

—he is "an aesthetic sham."[66]

However, it ought to be emphasized that Grosvenor, the "idyllic poet," is, at any rate, not a hypocrite on the lines of Bunthorne. Grosvenor is ridiculous because of his complete conviction that he has been "Gifted . . . with a beauty which probably has not its rival on earth";[67] as played by Barrington (who was not known for his wispiness of figure) such lines must have been irresistibly comic. He hates being the object of so much admiration, but he is "a trustee for Beauty"[68] and must endure it. He is, in himself, apparently a natural philistine, and his language is more mercantile than artistic: "Ladies . . . you have been following me about ever since Monday, and this is Saturday. I should like the usual half-holiday, and if you will kindly allow me to close early to-day, I shall take it as a personal favour."[69] When, threatened by Bunthorne, he transforms himself into "A commonplace type, / With a stick and a pipe, / And a half-bred black-and-tan,"[70] we believe in it because we have always known that was what Grosvenor was, underneath.

Both poets are philistines underneath but for different reasons. Each is as ridiculous as the other, though Grosvenor is the more likable of the two, and as a reward it is he who is allowed to marry Patience at the end. A circular issued by D'Oyly Carte in 1881 to advertise the opera claimed: "the authors of *Patience* have not desired to cast ridicule on the true aesthetic spirit, but only to attack the unmanly oddities which masquerade in its likeness."[71] This seems a little disingenuous, but it does appear to have been supported by the overall style of the original production. Jane W. Stedman says that "most critics agreed with the *Pall Mall Gazette,* which declared Gilbert's aesthetic costumes exquisitely beautiful, unlike the vulgar raw reds, yellows, and blues of the chorus's dresses when they become everyday young girls."[72] As Stedman says elsewhere, "Visually, *Patience* was very much on the side of aestheticism."[73]

So, again, we find Gilbert's attitudes not as clear-cut as they might at first appear. The plot of the piece places him firmly on the side of the ordinary people who ridiculed the drawing-room aesthetes, but on the basic matter of aesthetics, he was scarcely a philistine. And it is debatable whether Gilbert considered either of the Rival Poets any more contemptible than the briskly common-sense soldiers with whom they are contrasted. To quote Stedman once more, "the philistines of this opera, the Heavy Dragoons, are just as dependent upon the attractions of costume as are the poets."[74] Every man in the piece (except the nonspeaking Solicitor) is primarily concerned with the power of appearance in attracting women. As Colonel Calverley sings:

> When I first put this uniform on,
>   I said, as I looked in the glass,
>   "It's one to a million
>   That any civilian,
>   My figure and form will surpass.
>   Gold lace has a charm for the fair,
>   And I've plenty of that, and to spare,
>   While a lover's professions,
>   When uttered in Hessians,
>   Are eloquent everywhere!"[75]

The soldier postures before the looking-glass, and Grosvenor looks into a hand mirror, saying: "I am a very Narcissus!"[76] Which is the vainer of the two? The brilliant series of coups-de-théâtre that crowds the end of act 2 emphasizes this point: the soldiers dress as aesthetes, Grosvenor and the "Rapturous Maidens" become ordinary people. The two sides are interchangeable: there is no difference between them.

It would be wrong to overemphasize this point, however. The tone of the opera and the nature of the jokes that are made at the expense of the aesthetes throughout suggest an instinctive support of the honest vulgarity of ordinary life. As Bunthorne cries, setting aside his aesthetic mask: "What's the use of yearning for Elysian Fields when you know you can't get 'em, and would only let 'em out on building leases if you had 'em?"[77] (Notice, as with Grosvenor, the mercantile, materialistic imagery.)

There is one other point that needs to be discussed. In this opera it is Patience who is haunted by the absurd Gilbertian logic that had, in the previous operas, pursued the tenor heroes. She is told that love is "the one unselfish emotion in this whirlpool of grasping greed!":[78] and, of course, she believes this literally. She takes it on trust that true love is necessarily unselfish, but, she reasons, it is selfish to love anyone who is remotely attractive or pleasant to know, so she is trapped into loving only someone who is absolutely unlovable—Bunthorne, for instance. Only when Grosvenor has sworn that he "will always be a commonplace young man,"[79] at the end of the opera, does Patience allow herself to love him— another clear hit at the ugly fashions of the day.

But there is an interesting point behind this subplot, which challenges romantic assumptions about the nature of love, as set forth in many a melodrama. Gilbert finds it absurd to suppose that truly unselfish love is possible, or, indeed, desirable. Selfishness is seen as a good thing, at least in moderation. This casts an interesting light back on such plays as *Engaged*—though it does not necessarily imply that Gilbert endorsed the conduct of the characters of *Engaged*. Selfishness is a natural instinct that must be kept strictly in check.

The tone of the operas was now beginning to change: Gilbert was becoming less inclined to condemn characters outright. That is to say, while he still made his characters ridiculous, he did so in a less partisan spirit, not condemning specific classes of people but making a more general point about the absurdity of the human condition. I have already quoted William Archer's judgment that "The jester who railed at every one from king to scullion, offended no one."[80] He seems to suggest that a successful satire must offend. It is true that this is a good indication that the point has gone home, but in practice the offensiveness often comes from the portrayal of certain human types as despicable, morally worthless, perhaps less than human. Such satire contains the unspoken assumption that there is a kind of moral aristocracy of human beings, and that the satirist belongs to it, even if no one else does. There is something of this in the portrayal of Mr. Smailey in *Charity,* for instance. But as Gilbert's vision became more sophisticated, he became less inclined to judge harshly, and his satire became more democratic, so to speak, by emphasizing that human weakness is universal and also by suggesting that good and bad appear in human beings intermixed, not conveniently separate. The comedy of the main Savoy operas is not superior and dismissive but implies instead an acceptance of the leveling absurdities of the human condition.

In *Patience*, there is no really contemptible character—not even Bunthorne. He is crabbed and hypocritical, and at the end of the opera he is the only one excluded from the general pairing off, but his caustic wit, his bursts of candor, and the resignation with which he accepts his lonely state at the end all act in his favor. The fact that his role is played by the principal comedian also has its effect. Goldberg argues that aspects of Gilbert's own personality find expression through many of his characters: "He is, in *Patience*, both of the poets *simultaneously,* and never was a prettier example of unwitting self-exposure than in this libretto, in which Gilbert, ostensibly setting out to combat the aestheticals of his day, reveals the aesthetical in his own make-up."[81] Goldberg does not seem to realize that this capacity to inhabit more than one character's mind, to project aspects of oneself into several characters at once, is an extremely useful quality in a dramatist—and perhaps an essential one, but the only real problem with the above quotation is the use of the word "unwitting." It is entirely possible that Gilbert knew exactly what he was doing.

In *Iolanthe* (1882) Gilbert developed this idea still further. No single character "carries" the piece; it depends, instead, on ensemble playing. It may even be argued that the central characters are in fact none of the principal dramatis personae, but instead the two choruses. *Iolanthe* is the story of the conflict of two worlds, Fairyland and the House of Lords—the fanciful and the prosaic. At the end of act 1, the female fairies and the male peers sing defiance at each other, and they are, inevitably, paired off with each other at the end of act 2. That is the only really significant plot action in the piece.

Gilbert's fairies follow the conventions of stage fairies everywhere ("Tripping hither, tripping thither, / Nobody knows why or whither")[82] but candidly admit that "If you ask the special function / Of our never-ceasing motion, We reply, without compunction, / That we haven't any notion!"[83] This candor makes them prosaic and brings them (more or less) into the realms of the possible. Their existence is impossible, but their attitudes are entirely down-to-earth. In this respect, they contrast sharply with the Peers, members of real British society whose existence is entirely inexplicable—who have no rational function, and who accept, in the end, that they are more at home in Fairyland than in Westminster.

In one of the opera's main subplots, the Arcadian shepherd Strephon becomes a Member of Parliament with the aid of the Fairies; and, once there, his fairy powers enable him to carry every bill he chooses. Thus it is shown that reforming acts can only be passed with the help of a supernatural agency: Britain's primary legislative body is monstrously inefficient in doing the thing that it was formed to do. In this respect it is Fairyland that is practical and down-to-earth and Parliament that is impractical and unworldly. To this extent, at any rate, Gilbert is on the side of the Fairies—though there is a palpable note of amused affection toward the useless Peers throughout.

The conflict between the Fairies and the Mortals meets in the body of Strephon himself, the son of a fairy mother and a mortal father: he is "a fairy down to the waist—but his legs are mortal."[84] When urged to go into Parliament, he objects: "I'm afraid I should do no good there—you see, down to the waist, I'm a Tory of the most determined description, but my legs are a couple of confounded Radicals, and, on a division, they'd be sure to take me into the wrong lobby. You see they're two to one, which is a strong working majority."[85] I cannot help seeing this as a vivid image to describe Gilbert himself—a man divided between Tory and Radical ideas, his Tory brain being often overruled by his Radical legs, and always torn between the two contradictory impulses.

Sullivan's music has a similar effect here to that it had in *H.M.S. Pinafore*: it adds to Gilbert's sardonic ironies a level of genuine affection. When, in the song "When Britain Really Ruled the Waves," Lord Mountararat sings:

> When Wellington thrashed Bonaparte,
>   As every child can tell,
> The House of Peers, throughout the war,
> Did nothing in particular,
>   And did it very well. . . .[86]

it is easy to find oneself genuinely moved by the stirring music and to forget the precise meaning of the words. The song is the exact counterpart of Lord Mountararat's statement about the House of Peers being "not susceptible of any improvement at all":[87] it is both a condemnation and a boast. The opera is full of incisive satire at the expense of British political institutions, but one always feels that Gilbert has affection for the thing he condemns. He may believe that the House of Peers ought to be reformed and "a Duke's exalted station / Be attainable by Com- / Petitive Examination,"[88] but that does not debar him from liking the dim-witted Peers at a personal level. Indeed, in the song "Spurn Not the Nobly Born" the direction of his irony twists right round: he inverts the old melodramatic-sentimental assumption that "In lowly cot / Alone is virtue found"[89] so as to put in the desperate plea that "The Peerage is not destitute of virtue."[90] People sometimes have to be reminded that the doctrine of the Equality of Man works both ways, and that "Hearts just as pure and fair / May beat in Belgrave Square / As in the lowly air / Of Seven Dials."[91]

This ability to see both sides of the matter, and to ridicule each equally, runs through the whole opera. When Private Willis incisively sums up the House of Commons in eight lines, he realizes its absurdity but finds the alternative even more absurd:

> When in that House [i.e., the Commons] M.P.'s divide,
>   If they've a brain and cerebellum, too,
> They've got to leave that brain outside,
>   And vote just as their leaders tell 'em to.
> But then the prospect of a lot
>   Of dull M.P.'s in close proximity,
> All thinking for themselves, is what
>   No man can face with equanimity.[92]

The opera originally contained a song, "Fold Your Flapping Wings," which earnestly advocated social reform designed to abolish the crime created by poverty, but it seemed out of place and was quickly deleted. It was too realistic: for, despite all the political satire, the opera is set squarely in its own fantastic world, and in its last moments it comes firmly down on the side of fantasy, against dull real life.

There is a steady progression from *The Sorcerer* to *Iolanthe*: this is, perhaps, not easy to demonstrate, but we seem to move steadily away from a foundation in reality, until, in *Iolanthe*, we find ourselves in a hermetically sealed world, reflecting life but at no point really touching it. When the Fairy Queen exclaims at the end, "Then away we go to Fairyland,"[93] we may feel that the command comes too late, for we have been there throughout.

The plot of *The Sorcerer* could never be called realistic or probable, but it is set in a recognizable social world, and all the characters are real "types." Even the Sorcerer himself, J. W. Wells, is a real-seeming Victorian salesman, though the trade he plies happens to be impossible. *H.M.S. Pinafore*, too, may be set in the make-believe world of melodrama, but it has its reminders of reality; for instance in Josephine's "scena" "The hours creep on apace."[94] But from *Pirates* on (roughly speaking), the characters become less real-seeming and more whimsical, and the relationship with reality becomes more oblique. The point is, as I have said, not easy to demonstrate, but I believe it is true that the world of *The Sorcerer* is entirely different from that of *Iolanthe*. We are no longer in a world of simple parody, of simple satire, or of simple messages. A hundred ingredients are being skillfully mixed together to create a palatable dish: something more complex than mere rump steak and oyster sauce, and perhaps intended for more sophisticated consumers.

For it must be remembered that this is a period of transition in the theater and that the social class of the audience is rising all the time. The gods of the gallery are still there, but they are no longer such a focus of attention now that fashionable society is returning to the theater—a change that Gilbert and Sullivan opera did much to foster. The change can perhaps be expressed by comparing Gilbert's 1881 farce *Foggerty's Fairy* with his 1875 farce *Tom Cobb*. The central characters of each play are medical men: Tom Cobb is a surgeon and Freddy Foggerty an apothecary. In theory both are in straitened circumstances and looking for advancement. But whereas Tom Cobb suffers abject poverty and starvation in the course of his play, Foggerty is made to experience no such fundamental problems. His only real worry is how to marry the woman he loves. *Tom Cobb* is set in the shabby genteel world of the lower middle class, whereas the later play, *Foggerty's Fairy*, has a very upper-middle-class setting of affluence and Harley Street surgeries. This may be a reflection of Gilbert's own changing circumstances, but it also indicates the changing nature of Victorian drama, which by now was well on the way to the titled cast lists of the Society Drama of the 1890s. (The predominance of Peers in *Iolanthe* may be significant in this respect.)[95]

Hayter has noted that the first Gilbert and Sullivan operas (excluding *Thespis*) were all "set in Victorian England,"[96] but that "Beginning with *Princess Ida*, the operas are set in times and places increasingly remote from Britain in the 1880s."[97] The relationship between the action of the opera and the lives of its audience becomes more and more oblique after *Iolanthe*—though, as I have suggested, we can see the beginnings of such a trend as far back as *Pirates*. They become less openly satirical and more like pure entertainments. But this idea will be discussed in greater depth in chapter 7.

6

The Art of the Librettist

We have seen that in his early career Gilbert constantly gravitated toward the libretto form. Even in the early rhymed burlesques he was starting to think about the relationship between drama and music, though in comparatively crude terms. The recognizably Gilbertian style was developed in his librettos for the Gallery of Illustration, and when he experimented with topical satire in such pieces as *The Happy Land* (1873) and *Topseyturveydom* (1874), he found it the most natural thing in the world to intersperse dialogue with song. There are, of course, exceptions to this, but by and large it is only in the librettos that we find him speaking in his most characteristic voice.

I have suggested two reasons why this might be so. We can see, from some of the critical reaction to *Engaged* (1877), that Gilbert's ironic style could be thought inappropriate to the apparent realism of straight drama. But the introduction of song into Gilbert's plays breaks the illusion that he is presenting us with a direct reflection of real life; it emphasizes the artificiality of the experience, making us more sensitive to the critical elements of the Gilbert style. By this means he encourages the audience to step back a little from the dramatic action and perhaps to judge it a little more coolly. Naturally this effect can only be brought about in conjunction with the techniques of irony and parody that we have already seen in his style. In other hands, the libretto form is often a means of securing the emotional *involvement* of the audience, the music focusing the emphasis on the minds and feelings of the characters.

However, we have also seen that Sullivan's music often has precisely this effect of emotional involvement. The artistic aims of Gilbert and of Sullivan seem to disagree fundamentally on this point. The creative tension added a sense of depth to their joint products and should not be regretted. Still, it remains true that Gilbert generally used the libretto form to create a sense of ironic distance between the stage action and the audience.

126

The second reason I have suggested why Gilbert was attracted to the libretto form is that song provided a means by which he could reveal the essential truth of his characters to the audience. In *Princess Ida* (1884), King Gama sings: "If you give me your attention, I will tell you what I am."[1] This is the purpose behind many of Gilbert's lyrics, and not simply of the self-revelatory songs that became the trademark of the "Grossmith" roles. The songs in Gilbert's librettos usually involve a kind of stepping back from the specifics of the plot so that more general issues can be explored. Of course, as ever, there are exceptions: in the act 1 finales of the operas we find Gilbert writing versified dialogue, the main aim of which is simply to push the plot forward. But on the whole, the songs exist as a kind of commentary on what is taking place in the dialogue scenes.

A third reason might be added to this. Arthur Laurents, who wrote the "books" for such musicals as *West Side Story* and *Gypsy,* insists that the form of the musical demands absolute economy of dialogue: "Every line must make its point or you don't have it. A musical calls for the most economical writing there is in the theater."[2] This is a generally agreed-upon principle in the world of the twentieth-century musical. So, bearing in mind what I have said in chapter 2 about Gilbert's own style tending toward precisely this kind of economy, it is difficult to avoid the idea that the libretto was his most natural form of expression.

The role of the librettist has always been something of an anomaly: what he produces is not in itself a complete work of art but merely half of the combination of words and music that is called an opera. The librettist's relationship with the composer has varied over time: Metastasio (1698–1782) was regarded in his time as a master librettist and much more worthy of attention than his composers. Many of his librettos were set at different times by different composers. They were considered works of art in their own right.[3]

However, since Metastasio's heyday in the eighteenth century the position of the librettist in relation to the composer has been steadily falling. Lorenzo da Ponte, Mozart's famous librettist, did not command his composer as Metastasio had done; Mozart commanded him. And at the beginning of the nineteenth century Eugène Scribe played a vital role in creating a new style of libretto—based around powerful moments, grand climaxes, and spectacle. His verse was, in Patrick J. Smith's words, "at best hopelessly banal and at worse atrocious,"[4] but this was not really the point, since his task was simply to provide opportunities for the composer in the form of those dramatic *moments* that he was best qualified to create. The librettist has, broadly speaking, occupied this role ever since: he is the craftsman, and it is the composer who is the artist.

Gilbert is, in this context, an anomaly. The mere phrase "Gilbert and Sullivan" says it all: it is surprising enough that he should be mentioned in the same breath as his composer, but to put Gilbert *first!* The only comparable instance I can think of is that of Brecht and Weill—a comparison that may suggest why Gilbert should be in this position. Like Brecht, he was famous as a dramatist in his own right; like Brecht, he was a man of strong opinions about his works and great influence when it came to putting those opinions into practice. Gilbert's reputation ensured that his librettos were given an amount of critical attention not appropriate to others, and he also insisted that his words were as important as Sullivan's music.

The Gilbert and Sullivan operas are librettist's operas. The artistic vision was Gilbert's: he directed the original productions and supervised the creation of sets and costumes. Sullivan's role was secondary, merely providing incidental details for Gilbert's creations. Naturally, all this power was dependent on one basic fact: that Gilbert was able to write very good librettos—effective from the point of view of craft and containing an intellectual foundation that would give them an additional claim to serious attention. These elements were mixed together expertly to create something that also had that indefinable extra quality of artistry. He was much more than a mere copier of the existing conventions of libretto writing: he expanded the possibilities of music drama by (to take a well-known example) making the chorus an integral part of the drama rather than the usual singing scenery. Only by proving again and again that he could create high-quality librettos could he sustain his position of dominance at the Savoy Theatre.

Unfortunately I cannot here discuss in detail the way Gilbert structured his librettos. It is enough to say that he worked by rules that were essentially refinements of and improvements on the Scribean rules of the well-made play. As Jane W. Stedman observes: "More than his contemporaries, he adhered naturally to the unities of the French drama, including that of the single plot."[5] He also owed much to Meilhac and Halèvy, the Offenbach librettists, who gave to operetta a new tone, a sophisticated combination of satire and absurdity.

But Gilbert need not only be considered in relation to his predecessors: an interesting light can be shed on him by comparing him with his successors in that most twentieth-century of genres, the musical. He was considered by people such as Cole Porter, Ira Gershwin, and Alan Jay Lerner as the father of lyric writing: his influence on the development of the musical comedy and the musical is enormous. It is instructive to compare Gilbert's practice with some modern-day advice about the writing of the libretto for a musical, given in Stephen Citron's *The Musical: From The Inside Out.*

"The libretto of a musical is rarely written from beginning to end. It is generally created in sections which build one on top of the other."[6] We have already seen that Gilbert also wrote his plays in sections, a practice that forces the librettist to focus on creating a series of good moments rather than being diverted into concentrating on larger issues of structure. As I have mentioned, the book of a musical needs to be written with extreme economy—"every section of the libretto must count"[7]—and this kind of piecemeal construction helps here.

"The most obvious difference in the realm of the contemporary lyric stage is that the musical is divided into two acts";[8] very significantly, all but two of the Gilbert and Sullivan operas are in two acts. The typical European operetta of this era was either in one or three acts. It is true that a handful of Offenbach's operettas, such as *Orphée Aux Enfers* (1858) and *La Périchole* (1868), were originally two-acters, but this seems to have been primarily a matter of economy, and both were later expanded to three acts, when their success was established. Gilbert appears to have been the man who established the two-act structure as the norm. Stephen Citron says:

> The first act curtain . . . ought to leave the plot partially resolved but with its final outcome still in doubt. This is equivalent to the former third act curtain in a classic [five-act] play or the second act curtain in a contemporary three-acter.[9]

Gilbert did not conform precisely to this structure: in his librettos the balance between the two acts is much more equal. Act 1 tends to consist of exposition, the first great push in the plot occurring about two-thirds of the way through it, leading to a crisis at the end of the first-act finale; act 2 contains the bulk of the plot developments and a very brief resolution in the last few minutes. *The Mikado* (1885) is a very good example of this structure.

This binary structure is a natural expression of Gilbert's preoccupation with reversals and inversions. The second act is a deliberate contrast to the first—often taking place at night, while the first act took place in daylight. In such operas as *Thespis, The Sorcerer, The Gondoliers,* and *The Mountebanks* the contrast between the acts occurs at a deeper structural level. The first act presents us with the "normal" state of affairs; this is overturned at the end of act 1, and the topsy-turvy consequences are developed in act 2;

and in the last five minutes of act 2 the plot is resolved and the world is turned right way up again. Modern musicals are concerned less with this kind of systematic reversal and more with organic plot development. Citron quotes Mark Steyn as saying that the second act of a musical should develop the audience's "emotional involvement with the characters":[10] this is, by and large, not one of Gilbert's concerns.

So we begin to see differences between the modern musical and its Gilbertian prototype, but they are differences within an overall similarity. Gilbert, in working with Sullivan, had discovered a structure ideally suited to the operetta/musical form. (It is true that he first used the structure in *The Gentleman in Black* [1870], with Frederic Clay's music, but it was developed to its fullest only in later years, with Sullivan.)

Richard Traubner states in *Operetta: A Theatrical History* that Gilbert's librettos were "the *best* operetta books of them all, unequivocally."[11] It is difficult to imagine this statement disproved, though it may seem like damnation with faint praise, bearing in mind the quality of most operetta librettos. What is being praised here is essentially the combination of craft and intelligence that they display. They have "survived" the past century as no other comparable librettos have done, and, remarkably, they have been almost constantly available in book form for most of this century, as works of literature to be read. There are very few other librettos for which the same can be said.

LYRICS

It is easy for the academic Gilbertian to forget that, for most of those who enjoy the Gilbert and Sullivan operas, Gilbert's main achievement lay not in his satire, criticism of society, or philosophy, but simply in his being a great lyricist. This is Patrick J. Smith's assessment:

> Gilbert in his librettos went beyond what had theretofore been accomplished with the patter song, and he set a standard that has not been met since. This was because he was as good a comic poet as the libretto has produced.[12]

He was a profound influence on the twentieth-century lyricists. For instance, Alan Jay Lerner, the librettist of *My Fair Lady, Camelot, Brigadoon,* and other major twentieth-century musicals, called Gilbert "the Adam of modern lyric writing. P. G. Wodehouse, Lorenz Hart, Cole

Porter, Ira Gershwin, Oscar Hammerstein and their contemporaries and descendants all owe their lineal, genetic beginning to W. S. Gilbert."[13] Gilbert provided them with the example of a style of musical comedy in which literate, sophisticated lyrics could find a home. To quote Lerner again: "there is no doubt that Gilbert was the driving force [in the collaboration with Sullivan]. It was he and he alone who took operetta by the neck and raised lyric writing from a serviceable craft to a legitimate, popular art form."[14]

His skill did not lie only in outrageous displays of verbal dexterity, such as:

> I know our mythic history, King Arthur's and Sir Caradoc's,
> I answer hard acrostics, I've a pretty taste for paradox,
> I quote in elegiacs all the crimes of Heliogabalus,
> In conics I can floor peculiarities parabolous.[15]

This kind of trick rhyme wins easy applause, but his skill went much deeper than this. When, in his early days, he worked at *Fun,* writing Bab Ballads week after week, he learned how to fit a narrative into regular verse forms and often succeeded in doing so with stunning neatness. When he comments of his sailor-hero in "Joe Golightly":

> P'raps some Princess's son—
>   A beggar p'raps his mother.
> *He* rather thought the one,
>   *I* rather think the other.[16]

we are suddenly aware that this sardonic comment is expressed in the best possible words, with not a word wasted. There is no straining for rhyme, nor are there any of the awkward contortions of language that we often find when a writer tries to express such a subtle thought in such a strict rhyme scheme. The rhymed words are vital to the sense, and the fact that they are rhymed adds epigrammatic point to the quatrain.

We find the same kind of marvelous facility throughout the Gilbert and Sullivan operas. A well-known instance is the song, "Our Great Mikado, Virtuous Man,"[17] which tells, in three bravura verses, the story of the Mikado's law against flirting—information vital to the understanding of the plot as a whole. Or I might take a less celebrated example from *Ruddigore:* the sailor Richard Dauntless enters with his fiancée Rose Maybud, and he sings in the usual breezy sailor's manner:

> Happily coupled are we,
>   You see—
> I am a jolly Jack Tar,
>   My star,
> And you are the fairest,
> The richest and rarest
> Of innocent lasses, you are,
>   By far—
> Of innocent lasses you are!. . .[18]

To which Rose replies in exactly the same meter, but to completely different effect, as she recognizes a different image of the Jolly Jack Tar—the profligate womanizer:

> . . . I shall be left all alone
>   To moan,
> And weep at your cruel deceit,
>   Complete;
> While you'll be asserting
> Your freedom by flirting
> With every woman you meet,
>   You cheat—
> With every woman you meet![19]

The rhymes are unobtrusive, but precise, and Gilbert is never cramped by those little two-syllable lines, which give such an exuberant skipping effect to the verse. Indeed, he is able to use one of them to allow Rose to say "You cheat" almost as a throwaway—having set up the rhyme in three previous lines, of which only "Complete" sounds like a filler. These are the lyrics of a master craftsman: there is no sense of strain, and every effect slots into place with deceptive ease.

His skill as a lyricist is evident in the range he was able to command: I have already touched on patter songs, plot songs, and character songs; then there is the opening chorus of *The Mikado* in which the singers tell us, with disarming frankness, all we need to know about them ("If you want to know who we are, / We are gentlemen of Japan"),[20] and, of course, the obligatory love song. These last do not always avoid sentimentality but at their best can be charming and humorous without being cynical. For instance, Robin and Rose, the hero and heroine of *Ruddigore,* have no conventional love duet but do have a song in act 1 in which, too shy to express their love, they timidly consult each other about a fictitious friend:

Robin. I know a youth who loves a little maid—
   (Hey, but his face is a sight for to see!)
  Silent is he, for he's modest and afraid—
   (Hey, but he's timid as a youth can be!
Rose. I know a maid who loves a gallant youth,
   (Hey, but she sickens as the days go by!)
  She cannot tell him all the sad, sad truth—
   (Hey, but I think that little maid will die!)[21]

There are times when Sullivan's music seems to be working toward a different end from the words, but here Gilbert offers a perfect opportunity for Sullivan's simple, folk-song manner, which he takes up perfectly.

Gilbert had a great variety of style and form at his command. Bearing in mind his insistence that the words should be written before the music, his metrical ingenuity is amazing. He said, "Often a rhythm would be suggested by some old tune or other running in my head, and I would fit my words to it more or less exactly":[22] "I Have a Song to Sing, O!" from *The Yeomen of the Guard* (1888) being based on a Cornish carol, for instance. But to be able to keep such variety in his lyrics throughout such a long series of operas, and to repeat himself so little, is in itself a great achievement.

There is also another kind of lyric that we find throughout the operas. Stedman calls "Where the Buds are Blossoming" from *Ruddigore* (1887) "the loveliest of his Horatian lyrics, at least one of which had always graced each of his librettos, mingling happiness and sadness, an acceptance and a smiling resignation."[23] These meditative lyrics, in which the characters pause to take a longer view of life, and the temporary foolishnesses of the plot recede as the larger issues are contemplated, seem to have been written for Gilbert's own satisfaction and not for any commercial reason.

  Comes a train of little ladies . . .
   Wondering what the world can be?

  Is it but a world of trouble—
   Sadness set to song?
  Is its beauty but a bubble
   Bound to break ere long?

  Are its palaces and pleasures
   Fantasies that fade?
  And the glory of its treasures
   Shadow of a shade?[24]

"Is Life a Boon?" from *The Yeomen of the Guard* is a deliberate imitation of the Elizabethan style; Audrey Williamson compares "Whom Thou Hast Chained" from *Princess Ida* (1884) to Herrick and compliments its "Elizabethan shapeliness."[25] We have already seen that Gilbert admired the prose style of that period for its simplicity and clarity; the same qualities can be found in his imitations of its poetry.

A theme links these meditative lyrics, the idea of the impermanence of the things of this world:

> O'er the season vernal
> Time may cast a shade;
> Sunshine, if eternal,
> Makes the roses fade![26]

There is a kind of cheerful resignation in this, but in *The Mikado* Gilbert treats the same idea with a pessimism that is only semi-humorous:

> Joyous hour, we give thee greeting!
> Whither, whither art thou fleeting?
> Fickle moment, prithee stay!
> What though mortal joys be hollow?
> Pleasures come, if sorrows follow.[27]

This with the refrain "Sing a merry madrigal," "Fal-la"s and all, but *"Ending in tears,"*[28] to quote the stage directions.

One sometimes feels that Gilbert is, in these lyrics, partly revealing the dark side of his philosophy, the pessimism that is implicit in much of his comedy despite his attempts to mask it and deny it. The following, from *Princess Ida,* is ironized by the comments of the other characters, but Sullivan's setting hides these ironies, and perhaps, after all, this is the essential Gilbert speaking:

> The world is but a broken toy,
> Its pleasure hollow—false its joy,
> Unreal its loveliest hue,
> Alas!
> Its pains alone are true,
> Alas!
> Its pains alone are true.[29]

These are the attitudes of a Stoic, not of a Christian. There are no references to the possibility of another world after death; there is the constant implication that this life is all there is. There is also the illogical but morbidly appealing idea that worldly pleasures are phantasms, and that only pain, trouble, and misery are real.

These lyrics provide a serious anchor for the operas: they hint at worrying depths, though keeping them firmly in check. The idea embodied in these lyrics is not very original, but that does not mean it is not an idea worth expressing: essentially the lyrics are the equivalent of a whispered "Remember thou art mortal" directed at Gilbert's first audiences—a valuable reminder to the inflated Pooh-Bahs of that era.

This was only one mood among many. His best lyrics are generally comic, however, and his worst ones fail because of their sentimentality. His lyrics depend on logic rather than emotion, and usually avoid the cheerful acceptance of cliché that characterizes many of the opera lyrics of the Continental tradition. If Gilbert uses one of these clichés, it is usually to mock it—as, for instance, the rollicking drinking song in *The Sorcerer* (1877), which begins: "Eat, drink, and be gay, / Banish all worry and sorrow."[30] and only later turns out to be about tea. In *H.M.S. Pinafore* (1878) a song begins in a familiar-sounding way: "Fair moon, to thee I sing, / Bright regent of the heavens,"[31] but the next two lines take us away from ready-made poetic musings and into bathos: "Say, why is everything / Either at sixes or at sevens?,"[32] and the rest of the lyric is essentially a recap of the plot so far. A Gilbert lyric typically boils down to saying "this is what I think" rather than "this is what I feel."

Gilbert's best work usually depends on some kind of irony or unexpected twist, and this applies to his lyrics as well as to his larger-scale works. Thus the twist in one of his best lyrics, from *The Yeomen of the Guard*:

> Were I thy bride, ·
> Then the whole world beside
> Were not too wide
> To hold my wealth of love—
> Were I thy bride![33]

And so on through six more verses, and then the last:

> A feather's press
> Were leaden heaviness
> To my caress.
> But then, of course, you see
> I'm not thy bride![34]

It is interesting to find Ira Gershwin saying that "the trick or surprise ending" was "a structural device I have always liked"[35]—as in the last lines of his lyric for "But Not For Me":

> . . . When ev'ry happy plot
> Ends with the marriage knot—
> And there's no knot for me.[36]

This is another clear instance of Gilbert influencing the twentieth-century musical.

He wrote to William Archer on 5th October 1904:

> I have always held that English is (next to Italian) the very best of all European languages for singing purposes, provided that the song-writer will take into consideration the requirements of the singer & reject words & phrases that involve a hard collocation of consonants & a succession of close vowels. I wrote two of the songs in "The Yeomen of the Guard" ("Were I thy bride" & "Is life a boon") for the express purpose of proving this.[37]

This is the only occasion I know of in which Gilbert goes into the technical aspect of lyric writing in even the slightest detail. His words of warning about "a hard collocation of consonants & a succession of close vowels" remain good advice to the lyricist.[38] Gilbert often pretended to be musically illiterate, but he seems to have done this largely to play up to an amusing public image: he demonstrated, in an interview with Archer, a good knowledge of the light operas of the nineteenth century—as indeed he did when selecting music to relyricize for his early rhymed burlesques. Questioned by Archer about his lack of "musical faculty," Gilbert replied: "rhythm is one thing, and tune another—and harmony a third. I suppose I may claim a fairly accurate ear for rhythm, but I have little or no ear for tune."[39] But even this sounds like an exaggeration or a simplification.

There is no doubt that Gilbert was an extremely accomplished lyricist who knew as well as any, and probably better than most, the essential technical factors in the craft, though his patter songs sometimes seem to violate the matter of avoiding a "hard collocation of consonants." The fastest of these songs require a nimble tongue, but they are of course perfectly singable, even the notoriously fiendish "Nightmare Song" from *Iolanthe*: the comedians in amateur Gilbert and Sullivan groups prove this all the time. These songs, Gilbert's most obvious showcase, demonstrate Gilbert's facility with rhyme and rhythm, and only very occasionally does an overcrowding of consonants interfere with communication. One such example is found in "Nightmare Song": "In your shirt and your socks (the black silk with gold clocks), crossing Salisbury Plain on a bicycle."[40] "Black silk with gold clocks" is a jawbreaker.

Much could be said about the various techniques that are used in the lyrics, such as alliteration, of which Gilbert was particularly fond, though as a rule he never allowed the trick to become tiresome or let sound obscure meaning. But the essential point is that Gilbert's skill lay in keeping a balance between a large number of different elements.

7

1882–1889—The Pressures of Populism

Princess Ida: A Moment in Retrospect

PRINCESS IDA (1884) REPRESENTS A BREAK FROM THE PREVIOUS OPERAS, and not only because of its remote, fairy-tale setting. It is also unique in being in three acts, in being in blank verse, and in being based on a much earlier Gilbert play, *The Princess* (1870). That the change in direction was deliberate is surely indisputable, but the meaning of the change is less clear. The tone of the new opera was more serious and romantic than that of its predecessors; its satire on women's education must have seemed out of date, when women's colleges were a reality, and a successful reality. (This last fact surely added to the piece's remoteness from the world of its audience.) Gilbert later wrote to Sullivan (20 February 1889) that he much preferred "a consistent subject" to "the burlesque of *Iolanthe* or the *Mikado*."[1] *Princess Ida* may be seen as a first gesture of defiance to the public he considered lacking in taste.

Because *Ida* is such a close adaptation of *The Princess*, I shall not spend much time discussing its thematic importance. Though its continuing attraction to him at this date may be thought significant, it would be inappropriate to identify the Gilbert of 1884 too closely with the Gilbert of 1870.

The hostility to women's universities that is obvious in *The Princess* is, of course, carried over into *Princess Ida*. Love and marriage are considered the only reasonable ambitions of women. In *The Princess*, Ida is a ridiculous fanatic, incapable of logical reasoning. Though much of this character is retained in *Princess Ida*, she is given several arias that mock her neither in words nor music; these songs give her a dignity that is denied her in the dialogue. This suggests that Gilbert's position had shifted in the intervening fourteen years, and these songs give to Gilbert's attitudes to Ida an ambiguity that is familiar to us from the previous operas.[2]

It must be remembered, however, that several of Gilbert's early plays, such as *Ought We to Visit Her?* and *Charity*, suggest a much more sympathetic treatment of the "Woman Question." Both deal squarely with the different standards by which the sexes are judged by society: there is a distinct assumption that on this matter, at least, men and women should be treated as equals. There is, for instance, the scene in *Charity* in which Smailey, that pharasaical pillar of society, unexpectedly meets the woman he had "ruined" twenty years before:

> *Mr. Smailey.* . . . I have no desire to press hardly on any fellow-creature—
> *Ruth* (quietly). Come, that's kind, anyhow.
> *Mr. Smailey.* Perhaps, after all, you were not entirely to blame.
> *Ruth.* Well, p'raps not.
> *Mr. Smailey.* Perhaps I myself was not altogether without reproach in the matter. But in my case allowance should, in common charity, be made for follies that arise from extreme youth and—and inexperience. I was barely forty then.
> *Ruth.* And I was just sixteen. Well, I forgive you, along o' your youth, as I hope to be forgiven along o' my childhood.[3]

In Gilbert's most characteristic comedies, the women are usually the intellectual match of the men, and, though they may pretend to the conventions of Victorian womanhood that society expects of them, the knives underneath are never wholly concealed. The middle-aged women who run through the operas are deliberate reactions against the cliché ideal of the "angel in the house," and with their fierceness, frustration and anger they seem much more real than any of the fantasy heroines of Dickens. This is not to deny that these figures can become distasteful and the treatment verge on the misogynistic—for instance, in the figure of Lady Jane in *Patience*—but their power remains undeniable. Also, one must be careful that this distaste is not simply a symptom of outmoded notions of chivalry. Jane Stedman, in defending Gilbert's portrayal of middle-aged women, concludes pointedly that "protectiveness is no longer a practical mode of asserting male domination."[4]

Gilbert's attitudes on this subject changed from spot to spot. His views were undecided: he was against the sexual double standard, but he was also against female education. A clearer example could not be imagined of how Gilbert's attitudes simultaneously looked forward and back. He was unable to assimilate the full logic of the issue; he remade his attitudes with each individual case, in each instance reaching a different conclusion. He seemed clearer about what he was *against* than what he was *for.* His attitudes were defined by reaction against the bigots of both sides.

In the sequence of operas from *Pinafore* to *Iolanthe*, Gilbert developed the idea of balanced opposites that was so central to his way of viewing the world. In *Ida* he attempted to infuse the old play with this tried-and-tested balance, but in the event he was able to do so only imperfectly, and we may attribute the opera's comparative failure at least in part to this uneasy mixture of styles. (*Ida* lasted 246 performances in its first production, the briefest run for a Gilbert and Sullivan opera since *The Sorcerer.*) Since writing the original *Princess*, Gilbert had learned a way of satisfying all opinions, but in basing this opera on material written before he had learned the trick, he was unable to invest it with the same assurance he would have given to a work created from scratch at the time.

The Mikado: The Pressures of Populism

Princess Ida marks a break in the sequence of the operas, and each subsequent opera is to some extent a reaction against the previous one rather than a development from it. The reason for this change is not difficult to deduce. Both Gilbert and Sullivan became dissatisfied with the constraints of their collaboration from about 1884 onward, as can be seen from their increasing quarrelsomeness; and this, in turn, is easily explained.

Halfway through the run of *Patience,* in October 1881, the opera transferred to the newly built Savoy Theatre. The D'Oyly Carte Opera Company now had a purpose-built home. I have already mentioned the agreement made between Gilbert, Sullivan, and Richard D'Oyly Carte on 8 February 1883, binding Gilbert and Sullivan to produce an opera at six months' notice. On the same day this was signed, Gilbert read to his two partners the first part of what was to become *Princess Ida.*[5] Gilbert and Sullivan were becoming less of an artistic partnership and more of a machine for producing the money that could support them, Carte, the company, and the theater itself. Perhaps *Princess Ida* can be seen as a typical Gilbertian reaction to this situation: a deliberate reminder of Gilbert's early experiments. But what had been an innovation in 1870 was now rather old-fashioned; it was one of the few occasions when a Savoy Opera failed to match the mood of the times.

In the opening months of 1884, after the premiere of *Princess Ida*, a fundamental stress in the partnership opened up when Sullivan declared that he was resolved "not to write any more Savoy pieces."[6] He feared that his scores were "in danger of becoming mere repetitions of my former pieces,"[7] and he was hankering after a more serious or romantic subject in which burlesque and impossible elements would be absent. He rejected Gilbert's proposed plot for a supernatural opera (which was to see light as *The Mountebanks* in 1892). Throughout this dispute Gilbert took Carte's side, and naturally he did not understand Sullivan's objection to the idea of "Gilbertian" elements turning up in Gilbert's work. The argument was patched up, though it was to break out in different forms later, but its effects can be seen in the nature of the next opera, *The Mikado* (1885).

The Mikado is a much lighter, less satirical piece than any of its predecessors. In Nanki-Poo we have a tenor hero—but a hero whose only purpose is to love the heroine and be a docile counter in the plot. He has no social theories, no attitudes that can be satirized; he is nothing more than a pleasant face and a pleasant voice. The real, as opposed to the nominal, hero of the opera is the comic role, Ko-Ko. It is he who is the prime mover in the plot; it is he who creates and solves difficulties, rushes around, and gains the audience's attention and sympathies. Because he is the comedian, the woman he ends up marrying is not the heroine Yum-Yum but the comic battle-ax Katisha. Yet it is Ko-Ko, not Nanki-Poo, whom the audience remembers afterward. Nanki-Poo is a tailor's dummy, but Ko-Ko is alive.

The Mikado is a farce with romantic elements. It has moments of generalized satire, particularly where the archpluralist Pooh-Bah is concerned, but by and large it has no significant meaning for the outside world. There is indeed a theme binding the opera together: the idea of death. Death by beheading, by hanging, by burial alive, by boiling oil . . . the opera is obsessed with the notion. But its main purpose is simply to be the subject of black humor, and if there is a deeper significance it is only implied, and perhaps semi-conscious. The stoical philosophy that runs through so many of the lyrics ("Comes a train of little ladies," "Brightly dawns the wedding day," "See how the Fates their gifts allot," and others) is usually perceived by the audience only at a subliminal level.

The first production of *The Mikado* survived for 672 performances: thus it was from the first what it has been ever since—the most popular of the Gilbert and Sullivan operas. Its nearest rival in length of the original run was *Patience,* with 578 performances. The inevitable question must be, Why was it so popular? Several reasons may be suggested.

Firstly and most obviously, it is an excellent piece of theater. Its characters are motivated by the most basic desire there is: the desire to stay alive. Each character is rendered absurd or at any rate mildly laughable, but we never lose at least partial sympathy for any character, even for Pooh-Bah. Thus we are hooked, as an audience, from start to finish: we want to see Ko-Ko and the others extricated from their situation and are not satisfied in this desire until the opera's last spoken words.

Gilbert's "cynicism"—that is, his refusal to accept on trust the romantic assumptions of most Victorian drama—was widely condemned in his own day and was probably a source of genuine distaste for many playgoers. People went to the theater to be entertained, not to be preached at or to have their assumptions questioned. It was not an uncommon complaint of Gilbert's plays that "each speech / Seemed to reach / To a 'preach' / Near the end—d'ye see?"[8] But *The Mikado*, though containing much of the distinctive Gilbertian style, has genuinely romantic scenes in it. Nanki-Poo and Yum-Yum are really in love, and though their scenes together have wry and humorous lines, they say nothing to cast doubt on their love— unlike the lovers in *Iolanthe*, for instance. *The Mikado* places farce and romance—two very popular theatrical elements—alongside the expected elements of Gilbertian wit and Sullivanian tunefulness. The black humor is a typical Gilbert risk but one that paid off. At least one reviewer condemned it (William Beatty-Kingston of *The Theatre*), but it seems to have been accepted for the most part as mere good-humored fun.

However, I do not think these factors alone can explain the piece's great success. I believe the exotic element also played a vital role. In all the previous operas except *Thespis* (never revived) and *Ida* (a special case) the setting was contemporary England, and the actors were therefore restricted by the fact that their audience was familiar with the society they were reflecting—and Gilbert's comic method demanded at least a surface fidelity to the customs of that society. Even in the fairy-tale world of *Ida,* the Tennysonian origin, the blank-verse dialogue, and the comparatively serious tone all conspired to make the actors fearful of indulging themselves too much. But in *The Mikado* the actors were dressed in the kimonos of Japan, which must have been very freeing to Victorian men and women alike, accustomed to the restrictive corsets and collars of everyday dress. They were portraying a society about which hardly any westerners knew anything accurate, and though they were coached in their movements by a real Japanese lady, that can only have been a very thin veneer of "authenticity." By and large, the Japan of *The Mikado* is the burlesque Orient of pantomime—a playful reflection and distortion of England. This distortion is not really of the same kind as that in *Topseyturveydom,* because there is not the same kind of insistence on a satirical parallel with England. Ko-Ko is clearly an English cheap tailor, disguised in a kimono—not for satirical reasons but simply because it makes the character funnier. No consistent point is implied by the comparison of Gilbert's Japan with England: it is merely a technique used to boost the humor.

Gilbert had always been opposed to the old style of burlesque, which was pure vulgar frivolity without intellectual content, but *The Mikado* brought him, almost despite himself, into precisely that same world of burlesque, where there are no conventions and "anything is possible." The obviously "inauthentic" setting, the bantering reminders that we are not in Japan "really" (e.g., the topical references in Ko-Ko's "little list"), the unusual freedom of movement allowed by the kimonos—all encouraged the actors to treat the piece as a loosely built burlesque rather than the usual tight-knit opera.

Rutland Barrington, the first Pooh-Bah, interpolated many ad-lib lines into his part without Gilbert's sanction, such as "I'll give you such a Japanese smack in a minute," to Pitti-Sing in the middle of his verse of "The Criminal Cried."[9] Ian Bradley, in his *Complete Annotated Gilbert and Sullivan,* mentions many more such ad-libs for this opera than for any other; this is surely significant. George Grossmith, as Ko-Ko, was scarcely more innocent than Barrington in this respect. Jessie Bond, as Pitti-Sing, performed on the first night wearing a gigantic obi in order to set her apart from the other two "little maids"—this emphatically without Gilbert's permission.[10] And during the opera's first production a piece of physical business was developed in a scene in which Ko-Ko, Pooh-Bah, and Pitti-Sing were required to fall on their knees in front of the Mikado. Grossmith as Ko-Ko was pushed over by Bond as Pitti-Sing. And even more slapstick humor was later allowed into the scene.[11] Of course, Gilbert objected to all these additions when he learned of them.

But he was always fighting a losing battle: almost everyone else involved in the opera was against him. When *The Mikado* premiered in the United States, George Thorne, playing Ko-Ko, introduced much physical "business" that Gilbert would undoubtedly have condemned, had he been present. For instance, it was Thorne who originated a piece of pantomime concerning one of his big toes, which would suddenly spring upright from his foot at odd moments. Stedman tells us that Thorne "delighted audiences by turning a summersault whenever he sat down."[12] Carte supervised this "official" production and apparently approved such business. In addition, Thorne introduced a "dumb show verse" encore to "The Flowers that Bloom in the Spring," using an orchestration provided by Sullivan himself, who passed through New York during the run of this production.[13]

Gilbert tried, vainly, to restrain the excesses of the actors, but was opposed by both Sullivan and Carte—or at any rate was not encouraged by them. Yet it may be argued that the text of *The Mikado* is at least halfway toward such pantomime excess in any case: it is unashamedly a piece of pure entertainment, entirely commercial in intent and almost entirely lacking in identifiable "meaning." It looks like at least a step back toward the kind of burlesque that Gilbert had been at such pains to get away from at the beginning of his career. Why, then, should he object to the immensely popular alterations the actors made to the piece?

The most obvious answer is that Gilbert's ground rules in dramatic production were well known and that the most important of these was "No Ad-Libbing." He was not going to throw this rule out of the window for the sake of one opera. He would have argued that even the most frivolous of pieces must be produced within some kind of disciplined framework.

But is it too fanciful to suppose that he may have been in what amateur psychologists call "denial," that he was attempting to prove to himself that *The Mikado* was not the piece of pure froth that everyone else was clearly convinced it was? By attempting to rein in the excesses of the actors, he was applying to the opera a kind of artistic seriousness more applicable to the earlier operas—pieces that, though frivolous on the surface, had some serious underpinning to justify them.

It is important not to caricature Gilbert's position. He was always what we would call a commercial dramatist, in that he was determined to write plays that would attract a public and earn for him as much money as possible. But there is a clear difference between his position in his early years and his position now, in 1885. When he started out, the only question at stake was his own income, a matter that affected only himself and his wife. It was expected that most plays would last fewer than one hundred nights, and if a play failed, neither Gilbert, his wife, the theatrical manager, nor the actors would be ruined. But it is an entirely different thing to have a permanent company of actors settled in a specially built theater as part of a commercial Limited Company—and for all these elements to be dependent on the financial success of the products of your creativity. In the 1870s Gilbert could afford to take risks, though admittedly within a commercial framework. And as a result he produced daring experiments such as *A Sensation Novel, The Happy Land, Charity,* and *Engaged.* But as a member of the D'Oyly Carte Company, Limited, he was constrained from taking such risks—as much by his own sense of social responsibility as by outside pressure. His method of working was now much more cautious, as he explained in the 1885 article from which I have already quoted in chapter 2: "I had to make a dozen shots at the 'scenario' . . . before a course of action was decided upon [in the case of *The Mikado*]."[14] Every element of plot, dialogue, lyric, and witticism was painstakingly built up with absolute patience and care. As far as possible, nothing was left to chance. The radical reduction in Gilbert's output that took place at this time—forty pieces in the 1870s, ten in the 1880s—may be partly due to a natural slowing down of creativity, but his new, self-imposed carefulness of composition must also be considered a factor.

It would be demonstrably untrue to say that *The Mikado* was, as a result of this method, entirely bland and risk free. The black humor that lies at its center certainly risked revolting the audience instead of pleasing it. But the opera's lightness of tone, its romanticism, its appeal to the exotic, and its sheer frivolity do look like a concession to public taste. The following exchange, made in another interview also at the time of *The Mikado*, seems relevant:

> Interviewer: Where do you begin?
> Gilbert: Generally, I think by what is in demand, or I think is in demand.[15]

This sounds dangerously like trying to follow fashion rather than to lead it—though one must always be a little wary of giving too much importance to unweighed words spoken in an interview.

I am trying to avoid exaggerating the contrasts between the operas and the conclusions to be derived from them: after all, the differences in attitude are comparatively small. We are talking about a shift in emphasis, not a complete overhaul of Gilbert's ideas. Gilbert's character was made up of a mixture of conservative and radical elements in constant opposition; the tone of each opera changes only according to which side has gained a slight temporary superiority at that time. Thus when I say that in *Ruddigore* (1887) there is a partial return to Gilbert's earlier style, this does not imply a drastic departure from what we saw in *The Mikado*. It is only the emphasis that has changed.

FROM *Ruddigore* TO *The Gondoliers*

For the first few nights of its run, the opera's title was spelt *Ruddygore*—which, many agreed with *The Graphic,* was a "not very happily-selected" title.[16] It seems somehow indicative of the age that the public that had so enthusiastically embraced jokes about self-decapitation should have objected to such a title—and, indeed, that the difficulty should have been solved by the changing of a *y* to an *i*. Objections to the original spelling, and the booing that greeted the final curtain from some quarters, led to Gilbert testily suggesting as a new title *Kensington Gore; or, Not so Good as The Mikado*.[17]

The contrast with *The Mikado* is very clear—*Ruddigore* survived only 288 performances as opposed to *The Mikado*'s 672 performances. The new opera's darker tone was a clear disadvantage in commercial terms. That it revolves around torture and death is irrelevant, since *The Mikado* does precisely the same thing, but *Ruddigore* also insists on the reality of death by including a Chorus of Ghosts, who march and sing to some very dark music. It was also said that the opera's parody of melodrama was out-of-date, that it was deriding conventions that were already half-dead.

This is true: the world of *Ruddigore* is that of the early Victorian Gothic melodrama with elements of domestic and nautical melodrama thrown in. Melodrama still existed in 1887 but in a more sophisticated form. If the opera were nothing more than a parody of such melodramas, it would not be very interesting. But, as Max Keith Sutton has observed, "parody can become a form of satire,"[18] and in parodying the stock characters of the old melodrama Gilbert was criticizing the moral assumptions that underpinned them—and which, he implied, his audience still largely shared.

Ruddigore is an opera about morality: by what moral code should we live our lives? The "heroine" Rose Maybud lives according to the precepts of a book of etiquette; the "jolly jack tar" Dick Dauntless always acts upon his heart's dictates—which means that he only does those things that satisfy his selfish wants. The Baronets of Ruddigore are perpetually faced with a moral dilemma because they will die in awful agony if they fail to commit a crime every day. Thus Sir Despard Murgatroyd, who is naturally good-hearted, reveals: "I get my crime over the first thing in the morning, and then, ha! ha! for the rest of the day I do good—I do good—I do good!"[19] The "hero" Robin Oakapple is revealed to be the rightful Baronet of Ruddigore, Ruthven Murgatroyd, in disguise—and when this information is conveyed to the others, he immediately becomes a double-dyed villain. The whole of act 2 is concerned with his waverings between good and bad behavior.

The point of all this is impossible to miss. The breezy sailor-hero's apparent frankness is a mask for complete selfishness; the "hero" of act 1 becomes a villain and the "villain" of act 1 becomes a blameless district visitor. Even the "heroine" is at once priggish and heartless. The moral absolutes of the old melodrama are completely destroyed, and we are left stranded in a world where right and wrong are interchangeable. *Ruddigore* "could not have been written in a theologically secure society"[20] (to borrow a phrase of Stanley Kauffmann's regarding *Engaged*).

In act 2, in the scene in which the Ghosts of Sir Ruthven's ancestors question him on his daily crimes, they merely laugh when he says: "On Tuesday I made a false income-tax return";[21] they refuse to accept it as a proper crime because "Everybody does that. . . . It's expected of you."[22] The only act of his they accept as a crime is that of shooting a fox, for that is unsportsmanlike, which is much worse than being merely illegal.

At the center of *Ruddigore* is Robin Oakapple/Sir Ruthven Murgatroyd, the Grossmith role: if the opera has a meaning, it is here we must find it. Robin's character is dominated by fear, timidity, and a kind of arrogant modesty ("Ah, you've no idea what a poor opinion I have of myself, and how little I deserve it").[23] Faced with the possibility of inheriting the Ruddigore baronetcy, he runs away, leaving his younger brother to face the music. He had long sworn with Dick Dauntless that "come what might, we would always act upon our hearts' dictates":[24] but where Dick's heart counsels brutal selfishness, Robin's prefers to advise caution and strategic withdrawal.

Robin reacts to circumstances but never, until the very end, does he take the initiative and face those circumstances squarely. (There is a close similarity in this respect with such earlier farce heroes as Tom Cobb.) When, at the end of act 1, he is unmasked as Sir Ruthven, he accepts his new fate with resignation. He starts act 2 attempting to act the Bad Bart., but Rose Maybud need only plead with him for a minute and he becomes resolved to defy the curse. Immediately afterward, the portraits of his ancestors step out of their frames and lambast him for his lack of moral turpitude, and, faced with their tortures, he returns to his state of Bad Baronetcy. No sooner have they returned to their frames when the reformed Despard and Margaret enter and plead with him to reform. Under their influence, he agrees. And this weak vacillation between goodness and badness is only prevented from going on forever by his discovery of a legalistic quibble that dissolves the Ruddigore curse.

Robin is a man without any real moral center. He wavers to and fro; he is subject to the influence of whoever happens to be talking to him at the moment. It is notable that no one in the opera seems to act from a moral basis that is any more secure: Gilbert roundly mocks Rose Maybud and Dick Dauntless for their moral mainstays—the rigid rules of social conduct, and the "natural morality" of the conscience. Gilbert appears to be saying that there is no infallible guide to conduct. As G. Wilson Knight notes in discussing the Savoy operas, "We draw near to mad old Lear's

'None does offend; none, I say, none.'"[25] Gilbert scans the options and ridicules the standards of morality that he sees deserve ridicule, but he can find nothing that can better fill their place.

Edith A. Browne, in the first full-length study of Gilbert's life and work, noted that "it is Gilbert . . . the Justice of the Peace, who says that whenever he has a prisoner in the dock before him he always asks himself: 'What chance in life has this man had?'—Gilbert who frankly admits that he is an honest man because he has never had the temptation to be otherwise."[26] Should we see *Ruddigore* as an attempt to show what happens when a weak "good" man is subjected to this kind of temptation? It can certainly be so read, and this confirms the idea I have already expressed that Gilbert's characters are not scornful caricatures, no matter how sharp the unconscious self-condemnation of what they say. Robin's main character flaw is something Gilbert saw in himself. This idea is supported by the following verse from "Fold Your Flapping Wings," the song cut from *Iolanthe*:

> Take a wretched thief
> > Through the city sneaking,
> Pocket handkerchief
> > Ever, ever seeking:
> What is he but I
> > Robbed of all my chances—
> Picking pockets by
> > Force of circumstances?
> > > I might be as bad—
> > > > As unlucky, rather—
> > > If I'd only had
> > > > Fagin for a father![27]

This line of argument extends back to *Charity* (1874) and before and forward to *The Hooligan* (1911). It seems strange to associate *Ruddigore* with these "social-conscience" pieces—but Gilbert's point is clearly the same in all three. It is Robin's unfortunate ancestry that is the cause of all his woes—he shoots foxes by force of circumstances. Perhaps, having had "Fold Your Flapping Wings" excised from *Iolanthe* because of its too-serious tone, Gilbert resolved to find a comic way of expressing the same idea.

The end of the opera finds no solution to the moral emptiness that is Robin's real curse. The quibble that dissolves the Ruddigore curse, depending as it does on the fact that suicide was, in Gilbert's time, a crime, is appropriate because it is an example of what Gilbert certainly regarded as a legal absurdity: the law and morality have parted company. But we are given no suggestion as to how to bring the two together again. The moral certainties are dead and cannot be revived; and Gilbert, criticizing the old order, can find no acceptable new order to replace it.

The Yeomen of the Guard (1888) follows the pattern of reacting against its predecessor: it is the most "serious" of the series, in that, while it has humorous elements, the overall tone is romantic, and we are encouraged to care about the characters' fates. When Sullivan was read the plot in December 1887, he noted that it was a "pretty story—no topsy-turvydom, very human and funny also."[28] Gilbert's original idea for a successor to *Ruddigore* had been a new variation on the "lozenge plot" rejected in 1884, and Sullivan had rejected it again on the grounds that it was "a 'puppet-show' and not human."[29] The tone of *The Yeomen of the Guard* owes much to Sullivan's desire to break away from the old Gilbertianisms.

Nevertheless, *The Yeomen of the Guard* is a recognizable development from such other Gilbert pieces as *Dan'l Druce, Blacksmith* (1876). There is no reason to suppose that Gilbert was unhappy with writing in this style, which he regarded as more worthy of him than "the Jack Pudding nonsense with which my name is now associated."[30]

Two features of the opera must be mentioned here that are linked with the themes I have been attempting to draw out throughout this chapter. Firstly, the character of Jack Point has always been identified as a Gilbertian self-portrait (for instance, Leslie Baily calls Point "the tragi-comic jester in whom undoubtedly we may read more of W. S. G. himself than he put into any other of the creatures of his imagination"),[31] but he is certainly not portrayed in completely sympathetic colors. According to some unpublished memoirs of J. M. Gordon (who replaced Gilbert as stage director at the D'Oyly Carte when Gilbert died), Gilbert had intended Point to be "a *coward,* playing on his own grievances."[32] The truth of this is most obvious in the act 1 finale, in which, in response to Elsie's cry of "What have I done? Oh, woe is me!," he sings: "Oh, woe is *you*? Your anguish sink! / Oh, woe is *me,* I rather think!"[33] Audrey Williamson, too, notes this "touch of selfishness and self-pity" and adds that "Gilbert can hardly have been completely unconscious of what he was doing to Jack Point's character."[34]

Of course Gilbert was writing drama, not autobiography, and it would be simplistic to say that Jack Point "is" Gilbert, just as it would be simplistic to say the same of Robin Oakapple. But the ambivalences in this opera are particularly interesting because it is a piece from which the usual topsy-turvy elements are absent, and we might therefore expect it to exhibit a much more black-and-white attitude to the characters. Point is usually considered the central role of the opera, largely because of his "tragic" end, which dominates the act 2 finale, in which he *"falls insensible"*[35] of a broken heart. He gains our sympathies, but we are also forced to keep our distance from him because of his self-pity and also because of his ironic wit.

The nominal hero, Colonel Fairfax, is in some ways a much more unpleasant character: he torments the emotions of Elsie and Point during act 2 in a cruel and heartless fashion. There is a clear connection with the early tenor "heroes" of *The Sorcerer* and *The Pirates of Penzance* and with such characters as Prince Florian in *Broken Hearts*.

The overall plot structure deserves attention. *The Yeomen of the Guard*'s ending, in contrast with the deliberately artificial ones of its predecessors, allows events to develop to their natural conclusion, even though it results in misery for several of the main characters. Phoebe is forced to marry Wilfred, whom she hates, and Sergeant Meryll is forced to marry Dame Carruthers, whom *he* hates. Jack Point is deprived of his sweetheart Elsie and ends a broken man. The only couple who end happily are Elsie and Colonel Fairfax, the romantic hero and heroine to whose happiness everyone else must sacrifice everything.

In this, the most serious and straightforward of the operas, "happy endings" are the exception rather than the rule: only one or two "beautiful people" may find one, and everyone else must patch up a bad situation as best they may. The comforting final reversals of *Iolanthe* or *Ruddigore* are impossible: happiness and misery are distributed arbitrarily and without apparent order. We are shown a vision of an imperfect world, as we were in such plays as *An Old Score*. In Gilbert's comic universe the imperfections can be defeated and universal happiness established, but outside that avowedly artificial world simple and satisfactory solutions are not possible, and one person's "happy ending" means pain for someone else.

The Yeomen of the Guard, set in "heritage England," is not as uncompromising in its effect as Gilbert's serious plays of contemporary life, which had not succeeded financially, but the public response to even this partial change of direction made Gilbert cautious, as a letter to Sullivan (20 February 1889) shows:

> the success of the *Yeoman* [sic]—which is a step in the direction of serious opera—has not been so convincing as to warrant us in assuming that the public want something more earnest still. There is no doubt about it that the more reckless and irresponsible the libretto has been, the better the piece has

succeeded. . . . Personally, I prefer a consistent subject—such a subject as the *Yeoman* is far more congenial to my taste than the burlesque of *Iolanthe* or the *Mikado*—but I think we should be risking everything in writing more seriously still.[36]

Gilbert saw the issue as a straight choice between a serious subject (his personal preference) and an irresponsible one (the commercial option)— and, given this choice, he unhesitatingly preferred commercial success. The pressure to sustain the Savoy's sequence of success was beginning to affect what was being written.

The Gondoliers (1889), the last in the main series of Savoy operas, may be seen as a compromise between the kind of thing Gilbert wanted and what Sullivan preferred. Gilbert's old satirical tone can still be heard sporadically, but it coexists with an altogether lighter, more romantic, more "human" tone in which the influence of Sullivan is almost palpable. Audrey Williamson notes in it "a specially 'sunny' quality which is almost entirely devoid of shade,"[37] and this seems a just assessment. Charles Hayter notes that "*The Gondoliers* is much closer to a musical comedy than the earlier operas."[38] None of this is necessarily an adverse criticism of the opera, but it can hardly be denied that a change has occurred.

The most interesting element from a literary-critical point of view is the satire on "Republicanism": a return to the social-equality satire of *The Sorcerer* and *Pinafore*. The gondoliers are healthy and good-natured, but their belief in Republicanism is ridiculed mercilessly. Giuseppe explains:

> We are jolly gondoliers, the sons of Baptisto Palmieri, who led the last revolution. Republicans, heart and soul, we hold all men to be equal. As we abhor oppression, we abhor kings; as we detest vain-glory, we detest rank; as we despise effeminacy, we despise wealth. We are Venetian gondoliers—your equals in everything except our calling, and in that at once your masters and your servants.[39]

This, though rather simplistic, is not caricatured. But when it is revealed that either he or his assumed brother Marco is the rightful King of Barataria, Giuseppe's attitude changes immediately:

> Well, as to that, of course there are kings and kings. When I say that I detest kings, I mean I detest *bad* kings.[40]

As so often in Gilbert, abstract principles are a mask for self-interest. Marco and Giuseppe are impassioned believers in human equality so long as the idea has a chance of improving their personal lot, but as soon as they become monarchs they see the virtues of monarchy.

The satire is much kindlier than that in such previous works as *Engaged* or *Ruddigore*: there is no really unlikable character in the piece, not even the Grand Inquisitor Don Alhambra. A. H. Godwin's comment that "Gilbert's characters . . . are almost exasperatingly pleasant"[41] is, by and large, utterly false, but if we apply it only to *The Gondoliers,* there is justice in it.

The gondoliers' solution to their dilemma, the establishment of "A despotism strict, combined / With absolute equality,"[42] is a typical Gilbertian reductio ad absurdum, though it is not as thoroughly worked through as it might have been. The image at the beginning of act 2, of the kings occupying a more menial position than the courtiers who surround them, is a pure, good-natured absurdity: the sting is taken out of the earlier attitudes of Marco and Giuseppe because they are too innocent to take advantage of their new, exalted positions. If there is a serious point here, it is that they have been brought up to work and find their only fulfillment in serving others. As Giuseppe sings:

> Oh, philosophers may sing
> Of the troubles of a King,
> But of pleasures there are many and of troubles there are none;
> And the culminating pleasure
> That we treasure beyond measure
> Is the gratifying feeling that our duty has been done![43]

Marco and Giuseppe are innocents in the world of privilege and pleasure—so innocent, in fact, as to believe that they have duties as well as privileges. It is absurd to see them *"magnificently dressed . . . seated on two thrones, occupied in cleaning the crown and the sceptre"*;[44] but I wonder if it is only they who are the butt of that particular joke. Queen Victoria saw a royal command performance of the opera and apparently enjoyed it enormously, but it may be debated whether she can have been listening very carefully to the words. What, for instance, are we to make of this verse about the expected behavior of queens?

> And noble lords will scrape and bow,
> And double them into two,
> And open their eyes
> In blank surprise
> At whatever she likes to do.

> And everybody will roundly vow
> She's fair as flowers in May,
>   And say, "How clever!"
> At whatsoever
> She condescends to say![45]

Gilbert's attitude toward the privileged classes was never wholeheartedly supportive, and the opera demonstrates a submerged irritation for the useless pleasures of the Royal Family. I say submerged because Gilbert is palpably holding back the sharpest edge of his wit: one or two points are made with a brief, sharp edge, but the romantic tone overwhelms them. The most pointed satire is at the expense of nobles who supplement their income by sitting "by selection, / Upon the direction / Of several Companies' bubble" or by vowing "my complexion / Derives its perfection / From somebody's soap."[46] Even when the privileged people are not entirely idle, they are doing nothing more worthwhile than making money by promoting shady businesses.

Don Alhambra's song "There Lived a King," expresses at least one facet of Gilbert's own attitude to social organization. The song relates the parable of a King who "wished all men as rich as he . . . / So to the top of every tree / Promoted everybody"[47]—the result being:

> Lord Chancellors were cheap as sprats,
> And Bishops in their shovel hats
> Were plentiful as tabby cats. . . .
> And Party Leaders you might meet
> In twos and threes in every street,
> Maintaining, with no little heat,
>   Their various opinions.[48]

The moral is that social inequalities are inevitable in a structured society and that "When every one is somebodee, / Then no one's anybody!"[49] There is every reason to suppose this was Gilbert's own view. As Stedman has remarked, "Gilbert . . . saw no persuasive reason for any radical alteration of society, since any social framework must be filled by absurd mankind."[50]

Gilbert places no faith in either monarchy or republicanism in this opera; instead he defends the status quo, with its inequalities, simply because it exists and more or less works. The unusual amiability of the satire may be a concession to Sullivan, who was becoming more and more dissatisfied with Gilbert's "heartlessness": the result is pleasant but also a little anodyne—less distinctively "Gilbertian" than we have come to expect. The opera's fairy-tale ending is an unambiguous affirmation of the existing state of things. The harsh fact is that the satire is much less important to the opera than the romantic entanglements of the young couples.

Its dramatic structure is extremely simple, as Hayter, among others, has noted: "From this moment [at the end of act 1] to the end of the opera, there is little dramatic action. . . . The overall effect is that of marking time until Inez arrives with news that everyone has been waiting to hear."[51] *The Echo,* reviewing the original production, said, "It is not opera or play; it is simply an entertainment."[52] It has sometimes been compared in tone with musical comedy,[53] and with justice. Despite the touches of satire, the libretto is simply much less "significant" than any of its predecessors—even *The Mikado.*

Gilbert may have felt after this that he had conceded too much, and this may in turn have contributed to the force of the explosion that was temporarily to break up the partnership—the notorious "Carpet Quarrel." However, to put aside such desperate speculation, it is generally accepted that the main sequence of the collaboration ends here, and that the last two operas (with which I shall deal in the next chapter) were mere damp squibs after the main display. Their tone is certainly different. Given the stresses that were evident in the partnership from *Ida* on, we might be surprised that the collaboration lasted so long were it not for the all-conquering need for financial success.

ART AND MAMMON

The librettos Gilbert provided for Sullivan to set changed in their nature as the years passed. Of course they did; the wonder would have been if they had not. But when we look at the nature of these changes, it is difficult to explain them without recourse to facts that lie outside the "four corners" of the text: to Gilbert's relationship with his collaborator Sullivan, and, just as importantly, to his relationship with Carte, who fulfilled the wonder-working role of The Man With The Money. Gilbert accommodated his artistic ideas with those of Sullivan, and such an artistic compromise is not to be scorned, but one cannot resist the notion that the essential fact behind this compromise was not always the creation of the best possible opera but instead was the creation of the most commercial "Gilbert and Sullivan" product. Carte was the least obviously necessary member of the triumvirate of Gilbert, Sullivan, and Carte, but his influence can be traced clearly in some of these later operas, and perhaps it may be said that this influence was not always to the good. Gilbert was an artist as well as a craftsman, and everything he wrote for Sullivan has much to recommend it: he is never less than entertaining, and if in a piece such as *The Gondoliers* we sometimes feel he is holding back the full force of his satirical intelligence, that does not mean there is no wit or intelligence to be found in it. And the compensating surge of human warmth that floods the opera is no mean substitute.

The idea that I have suggested as the key to the understanding of Gilbert's best work—"The Land Where Contradictions Meet"—no longer quite fits. The robust contradiction between the warring halves in *H.M.S. Pinafore* is very different from the compromise of *The Gondoliers*. The pressures exerted by the third collaborator, Carte, were beginning to show in some of the operas, and that resulted in a blurring of the artistic vision. Sullivan was the more vocal railer against what he saw he was being forced to do to fit into the commercial "Gilbert and Sullivan" mold; Gilbert, the good professional dramatist, expressed himself more than content with the situation. But I suggest that the librettos he wrote for Sullivan after *Iolanthe* betray a deep disquiet at the situation. The startling swing of tone between each libretto and its successor suggests that Gilbert was fighting against a sense of dissatisfaction that could not be assuaged. The sense of a growing artistic vision, observable in the sequence of operas from *The Sorcerer* to *Iolanthe*, has been lost.

Perhaps, after all, it is not so fanciful to see this as the story of a conflict between Art and Mammon; for even commercial dramatists can have their own notion of art. And we may suddenly see in a new light the cataclysmic event in Gilbert's life that followed the premiere of *The Gondoliers:* I mean the acrimonious dispute with Carte that today we call "The Carpet Quarrel." Perhaps in terms of dull biography the quarrel was, after all, not some great heroic onslaught against boorish Mammon, but we may be forgiven for murmuring: "Well, it should have been." It seems so artistically right that some such conflict should have broken out at this point of the story.

In many ways, this is where the story ends. After the quarrel, Gilbert's literary output declined in both quantity and quality, and with alarming swiftness; one might argue that all there is left to relate is a sort of extended epilogue. But Gilbert has not quite finished telling us all he has to say, and in these last flawed works there is indeed much that it is worth pausing to hear.

8

1890–1911—Last Plays

In the central Savoy period, Gilbert refined the ideas of his early years and created works that were ever more carefully polished before he sent them out into the world. Sometimes, in the years approaching 1890, we can see him beginning to overwrite, but the tendency became obvious only now in this, the last period of his career. His creative juices were starting to run low: in these last twenty-one years he wrote only nine stage works. (I exclude *Rosencrantz and Guildenstern,* first performed in 1891, and *Trying a Dramatist* from 1911: both were written, in all essentials, in the 1870s.) His plots began to lose the simplicity and unity of his best earlier works, and he began to repeat himself. When a character of his sings in *His Excellency* (1894) that "the mine of jocularity is utterly worked out,"[1] we feel that Gilbert was writing from the heart.

Maybe the enthusiasm was still there, and it was simply the ability to match the old standards that was failing. Jane W. Stedman quotes a letter written by Gilbert to a Mrs. Stephenson on 7 January 1892, just after the premiere of *The Mountebanks:* "this is the worst libretto I have written. Perhaps I am growing old."[2] Perhaps indeed. He was fifty-five years old when he wrote these words, and his literary talents were growing inflexible.

However, this decline was neither immediate nor absolute, and there is much in these pieces worth examining. It is, for instance, interesting to see Gilbert responding to the new atmosphere of the 1890s. His style was beginning to seem antiquated, but he retained to some extent the ability to sniff the air and create works that reflected the prevailing atmosphere.

Five Librettos

The line of Savoy operas was broken in 1890 with the "Carpet Quarrel," which was essentially a dispute between Gilbert and Richard D'Oyly

Carte over production expenses. Sullivan sided with Carte, and so he and Gilbert became for a time opponents at law. Though the three patched up their differences later, creative trust was broken, and it is generally accepted that the last two Gilbert and Sullivan operas are not up to the old standard.

However, the split with Sullivan did at least give Gilbert the liberty to collaborate with another composer, for the first time since *Princess Toto* in 1876. Thus was produced *The Mountebanks* (1892). This was the long-delayed fruition of Gilbert's "Lozenge Plot," presented to Sullivan in 1884 and refused by him on the grounds that it was "unreal and artificial."[3] In the end the music was written by Alfred Cellier, who had previously collaborated with Gilbert on *Topseyturveydom* (1874); however, Cellier died before the music was quite completed, and the finished product was affected by the necessity of cutting unset lyrics out of the libretto.

The libretto has an unsatisfactory feel to it: Gilbert's assessment of it as being his worst libretto seems harsh, but the overlong gestation period, combined with the last-minute patching up that took place, certainly blurred the overall structure.

The plot consists of a simple binary structure, of the type we have seen before in such pieces as *The Gentleman in Black* (1870) and *The Sorcerer* (1877): the normal conditions of life are reversed by supernatural means at the end of act 1, and the consequences of this are seen in act 2, with a brief coda in which the status quo ante is restored, though a few extra happy endings are quietly added as a garnish.

In this case, a cast of brigands, mountebanks, and villagers inhabiting a Gilbertian Sicily are thrown into confusion when they drink a potion that, as the label on the bottle says, makes *"every one who drinks it exactly what he pretends to be."*[4] The brigands were disguised as monks, and so become monks; a young woman in their band was disguised as an old crone, so she becomes one; two of the mountebanks were passing themselves off as clockwork figures, so they become clockwork in real earnest. In an oddly melodramatic and sentimental final scene, the bottle's label is burned and the potion's spell thereby nullified.

The plot seems unsatisfactory because it fails to address properly the theme stated on the bottle's label: *"Man is a hypocrite, and invariably affects to be better and wiser than he really is."*[5] This idea is not borne out, or even pointedly refuted, by the plot: it is simply left lying there, while a sequence of purely trivial consequences is worked out. The only moment when the theme of satire on the human condition is properly addressed is the act 2 duet "Put a Penny in the Slot," in which the mounte-banks Bartolo and Nita, now turned into the clockwork figures they were pretending to be, assure us, the audience, that we are no different from them:

> *Bartolo*. Clockwork figures may be found
>   Everywhere and all around.
> *Nita*.Ten to one, if we but knew,
>   You are clockwork figures too.
> *Bartolo*. And the motto of the lot,
> *Nita*."Put a penny in the slot!"[6]

This is almost the only coherent remnant of what must have been Gilbert's original idea. The rest of the libretto contains many amusing scenes, but the intellectual unity of his best librettos is absent. The combi-nation of ideas is not coherent enough to fit into the framework I have sug-gested for the main Savoy operas: we are no longer in the Land Where Contradictions Meet. Some of the ideas are clearly borrowed from his translation of *The Brigands* (1871), and I have mentioned how the overall structure was an ancient favorite of Gilbert's. The old style is beginning to feel stale, and the whole seems less than the sum of its parts.

As Stedman notes, "The post-1890 librettos . . . (except for *Haste to the Wedding*) have multiple plots."[7] She also draws attention to "the sugges-tion of diffuseness in the structure"[8] of *The Gondoliers* and its successors. Gilbert is beginning to go back on his own principle of adherence to the idea of the single plot. But this, like the increasing windiness of the prose style, can be put down to creative exhaustion rather than to a conscious policy.

Little need be said of *"Haste to the Wedding"* (1892), Gilbert's next li-bretto: it was a reworking of *The Wedding March* (1873), his translation of the Labiche farce *Un Chapeau de Paille d'Italie,* the new lyrics being set by George Grossmith. It is surely significant that Gilbert should now turn back to this ancient triumph, which he had viewed at the time as a piece of purely commercial hackwork: he was beginning to find original ideas hard to come by. We have already seen that the idea of *The Mountebanks* dated back to the early 1880s.

Utopia, Limited (1893), with which Gilbert resumed the collaboration with Sullivan, has all the defects of plot and style that had begun to emerge, but it does at least have the advantage of containing a number of vigorous ideas. It contains many reminiscences of earlier works, but the plot was at any rate new-fashioned for the occasion. The belligerently satirical tone looks back to *The Happy Land* (1873), suggesting that Gilbert was reacting in typically contrary manner to the nostalgic terms in which the press greeted the return of Gilbert and Sullivan.

Gilbert's Utopia is, like Topseyturveydom or the Fairyland of *The Happy Land*, a distorted reflection of the England in which he lived. It is ruled by the Anglophile King Paramount; two of his daughters have been "finished" by a straitlaced English governess, and his eldest daughter Princess Zara has been sent to Girton. Zara returns to Utopia, bringing with her six representatives of British success, the "Flowers of Progress," to complete the remodeling of Utopian society. These include Mr. Goldbury, who recommends the creation of Limited Companies as a panacea for all ills. It is he who turns the island into Utopia (Limited) and extends the idea to all its inhabitants. ("There is not a christened baby in Utopia who has not already issued his little Prospectus!")[9] This tone of topical, and sometimes bitter, satire lies at the heart of the opera.

Ironic inversion is, as ever, the main satirical technique: Gilbert now felt so assured that everyone was familiar with his style that he could afford to make the ironies a little less obvious. For instance, everyone refers to Great Britain in fulsomely complimentary terms ("the greatest, the most powerful, the wisest country in the world,"[10] etc.), but the more flattering the terms, the less appealing Britain appears. By the time we reach the act 2 finale, what might have appeared to be a straight compliment seems much more jaundiced, and the threat in the refrain becomes much more obvious than it might otherwise have been:

Zara. There's a little group of isles beyond the wave—
   So tiny, you might almost wonder where it is—
That nation is the bravest of the brave,
   And cowards are the rarest of all rarities.
The proudest nations kneel at her command;
   She terrifies all foreign-born rapscallions;
And holds the peace of Europe in her hand
   With half a score invincible battalions!
    Such, at least, is the tale
    Which is borne on the gale,
     From the island which dwells in the sea.
    Let us hope, for her sake,
    That she makes no mistake—
     That she's all she professes to be![11]

This verse explains pretty clearly one of the opera's main points. The argument runs thus: Great Britain says that it is the best country in the world and that its inhabitants are the natural superiors of all others. Very well: if so, then Britain has the perfect right to rule all other nations, since Britons are a race of gods walking among mortals. But if not—if Britain is not all she professes to be—then it will be the worse for Britain as well as for the rest of the world. Or, as Gilbert wrote in a final refrain for this finale, cut in preproduction:

> But supposing instead
> That we've all been misled—
> What a kettle of fish there will be![12]

As a critique of the colonial mentality this still seems frighteningly valid as we look back on the past century from our present safe vantage.

George Bernard Shaw, reviewing the opera, noted: "There is, happily, no plot":[13] and it is true that the structure is highly fragmentary. The satirical subplots are full of jokes and ideas but do not fit together properly; a romantic subplot between Zara and Captain Fitzbattleaxe resolves itself in act 1 and has nowhere else to go in act 2. Considered as a well-constructed libretto in the old style, it fails completely; but Shaw chose to think of its formlessness as an advantage, and perhaps it is best seen as a series of linked satirical sketches, a kind of large-scale revue.

Shaw's review of *Utopia, Limited* was entirely positive, and indeed the tone of political satire must have been highly congenial to him, though he draws no special attention to it. One suspects that Shaw was half-remembering *Utopia, Limited* in such late plays as *The Apple Cart* (1930) and *On The Rocks* (1934). The 1890s were characterized by, among other things, a flourishing political awareness that was to have a vital influence on the development of the "New Drama" of the turn of the century. It was a prescient move of Gilbert's to emphasize this aspect of his work at this moment, *before* such firebrands as Shaw and Granville Barker burst on the theatrical scene. This was a period during which the nation was criticizing its own nature and influence more seriously than ever before: what better moment to present it with a "State of the Nation" opera, which is essentially what *Utopia, Limited* is? It is highly unfortunate that the execution of the piece did not quite come up to the conception.

One of the most interesting figures in the opera is King Paramount, nominally a "King of autocratic power"[14] but actually held under the thumbs of two Wise Men, who, according to the Utopian constitution, can

Rutland Barrington as King Paramount in *Utopia, Limited*. (The Raymond Mander and Joe Mitchenson Theatre Collection.)

have him blown up if he abuses his power. (One character calls it "Despotism tempered by Dynamite."[15]) The Wise Men use their power corruptly to further their own interests and sadistically to humiliate the King. They make him write anonymous denunciations of himself in the Utopian scandal sheet *The Palace Peeper;* they make him write a comic opera satirizing himself entitled "'King Tuppence; or, A Good Deal Less than Half a Sovereign.'"[16] The King's desperate response is to laugh at his own misfortunes: "properly considered, everything has its humorous side—even the *Palace Peeper.*"[17] But his laughter soon becomes uncertain and bitter, and at this point his predicament ceases to be comic.

He is the opera's central character; Captain Fitzbattleaxe, the tenor in love with the heroine, is by comparison nowhere. Gilbert, now in his late fifties, could work up very little interest in stories of young love and was much more concerned with the problems of men such as King Paramount, who seems to be suffering a sort of midlife crisis. The early Savoy operas revolved round the tenor hero, but the last two of the series (*Utopia, Limited* and *The Grand Duke*) have as their heroes characters played by the stout, middle-aged comic baritone Rutland Barrington. One must, of course, be very careful about this sort of identification, but King Paramount does appear to be a kind of Gilbert figure.

There is an uncertainty of purpose in Gilbert's treatment of the six "Flowers of Progress": when they are first presented to us, in an act 1 finale that is like a satirical masque, their songs reveal to us their stupidity and corruption. Their influence on Utopia can only be destructive, on the basis of what this sequence tells us, and indeed several scenes in act 2 suggest precisely this:

> *Phantis.* Are you aware that the Lord Chamberlain, who has his own views as to the best means of elevating the national drama, has declined to license any play that is not in blank verse and three hundred years old—as in England?
> *Scaphio.* And as if that wasn't enough, the County Councillor has ordered a four-foot wall to be built up right across the proscenium, in case of fire—as in England.
> *Phantis.* It's so hard on the company—who are liable to be roasted alive—and this has to be met by enormously increased salaries—as in England.[18]

But this is contradicted by the opera's final scene, in which the Utopians revolt on the grounds that the Englishmen's reforms have been too successful:

Scaphio. Our pride and boast—the Army and the Navy—
  Have both been re-constructed and re-modelled
  Upon so irresistible a basis
  That all the neighbouring nations have disarmed—
  And War's impossible![19]

This idea is introduced to prepare the way for Gilbert's last barb, that Utopia ought to guard against the perils of efficiency by introducing the most important element of the British system, Government by Party:

> *Zara.* No political measures will endure, because one Party will assuredly undo all that the other party has done; and while grouse is to be shot, and foxes worried to death, the legislative action of the country will be at a standstill. Then there will be sickness in plenty, endless lawsuits, crowded jails, interminable confusion in the Army and Navy, and, in short, general and unexampled prosperity![20]

This is clever in a bitter way, but it fits in with nothing of what has gone before. The world of *Utopia, Limited* has no self-consistent reality. It works very well at the level of satirical comment, but at the structural level it is disconnected and unsatisfactory.

We have seen how Gilbert was able, in the best Savoy librettos, to balance contradictory ideas against each other, thus expressing the half-acknowledged doubts in his mind, which were also reflections of the doubts of his age. But the contradictory ideas in *Utopia, Limited* have not been artistically assimilated to anything like the same extent; they can only be perceived as annoying inconsistencies. Again, this can be put down to Gilbert's waning creative powers.

His Excellency (1894) is much more satisfactory in structural terms. It concerns George Griffenfeld, the Governor of Elsinore in Denmark, who delights in tricking and humiliating the people he governs. He makes his guard drill as ballet girls, sets up butter slides, and carries out such elaborate deceptions as making his daughters' suitors think the King has given them moneymaking appointments. The Prince Regent happens to arrive in Elsinore, disguised as a vagabond, and the Governor, noticing his resemblance to the Prince Regent, pays him to impersonate the Regent in the cause of another practical joke. At the start of act 2 the Regent hands out happy endings to everyone except the Governor, whom he degrades to the ranks, and the rest of the opera builds up to the moment when the Governor realizes that the Regent really is the Regent, and that all happy endings and acts of justice do indeed have full effect. The opera ends with the happy couples dancing off, leaving Griffenfeld to stand sentry at the gates of the castle he once occupied.

The opera is itself a kind of practical joke: a series of ridiculous events that take place for no deeper reason than the fun of it. We know from the start that the vagabond is the Regent, so there is no surprise in the ending, nor is there any dramatic tension in the process of reaching it. There is an air of charade about the whole thing: because the end is assured and the fates of the characters we most like are never in doubt, the reader/spectator remains curiously uninvolved.

(It is interesting to note, however, that just as *The Mountebanks* concerned characters who turned into the people they were pretending to be, so in *His Excellency* we have the deceptions of a practical joke turning into reality. There is an appropriate theatricality in this theme, which is, unfortunately, not coherently explored in either piece.)

Nevertheless, this is the best of Gilbert's 1890s librettos, from a technical point of view. The tone is humorous rather than satirical, and it even contains one or two likable human beings. Governor Griffenfeld is an interesting character because he is the opera's major figure and also its villain, in so far as it has a villain. He is a combination of humour and cruelty (like the Mikado?)—not without a certain charm but only capable of seeing a joke when the butt is someone else, and perhaps not even quite understanding how humiliating his jokes really are:

> *Griffenfeld.* Upon my word, there's no such thing as gratitude. I do all I can to make my soldiers amusing—I place them in all kinds of ridiculous situations—I make them a source of entertainment to a whole township of attractive girls, and instead of being pleased and grateful for the attention, they growl like so many sore-eared bears![21]

Gilbert's view of the matter is expressed by Harold, one of Griffenfeld's soldiers: "The fact is, the point of a joke is like the point of a needle—hold the needle sideways and it's plain enough, but when it is directed straight at you—well, it's not always very easy to see the point of it."[22] This argument against the cruel humor of the practical joke, with its implied plea for mutual tolerance, is very sane and sensible, but it must be admitted that it is not the most profound theme in the world, and this adds to the opera's lightness of tone.

There is a nice parallel to be drawn between Governor Griffenfeld and King Paramount of *Utopia, Limited.* Both are authority-figures to whom humor is important; they are what one might call Joker Kings.

There is, however, a fundamental difference between them. Paramount's humor is a defensive device to allow him to cope with subjugation to the whims of the Wise Men; his is the despairing laugh of the pessimist. Governor Griffenfeld, however, is the man in control, and he uses his power sadistically, much as the Wise Men did in *Utopia, Limited*. Humor is for him offensive rather than defensive: a sword, not a shield. And, interestingly, he is punished for his cruelty in the end, as the Wise Men were. This kind of explicit moral judgement is unusual in Gilbert's comic librettos.

The idea of the Joker King is taken up again in *The Grand Duke* (1896), as is the idea of the ruler whose grasp on power proves insecure—a very fin de siècle theme. King Paramount was under constant threat of deposition by dynamite; Governor Griffenfeld was suddenly degraded to the ranks. So in this opera (Gilbert's last collaboration with Sullivan) the whole plot is constructed round a conspiracy to dethrone the Grand Duke of a small German state.

The opera feels like a deliberate attempt to assume a "Gilbertian" style that Gilbert was no longer able to use with any enthusiasm. The plot contains many reminiscences of his earlier works: of *Thespis, Tom Cobb, The Gondoliers*, and *The Brigands*. The plot is much too complex to describe in detail here. It is enough, for the moment, to say that Ludwig, the principal comedian of a theatrical troupe, becomes, for one day, the Grand Duke of Pfennig Halbpfennig by a particularly absurd kind of bloodless coup. Max Keith Sutton has drawn attention to the similarity of this to ancient fertility ritual:

> The decrepit Rudolph has the role of the Old King whose death signifies the end of the year, the defeat of Winter in the ceremonial contest with Spring. . . . Rudolph undergoes legal death in the mock duel—the moment of ritual sacrifice—and the plump, sausage-devouring comedian takes over as duke for a day and Lord of Misrule.[23]

This comparison is surprisingly exact, as is an associated comparison Sutton makes with Aristophanic comedy: the battle of words between Rudolph and Ludwig in the act 1 finale ("Big bombs, small bombs, great guns and little ones!")[24] being equivalent to the Agon, and Ludwig's act 2 patter song "At the Outset I May Mention,"[25] with its confidential addresses to the audience, bearing comparison with the Parabasis. A taste for ancient Greek things was one of the fashions of the day, as Ludwig's patter song emphasizes:

> At this juncture I may mention
> That this erudition sham
> Is but classical pretension,
>   The result of steady "cram.".…
> And of course I'm only mocking
>   At the prevalence of "cram."[26]

The use of Aristophanic structure may therefore have been deliberate.

The connection between the "Lord of Misrule" and the Joker Kings of *Utopia, Limited* and *His Excellency* is obvious. Ludwig makes his court wear extravagant ancient Greek costumes, for no immediately relevant reason, and plays a very childish practical joke on the visiting Prince of Monte Carlo and his suite. He is not embittered or self-pitying, like King Paramount, or unpleasantly malicious, like Governor Griffenfeld, but has similarities with both. The question about these Joker Kings must be, of course, What is their significance? One cannot resist the conclusion that they may be regarded as being to some extent reflections of Gilbert as he saw himself. As Gilbert was in absolute artistic control of the Savoy, so his Joker Kings rule: sometimes feeling under attack, sometimes showing a malignant streak, sometimes puckishly irresponsible. Ludwig's association with his theatrical troupe reinforces this identity.

One of *The Grand Duke*'s great problems is that too many plot ideas are mixed together without gelling properly. Sutton has also drawn attention to the "role-playing" aspect of the plot. Julia Jellicoe, the "leading lady" of the theatrical company, is destined to be Grand Duchess after the revolution, for no better reason than because it is the most important female role in that "situation." To her, the distinction between the theater and life has become blurred. Ludwig's court wears Greek costumes from the troupe's projected production of *Troilus and Cressida;* theatricality, role-playing, and make-believe are a constant theme throughout. This connects with similar ideas I have noted in *The Mountebanks* and *His Excellency.* I said that the theme is not properly explored in those other pieces, but it is all-pervasive here: one might say Gilbert overexplores it. The emphasis on surfaces, on decadence "in the literal sense of . . . physical and mental, moral and political decay"[27] (to quote Sutton again), is in keeping with the tone of the times. The opera has a feeling of overripeness on the verge of "going off"; it has some of the stifling lushness of a Beardsley drawing (though without any of its concomitant crudities).

The world of *The Grand Duke*, like that of *Engaged*, has lost its moral certainties, but *The Grand Duke* has in it a sense of moral stagnation that was absent from the earlier piece. This can probably best be explained by saying that the characters in *The Grand Duke* make no attempt to hide the selfishness that in *Engaged* was disguised in noble language. They show their feelings as clearly and simply as children:

> *Ludwig.* But when I inform your Highness that in me you see the most unhappy, the most unfortunate, the most completely miserable man in your whole dominion—
> *Rudolph (still sobbing).* You the most miserable man in my whole dominion? How can you have the face to stand there and say such a thing? Why, look at me! Look at me! *(Bursts into tears.)*
> *Ludwig.* Well, I wouldn't be a cry-baby.
> *Rudolph* A cry-baby? If you had been told that you were going to be deposed to-morrow, and perhaps blown up with dynamite for all I know, wouldn't you be a cry-baby?[28]

In *Engaged* a character in a parallel situation would have put on at least a show of dignity, though his real views on the matter would have been just as clear.

Gilbert had, in the 1870s, been part of the generation that was questioning the old certainties. He took the assumptions of the age and examined them in a skeptical spirit in such pieces as *Charity, The Happy Land*, and *Engaged*. But throughout these plays, frivolous though the tone might sometimes be, there is always the underlying assumption that the issues being tackled are, after all, of importance, that there is a difference between right and wrong that it is vital to understand.

But the generation that came to prominence in the 1890s was taking its skepticism to even greater extremes. In the words of Holbrook Jackson: "An imp of disquiet was abroad. . . . The young men enjoyed the fun as they rushed about smashing up the intellectual and moral furniture of their parents."[29] The Decadents, taking for their justification Walter H. Pater's adjuration to experience life and to reject any "theory, or idea, or system, which requires of us the sacrifice of any part of this experience,"[30] suggested that good and bad were, after all, nothing more than arbitrary distinctions that prevented the full experience of life. This was to cut down to the fundamental assumptions of civilized life, and onlookers might be forgiven for fearing that to act thus was to risk setting the whole structure of society tottering. There were those (of whom Oscar Wilde is the most obvious example) who suggested that the life of the moment was the only vital thing: that it was, for instance, more important that a sentence should be perfectly achieved than that it should be true. This was, indeed, an Age of Surfaces.

Gilbert certainly did not approve of these aspects of the age, but he was nevertheless affected by them, as *The Grand Duke* shows. The characters experience life and react to it entirely as their immediate desires demand: they scarcely even pay lip service to morality. In act 2, Ludwig is perfectly willing to commit polygamy, and no one else thinks of this as anything more than an unfortunate peccadillo.

There is a constant emphasis on the simple sensual facts of existence. Ludwig describes his bride-to-be as "Pretty Lisa, fair and tasty";[31] there is a song about sausage rolls ("It's a greasy kind of pasty, / Which, perhaps, a judgment hasty / Might consider rather tasty");[32] another song describes in detail the sensations of illness:

> When your lips are all smeary—like tallow,
> And your tongue is decidedly yallow,
> With a pint of warm oil in your sw*a*llow,
>   And a pound of tin-tacks in your chest—. . .
> Then you've got to a state which is known
>   To the medical world as "jim-jams."[33]

All this helps to create the slightly sickly atmosphere of the whole.

Interestingly, in these librettos of the 1890s Gilbert was beginning to use a new kind of humor—a naively frivolous species of wordplay. In *Utopia Limited*, Princess Zara comforted the tenor for the fact that his singing was suffering because of his love for her by saying: "Who thinks slightingly of the cocoanut because it is husky?"[34] This kind of thing can be charming, but it is a break away from Gilbert's earlier style of wit, in which almost every joke could be dissected to find a serious moral meaning. In *The Grand Duke* this new humor becomes rather elephantine:

> *Ernest (angrily)*. When you come to think of it, it's extremely injudicious to admit into a conspiracy every pudding-headed baboon who presents himself!
> *Ludwig*. Yes—I should never do that. If I were chairman of this gang, I should hesitate to enrol *any* baboon who couldn't produce satisfactory credentials from his last Zoological Gardens.[35]

We may imagine that this new style was being developed as a result of Gilbert's increasing dissatisfaction with the old "Palace of Truth" style.

The plot is too complex, but the invention is too tired; the humor is at the same time too lumpen and too thin; it might be said that the tone fits the age *too* well, in that it picks up something of the atmosphere of moral irresponsibility that was one of the more perishable aspects of the 1890s. Gilbert's prose style was becoming more prolix, and *The Grand Duke* contains many sentences that are just long enough to become tedious. Worse, the quality of his lyric writing was deteriorating a little, too: the opera contains such desperate rhymes as "leftly/deafly,"[36] "lowest/ghoest,"[37] and "quiver/diskiver."[38] There are good things in it, of course, but enough elements were sufficiently wrong to make it the least successful Gilbert and Sullivan opera since *Thespis: The Grand Duke* ran for only 123 performances.

Shortly after the premiere, Gilbert wrote of the opera thus in a letter to Mrs. Bram Stoker, dated 9 March 1896: "I'm not at all a proud Mother, & I never want to see the ugly misshapen little brat again!"[39] In this comment his sense of weariness at the whole nerve-racking business of theater is obvious, and it is not surprising that he announced his retirement as a dramatist the next year, after the failure of *The Fortune-Hunter.* And though he wrote three more plays in his "retirement," they were nothing more than occasional pieces or "sins of old age." He had begun to accept that his best days were now behind him.

Four Last Plays

The Fortune-Hunter (1897) was Gilbert's first "serious" play since *Brantinghame Hall* in 1888—and even the latter, it seems, had been a play written much earlier and hastily revamped.[40] Between those dates Gilbert had devoted himself entirely to the writing of librettos, and the fashionable style of drama had changed. The demographic profile of theatrical audiences had changed much in the years since Gilbert first started writing for the theater: the theater was now a place for the fashionable folk to see and be seen, as it never was in the 1870s. And this change was reflected in the plays that were being produced: as the early Victorian drama was, in general terms, centered on the problems of the working and lower-middle classes and mid-Victorian drama on the solid middle class, so late Victorian drama focused on the upper classes—the aristocracies of birth and wealth. The society melodramas of Wilde, and such Pinero plays as *The Second Mrs. Tanqueray* (1893), were exclusively concerned with the titled and the moneyed, who, having nothing more important to concern them, agonized over the morality of their personal behavior: particularly, of course, their sexual behavior.

The influence of Ibsenism, as it was understood at the time, was also felt, not only in the new willingness to air issues of sexuality (in a roundabout way), but also in the trend away from the old theatrical conventions of rhetoric and toward a much more "psychological" and understated approach to dramatic writing and acting. However much the Ibsenite drama was decried by the traditionalists, it could not be ignored, and it had a significant effect on even such dramatists as Pinero: it provoked a movement toward a new style of drama, which was not only "realistic" in subject matter but also "naturalistic" in treatment.

Many felt at the time what has since become generally accepted, that the 1890s marked the point when British drama emerged out of the wilderness and freed itself from the banal conventionalities in which it had been bound, an idea Clement Scott vehemently denied in his anti-Ibsen review of *Ghosts* (in *The Illustrated London News,* 21 March 1891):

> Are not Gilbert, Pinero, Henry Arthur Jones, as unconventional and as free in their method as any dramatists in the memory of living man? And now, having attained this important point, after years of struggle and labour, we are to be airily told that Ibsen and the founders of the Independent Theatre are the chosen apostles to free the neglected stage from the fetters and manacles of conventionality![41]

Scott was overhostile to the rising generation, but this is a legitimate point, though overstated. This marvelous new generation no more sprang out of nowhere than did Tom Robertson, Gilbert, or Pinero. Their works were, as ever, a development of what had gone before. The techniques of melodrama did not disappear but turned up in new, less bombastic guises. William Archer, reviewing Wilde's *A Woman of No Importance* (in *The World,* 26 April 1893), wrote rather mischievously of the big scene at the end of act 3:

> It would be a just retribution if Mr Wilde were presently to be confronted with this tableau, in all the horrors of chromolithography, on every hoarding in London, with the legend 'Stay, Gerald! He is your father!' in crinkly letters in the corner.[42]

But in theory if not quite in practice, unconventionality and truth to life were the latest watchwords in drama. *The Fortune-Hunter* makes some attempt to come to terms with some of these new trends, though it is all too obvious that it was written by a man of an earlier generation. Gilbert could only have accommodated himself to the times with a complete reinvention of his style from fundamentals, which, at the age of sixty, he was both unwilling and unable to do.

The play is constructed around an article in the French *Code Civile* that states, in the words of Gilbert's prefatory note to the play, that

> a Frenchman who is under the age of twenty-five CANNOT LEGALLY CONTRACT MARRIAGE UNLESS HE HAS OBTAINED THE CONSENT OF HIS PARENTS IF THEY BE LIVING. If, dispensing with this consent, he should go through the form of marriage, that marriage may be attacked by his parents or by himself. It is open to his parents to give a post-nuptial consent to such a marriage, but he is not bound by such consent, and is entitled nevertheless to apply to the Courts for a decree of nullity on his own responsibility.[43]

The Marquis de Bréville, a charming young Frenchman, marries a rich Australian heiress, Diana Caverel. However, on discovering that she is not as wealthy as they both thought, he grows cold toward her and decides to use the article in the *Code Civile* to have the marriage nullified. He knew that his parents would not approve of his marrying anyone of less than aristocratic background, so he has not told them. He says that he wishes to shield his parents from the disgrace of applying for the nullification of their son's marriage, so he does so himself. However, when his parents learn of the marriage, they say that, though they disapprove of it, they never thought of invoking the article—for "that law is as infamous as he who would resort to it."[44]

In the last act de Bréville discovers—"to my surprise, I admit"[45]—that he is not capable of carrying out his scheme, especially since he discovers that his wife, from whom he has become separated, has borne them a son, who "will go through the world a bastard"[46] if the marriage is nullified. But it is too late to stop the court proceedings, as they are to take place that very afternoon; the only way they can be halted is by de Bréville's death, so he hastily provokes a duel and deliberately allows his opponent to kill him. Thus he redeems the honor of the family.

The play is, unashamedly, an old-fashioned well-made mechanism with a carefully contrived final twist, though the taste of the day was moving away from such overt neatness, as we have already seen in Archer's "Real Conversation" with Gilbert, quoted in chapter 2. The style of dialogue, too, is absurdly at odds with the new naturalism:

> *Sir Cuthbert.* I am ready to receive proofs that I have done M. de Bréville an injustice, but in fairness to myself, I should tell you that his father has stated in my presence that no consideration would have induced him to take proceedings which, although sanctioned by the laws of his country, he denounced as infamous beyond expression.[47]

Such a style is acceptable in Gilbert's ironic comedies, which are partly parodic in intent and in which there is no pretense of stage simply mimicking life, but *The Fortune-Hunter* is a "serious" drama, and such highly wrought speeches do not fit the genre conventions as they were understood in 1897. Also, Gilbert's style here is much more stilted than it was in such 1870s equivalents as *Charity*.

However, despite these old-fashioned elements, it is clear that Gilbert was making a genuine attempt to reflect some of the concerns of the age. Stedman has drawn attention to the "independent, unconventional"[48] heroine Diana Caverel, who "frankly, with the language available to her, describes the way in which her unmistakably sexual passion has subjugated her individuality."[49] Stedman is clearly referring to such speeches as:

> I am a fool to give myself up to you thus. Go your way—who are you that you are to be so loved? Are you so much better, wiser, braver, fairer than other men that they are to be as nothing to me, and you are to be as all in all? Are you so—(*suddenly breaking down*). Yes, yes—God help me, you are the life that is in me, and I love you till I hate and abhor you for the fearful thraldom in which my senses are held![50]

This is very strong meat for Gilbert; the nearest parallel I can think of is with some of Selene's speeches in *The Wicked World* (1873), which had in any case been somewhat tamed by the blank verse. Diana's desire for unusual freedom is suggested in passages such as this:

> I must move about the world, or I am as a caged prisoner. I want fire and heat and colour—blue skies and bright sunshine—the bustle and movement of great cities—the whirl and torrent of rapid travel—and the give and take of bright brains.[51]

This suggestion of independence of mind also has a predecessor, in Jane Theobald, the actress heroine in *Ought We to Visit Her?* (1874). Diana's behavior is made more acceptable, however, by her being an Australian, and so by implication naturally wild and untamed.

Still, Diana is treated sympathetically, unlike the comic snobs the Coxe-Coxes, who are mercilessly ridiculed for their petty-mindedness. Another major character, the breezy American Duchess of Dundee (*"née Euphemia S. Van Zyl, of Chicago,"* as the cast-list notes),[52] is an unashamed fortune hunter who earns respect because of her straightforwardness. If we put Diana and the Duchess alongside the French semihero the Marquis de Bréville, who despite past errors redeems himself in the end (like Sidney Carton), then we have a startlingly international set of characters. Of the nationalities, the English come out the worst, the only decent Briton of the lot being the rather colorless Sir Cuthbert Jameson. This seems to be associated with the idea Gilbert had explored in so many of his comic pieces, the idea that English characteristics may be defined by comparison with foreign societies and people.

This is particularly relevant to the character of the Marquis de Bréville: in some ways he lives up to the stereotype of the dashing young Frenchman, but he mocks Sir Cuthbert when the latter assumes the stereotype to be true:

> [M]y respectable John Bull, you hate a Frenchman as you hate a bright Sunday. We are all vain, frivolous, egotistical. Is it not so—hein? But we have our *rôle*—we send you actors, singers, fiddlers, painters—we amuse you and we decorate your wives—that is our *rôle*. And while you pity the funny, ingenious, poor foreign devils, you are ready enough to laugh at their capers and to pay them handsomely for cutting them. My good, respectable, church-going John Bull, you are wrong, wrong, wrong! A word in your ear—but it is in confidence. There are men in France who are not mountebanks![53]

De Bréville is an interesting figure because of his ambiguous role in the play: he is presented to us from the start as genuinely charming and likable, and yet his action in seeking to nullify the marriage for financial reasons is the action of a conventional villain. His change of mind in the last act is, for Gilbert, surprisingly psychological:

> *De Breville.* . . . It is not to be wondered at that you do not quite know me, for I do not quite know myself. I fancied that I was committing myself to an act of villainy to which I was equal: it at no time seemed easy, but at one time it seemed possible. Well, I was mistaken.[54]

Like Robin Oakapple in *Ruddigore*, he is unsure for a time whether he is a hero or a villain: then, rather to his own surprise, he comes down on the side of the angels. This is not quite psychological complexity—we are always aware that Gilbert is using, and toying with, the theatrical conventions—but it does recall the controlled contradictions and ambiguities of Gilbert's earlier work.

The Fortune-Hunter is an "interesting" rather than a good play. It toured the country but was never produced in London. Gilbert later revised it and sought a producer for it, without success. As Stedman says, "By then, it was far too old-fashioned in form, though perhaps not in content."[55] But the quality of a play is not judged solely by its ideas.

The first play of Gilbert's "retirement," *The Fairy's Dilemma* (1904), reverts to an older theatrical tradition: it is a playful mockery of the kind of pantomime with harlequinade that had by that date all but died out. Gilbert himself recognized that it was an anachronism. In a letter to Mr. Bourchier (2 August 1904) he wrote: "The piece came too late—it should have been produced forty years ago, and then people would have appreciated its intention."[56] Sutton has pointed out that Gilbert had long been interested in the possibilities of making the harlequinade an integral part of the pantomime, rather than a mere tacked-on extravagance.[57] Such Gilbert articles as "On Pantomimic Unities" (*Fun,* 20 February 1864) and "A Consistent Pantomime" (*Graphic,* 16 January 1875) explore the idea, but he never put these ideas on the stage until *The Fairy's Dilemma* (subtitled "An Original Domestic Pantomime").

The play is, in conception at any rate, extremely ingenious. Two characters from the pantomime-supernatural world—the Fairy Rosebud and the Demon Alcohol—pool their resources to interfere in a romance in the London of 1904 but succeed only in creating havoc. They assume that Sir Trevor Maulverer, being a Baronet, must necessarily be Bad, and his intentions to the nurse Jane Collins dishonorable. (Jane Collins is really Lady Angela Wealdstone in disguise, for a reason more complex than explainable.) The Demon Alcohol abducts Clarissa Whortle (at that moment disguised as a nurse) and deposits her in Sir Trevor's Whitehall Mansions flat—though the honorable Sir Trevor immediately returns her. In short, the two immortals make a disastrous mess of everything, and the only way they can think of resolving matters is to use the standby solution of transforming everyone into the harlequinade characters. In the last sequence we see the traditional harlequinade sketches unwillingly enacted by these respectable establishment figures. For instance, the priggish Rev. Aloysius Parfitt is transformed into Harlequin, and, being utterly ignorant of his duties in this role, is instructed by Lady Angela:

> *Lady Angela.* . . . You'll have to change things into other things. For
> instance, a man comes along in a fifteen hundred pound motor-car with
> "FISCAL POLICY" on it. You slap the car with your bat, and it changes into
> a coster-monger's barrow labelled "FREE FOOD FOR EVERYBODY."
> *Aloysius.* But that is not at all in accordance with my political views![58]

The comedy here comes from the spectacle of these self-important pil-
lars being reduced to enacting all the old amoral, anti-authority routines.
Or perhaps it is best seen as a deliberate reminder to these polite "New
Drama" characters of the vigorous, vulgar early Victorian drama that the
"New Drama" was so eager to forget.

> *Sir Trevor.* . . . I perceive a nursemaid approaching wheeling a
> double perambulator, and accompanied by a Corporal Major of my own
> regiment of Household Cavalry. Conceive my distress when I tell you that
> I instinctively feel that it will be my painful duty to trip up that Corporal
> Major, and rob the poor girl of her hat, boa, and other cheap finery, while
> you sit upon the perambulator, and squash her helpless innocents!
> *Judge (horrified).* No, no! I am a father—I cannot do it—I cannot
> do it![59]

This sequence is the most effective in the play: the overwritten and rather
static drawing-room comedy of the mortals is whisked away and we are
transported, via "The Revolving Realms of Radiant Rehabilitation," to a
brightly colored world of pratfalls and few words.

> [SIR TREVOR *slaps three times on door post, then lies*
> *across doorway.* PASTRYCOOK *comes out and tumbles over him.*
> *Sir Trevor* (with his hand on his heart). Oh, I beg yer parsnips!
> [PASTRYCOOK *very angry, and expresses his feelings in*
> *gesture.* SIR TREVOR *takes him confidentially by the arm.*
> *Sir Trevor* I say, do you want a handy young man?
> [PASTRYCOOK's *anger vanishes, and he expresses that*
> *he does.*
> *Sir Trevor.* Then I'm the chap for you! Tuppence a month, paid the
> year before next, and find my own motor-car![60]

This reads like a documentary reproduction of the old routines. Gilbert's
treatment of them is a criticism of their amorality, but a real affection for
them also shows through.

Of course, as ever with such Gilbertian reversals, there must come a
time when normality is restored. The Fairy Rosebud and the Demon

Alcohol have a fit of conscience at taking this "monstrous liberty"[61] with the lives of the mortals and restore them to their original conditions, asking in return that the Reverend Parfitt marry the Fairy and the Demon to each other. This marriage of good and evil tells us much of Gilbert's view of the world. He did not believe in the established moral absolutes, and he delighted, as we have seen, in confusing the melodramatic stereotypes of hero and villain. In the first scene of the play the Fairy and the Demon decided to give each other work by agreeing on a set of mortals on whom to impose their own respective ends—the Fairy Rosebud sure in the knowledge that "I'll interfere just in time . . . and restore her [the heroine] to the arms of her faithful clergyman."[62] This is oddly reminiscent of the opening chapters of the Book of Job, one of Gilbert's favorite works of literature. It would be absurd to draw a close comparison between the two works, but there is a real implication that good and evil are opposing forces that nevertheless work together.

By and large, the supernatural and pantomimic scenes are the liveliest parts of the play. However, even in the duller drawing-room sections there are moments when the old wit shows through the wordiness. Gilbert has his moment of revenge for all those years as a librettist when Sir Trevor, musing alone upon the mistaken reputation Baronets have, says:

> *Sir Trevor*. . . . In my moments of leisure I have composed a lament upon the subject which may tend, not infelicitously, to correct this unfortunate misconception.
> [*Symphony in orchestra. He takes music from his pocket and comes down as if to sing. At this moment enter* ALOYSIUS *and* CLARISSA. . . .[63]

And Gilbert is clearly having a little in-joke when he has the Reverend Aloysius Parfitt "discovered" at the start of act 1, scene 2, seated at the harmonium and playing Sullivan's "Lost Chord."[64]

The world of this play is the one in which Gilbert was most comfortable—the world of theatrical parody. As in *A Sensation Novel, H.M.S. Pinafore, Ruddigore*, and many others, he holds up a mirror, not to the world but to another mirror; but the intention remains the same, to reveal unusual truths about the world—to use these two mirrors to show it its metaphorical bald spots.

Unfortunately, the "real world" criticized in the play seemed as anachronistic in 1904 as the parody of pantomime, to judge by Max Beerbohm's review of the piece:

For the mortal characters "date" not less obviously than the fairies. There *are* no mild young curates, with side-whiskers, and with a horror of the stage, nowadays. There *are* no young military baronets who compose love-verses and sing them with a piano-accompaniment, nowadays. There *are* no ladies who sit at their toilet-tables combing tresses of false hair, nowadays. Such ladies ceased to exist when chignons ceased to exist.[65]

And Mr. Justice Whortle is a "Judicial humorist" of the type that Gilbert had attacked almost twenty years before in *The Mikado*.[66] *The Fairy's Dilemma* is a play that satirizes the dead past, so it works best when it gives itself up to frank fantasy and nonsense. It is amiable, and pleasantly nostalgic—there are passing reminiscences of such past glories as *Pirates* and *Patience*—but it fails to be anything more.

Fallen Fairies (1909) was Gilbert's last libretto: one might also call it his last Savoy opera, since it was first performed at the Savoy Theatre, though the composer was not Sullivan, who had died in 1900, but Edward German. The opera was a reworking of *The Wicked World,* and there is little to be said about it that I have not already touched upon in discussing the earlier play. The three acts are condensed into two, but most of the dialogue in *Fallen Fairies* comes from *The Wicked World,* though the sequence of some of the scenes is changed. The main difference lies, of course, in the songs. The Fairies' songs tend to the insipid, but those of the three men do at least have a kind of crude humor. These songs give the men a more prominent place in the opera than they had in the fairy comedy, though they scarcely make the men more sympathetic. The songs are celebrations of "mortal love": they are hypocritical avowals, denunciations of corrupting womanhood, comic and slightly leering affirmations of the importance of Woman to Man; or, as here, shameless exploitation of the innocence of the Fairies:

> *Ethais.* When homage to his Queen a subject shows
> (A Queen that's duly crowned),
> He puts his arm around
> That monarch's waist—like this,   (*Doing so.*)
> And plants a very long and tender kiss
> Sometimes upon her cheeks of creamy rose,
> But, preferably, just below the nose![67]

The Fairies, on the other hand, sing songs speculating on whether love is a blessing or a curse, and, when mortal love strikes them, songs of jealousy and overwrought agony. In the end, one is left with a vague wish that they would find something else to sing about for once.

The songs are appropriate in that they reflect the small compass of subjects in the original play, but by doing so they expose the play's weakness. Also, the lyrics show an overreliance on iambic pentameter (understandably) and are in general competent but unmemorable. One is not surprised to learn that the opera ran for only six weeks. But it is interesting in showing the persistent hold this plot had over Gilbert: its themes of idealized womanhood and brutal Man, and of "mortal love" being at the same time destructive and necessary, have a somewhat disturbing power; and the idea of portraying strong women who are not merely appendages to men is something that runs through much of Gilbert's more serious work.

These last plays seem almost like a deliberate recapitulation of Gilbert's various styles. First the serious "issues" drama of *The Fortune-Hunter*; then *The Fairy's Dilemma,* a return to the old Gilbertian style; and *Fallen Fairies,* a reminder of the fairy comedies and also his last libretto. Gilbert was now almost a "classic" in his own lifetime: the Savoy operas were being revived; in 1907 he was knighted and also honored with his first full-length biography. His biographer, Edith A. Browne, wrote critically and unenthusiastically about his prose dramas and fairy comedies and reserved her praise for the Savoy operas, much to Gilbert's annoyance. He must have been pained by passages such as this:

> one last word of the artist to whose heart *The Wicked World, Broken Hearts,* and *Gretchen* are dearer than the Savoy Operas. As we think of his favourite plays and our favourite comic operas . . . do we not reflect on the curious fact that many a successful man would fain owe his success to some medium other than that by which it has been attained, many a genius would, if given his choice, choose to be a genius of a different type![68]

Gilbert, in a letter to Browne dated 10 March 1907, wrote: "I can hardly believe that I owe the compliment [of being the subject of a biography] to the easy trivialities of the Savoy *libretti.*"[69] But already these were regarded as his sole claim to fame: his early diversity of achievement was all but forgotten. So in these last plays he insists on demonstrating that his talents do not lie only in the creation of "easy trivialities": when he returns to the libretto form, he does so with a piece that is a complete break from the accepted Savoy style. Such a gesture of defiance is entirely characteristic.

The Hooligan (1911), his last play, is the best of these last works. Again, the style is not typically "Gilbertian": it is a rather grim study of a criminal awaiting execution. Yet it does use some of the ironic techniques that underlie his best comic pieces, and this may be one of the reasons it succeeds. Another reason may be found in the circumstances of its composition: written as a music-hall sketch for the Coliseum star Jimmy Welch, it was necessarily brief, and Gilbert's verbosity was kept firmly in check.

In it, a young hooligan called Nat Solly wakes up on the morning of his execution. He is petrified and self-pitying. He had only meant to "cut" his girlfriend, he says, but his hand slipped, "on account of youth and inexperience."[70] He rambles on, alternately maudlin, angry, and terrified; he pleads for clemency on account of his weak heart and his weak head; he recounts a vivid nightmare about his trial. At last there is a noise at the door and he lapses into hysteria: however, they are not there to take him to execution but to say his death sentence has been commuted to one of life imprisonment. And Nat Solly, shocked by this sudden relief, collapses and dies of heart failure.

The play is subtitled "A Character Study," and indeed it is much less plot-led than most of his other plays: its main concern is to portray Nat Solly's changing moods and increasing terror, though Gilbert's concern for plot does reappear in its last moments. And the portrayal of Nat Solly's character deserves a little examination.

The Hooligan engages with a live issue of the day as Gilbert had not really managed to do in *The Fortune-Hunter*, and had certainly failed to do since then. John Galsworthy's controversial play *Justice* (1910) had shocked its audiences by showing the terrors of a man in an isolation cell; and now Gilbert was doing the same thing with the condemned cell (though in a different style). Beerbohm's review of *Justice* (*The Saturday Review,* 5 March 1910) makes an important point that also applies to *The Hooligan:*

> Mr. Galsworthy . . . carefully eschews any show of sympathy with one character. . . . In showing us a young criminal caught in the toils of law, he shows us no hero, but a rather uninteresting youth with a tendency to hysteria, who does not, when he is confronted with the cheque that he has forged, hesitate to let suspicion fall on an innocent colleague. . . . [Galsworthy] knows that a suspicion of special pleading would jeopardize his case.[71]

Galsworthy's purpose is to expose the brutality of the use of the isolation cell as a punishment: he is, as Beerbohm notes, presenting a "case." Similarly, Gilbert's play seems in part intended as propaganda against capital punishment on the grounds of causing inhumane distress. And, like Galsworthy, he deliberately chooses not to make his hero in any way heroic, because it would weaken his argument if he seemed to be making an unsafe generalization from a special case. So Nat Solly is presented to us as a weak, self-pitying, casually violent young man whose pleas for clemency are transparently nothing more than wild attempts to save his skin. His character has no real redeeming features, and yet reader and audience sympathize with him, and there can be no reason why this should be so except the elemental fact that he is terrified. And the ending—the reprieve and heart failure—also has a "message" in it: the play is arguing that the inhumanity of capital punishment does not lie in the execution itself so much as in the anticipation of it.

In showing us the character of Nat Solly, Gilbert uses some of the techniques of his ironic comedies. Solly's longest speech is a self-pitying justification for his acts, every word of which is, though he does not realize it, a condemnation of his character: like a man in the Palace of Truth, he is condemned to be honest almost in spite of himself. It is here that we see most clearly the recognizable Gilbert style, the sense of distance between writer and character:

> An' one night I comes out an' I finds 'er [his girlfriend] wivvout 'er pal; she'd bin on the razzle and was staggerin' along singin' and 'owling, and I covers my face and goes behind 'er an' I did wot I swore I'd do. But I never cut a gal before—not in the 'ole course of my bloomin' life I didn't (and that's in my favour, mind yer), and my 'and slipped on account of youth and inexperience. . . . And 'im wot called me a 'eap o' tea-leaves and kicked me silly—I showed 'im manly-like wot a 'eap o' tea-leaves can do when 'e's put to it! And 'im to go and give evidence of freats—'im wot I could ha' put away a dozen times if I'd a mind to it.[72]

It sounds almost like a low-life version of *Engaged*. But it is quite believable in a naturalistic sense, if we bear in mind how worked up Solly is by this stage. He has lost control of the screening mechanism by which people prevent unfortunate admissions from slipping out.

The style is as realistic as Gilbert was capable of making it. Solly's cockney accent is tiring to read in bulk and is more an impression than a closely observed reproduction of real cockney speech. But the speeches— even Solly's big monologues—are written clearly and simply, without those clogged, complex sentences that were such a feature of Gilbert's late style. The limitations of the piece forced him to cut everything down to the minimum so that the effect, too, is made clear and simple. The play was genuinely shocking to its first audiences—"It was so gruesome that women had gone out fainting"[73]—which is not bad for a seventy-four-year-old dramatist addressing an audience inured to the outspoken "New Drama."

We know how important Gilbert felt endings to be: "The dramatist's real problem is, and must always be, the solution in the last act."[74] He held that ending a play on an anticlimax was not "sound art,"[75] though he recognized the precedents. So even this "character study" ends with a twist—or rather two twists; though these twists are, in their way, the natural culmination of everything that has gone before. The final crisis is a peripeteia, a reversal of fortune: the man at the door is not there to lead him to execution but to tell him he is to live. We, the audience, react with relief to this sudden end to the grim intensity of what has preceded this moment, and yet at the same time we may suddenly suspect the *other* twist, Solly's death, since the weakness of his heart has been carefully set up for us. But we have been fooled for a moment that the piece might be, formally speaking, a comedy: and this adds to the shock of the realization that it is not. It is an artful play, a surprisingly good swan song, bearing in mind the pieces that had preceded it. It succeeds because it uses Gilbert's long-practiced techniques to new ends: and though some of his last plays suggest that he was stuck in an overworn groove, he could still be jolted out of it.

It is, after all, no surprise to learn that a writer's style, like his limbs, may become stiff in later years. A similar stiffening occurs in the later works of such long-lived writers as Shaw and P. G. Wodehouse, sometimes to the point of self-parody. And yet this does not imply that there is nothing worthwhile in these later works, simply that one must make more and more allowances for age in assessing them. Gilbert, writing to a friend about *The Fairy's Dilemma,* said, "I think you'll call it rather 'young' for a wretched old josser in his sixty-eighth year,"[76] which is, in its way, true enough; but whether it would be considered "young" if written by a younger man is not so easy to say. There are many good ideas in these last plays and librettos; their main problem lies in the manner of execution.

Another difficulty arising from Gilbert's increasing age is that he gradually lost that sense of engagement with the issues of the day that is evident in most of his work in the 1870s and 1880s. In the 1890s and beyond he became the "old guard," enjoying such privileges of age as the right to grumble at the degenerate younger set. In some ways Gilbert prepared the way for the dramatic revival that was one of the main features of that period, with his "problem plays," his pessimistic ironies, and his use of "general ideas" as the foundation of his plays. But, perhaps inevitably, he was not pleased with the new dramatists with their "inartistic" unconventionalities. He could not mimic them: the naturalistic style was something alien to his theatrical assumptions. He was condemned, instead, to recapitulate his previous achievements until, by chance, in the last year of his life, he found a way of writing that could use his old techniques to the accepted new ends. *The Hooligan* is not a masterpiece, and to some extent the way one sees it is colored by knowledge of Gilbert's age when he wrote it, but this brief sketch does give one a tantalizing glimpse of new possibilities. There are many ways of describing the difference between a craftsman and an artist, but one way of putting it is that an artist always retains the capacity to surprise.

Conclusion: Contradiction Contradicted

A Child of the Age

Gilbert was born of the generation that came to maturity in the late 1850s at a time when the religious and moral certainties of the early Victorian age were being challenged, most obviously by Darwin's *Origin of Species* (1859) but also by such works as the theological *Essays and Reviews* (1860), by the working through of the social instability of the "hungry forties," and by the crisis of the Crimean War (1853–56). Throughout the 1860s new questions were asked, and a change in the tide of mass thought was felt, as G. M. Young notes:

> Religion, conceived as a concerted system of ideas, aspirations, and practices to be imposed on society, was losing its place in the English world. . . . The ethical trenchancy of the Evangelicals was passing over to the agnostics, who in their denunciation of the Sin of Faith, their exaltation of scientific integrity, could be as vehement, as dogmatic, and at times as narrow, as any of the creeds which they believed themselves to have supplanted. Agnosticism had the temper of the age on its side.[1]

Uncertainty is a terrible thing to acknowledge, and many years would pass before a true agnostic spirit would work its way into the mainstream of society. In the meantime, for many, uncertainty expressed itself in an overemphasized certainty, as if an idea might be transformed into fact by sheer force of personal opinion.

If Darwin and the Bible critics were to be believed, then the Scriptures, the foundation of Christian belief and morality, could no longer be taken on trust: they had to be critically reassessed, their literal truth cast into doubt. The fabric of English society, which was based so completely on Christian belief, was weakened not so much by any general acceptance of the critical things that were being written as by the simple fact that these things were being written at all. Questions, deep and fundamental questions, were being asked; they could not yet be answered with any certainty, but their mere existence was destabilizing enough.

Anthony Trollope's *The Way We Live Now* (1874–75) expresses Trollope's shock at the changes he found in English society on returning to England in December 1872 after one and a half years abroad. He felt that the old social order had been undermined by a cynical acceptance of money as the all-powerful good in life. The traditional class structure, upheld by the church, was as vitally affected as Christianity itself by this mood of doubt; and Trollope saw a new tendency among the aristocracy to make the most of its privileges and to ignore the compensatory duties and responsibilities. It would be oversimplistic to say that these things were the unique and sudden product of this particular time, as if previous generations had been strangers to doubt, but in terms of broad tendencies the idea that the atmosphere of English society changed at this time is inescapable. In the words of George Kitson Clark:

> The intellectual and spiritual histories of these people seem to confirm Young's view that round about 1860 there was a change in nineteenth-century culture, after which traditional beliefs and loyalties became less generally acceptable and were rejected by men who earlier would have been unlikely to question them.[2]

But what was there to replace these discredited beliefs? Liberal humanism, possibly: Christian morality without Christian religion? A belief in science: a Gradgrindian pursuit of fact which, as the emergence of Eugenic ideas at the turn of the century suggests, was not without its drawbacks? A purely materialistic philosophy: a philosophy which can, all too easily, degenerate into mere selfishness and cynicism? These were utterly fundamental choices, the consequences of which we are still working out today. And it was in this rudderless society that Gilbert emerged as a writer for the theater. A child of his age, he grappled with these questions and sought a way of expressing these doubts, the doubts of his age that were also his own doubts: and he also tried to find a way of doing these things within the constraints of commercial drama.

I do not mean that he "tried" to do all this at the conscious level, that he sat down at his desk and attempted to write plays that would summarize the spirit of the age. But Gilbert was sensitive to the atmosphere he lived in, and he was fastidious enough to be always probing the ideas behind events. He wrote to make money, but what he wrote, even his most frivolous and obviously commercial works, reflected his personal concerns and expressed his ideas about the things that were happening around him. He could not do otherwise.

THE DEVELOPMENT OF A STYLE

Gilbert did not immediately find a style in which all this could be done: that took time. When he began to write for the theater, he was inevitably an imitator: he clutched at the popular form that approached nearest to what he wanted to do in drama—that is, the rhymed burlesque/extravaganza— and by experimenting with the form came to a firmer understanding of what he could do within its confines.

It was a confessedly "low" dramatic form, the great and only purpose of which was to entertain: to delight and to amaze. The actual script had a merely subordinate role to the necessary "turns" of the various performers and the spectacular effects that the piece was to exhibit. The script's main purpose was to tell a familiar story in a light, unfussy, and pun-laden manner. Parody and satire (or, at any rate, topical "digs") were always part of the extravaganza form, but these were never more than incidental features. Gilbert, in his excursions into the form, quickly latched onto these elements as the ones in which he might best speak in his own voice. Though he was able to develop the satirical elements a little in the later extravaganzas, the restrictions of the form prevented him from making them more than a minor element in the whole. It quickly became obvious that he had to move on.

In the blank-verse fairy comedies he exchanged rhymed couplets for blank verse, used more original stories, and jettisoned the puns. However, by keeping the remote settings and vaguely fairy-tale atmosphere he was able to tackle important issues of human behavior without the tone becoming too "near the knuckle." The plays, though sometimes seeming to betray the superior attitude of a god amusedly watching the antics of frail mortals, do come to the interesting conclusion that these frailties are in some respect virtues, in that they are integral to what makes us human. For instance, by showing the chaos that ensues when humans are deprived of the ability to lie, in *The Palace of Truth* (1870), Gilbert is able to demonstrate how important that ability is. Human faults are forgiven and even justified, though the author ensures that he and the audience are kept safely superior to the antics of the characters on stage.

In his prose dramas he used realistic settings and recognizable characters to reflect more obviously what he saw around him. In the best of these, such as *An Old Score* (1869), he portrays the hypocrisy of the respectable and shows how those who might seem, on the surface, less deserving—those lacking in social grace, those lacking wealth and power, those occasionally guilty of bohemian dissipations—might still prove to be made of better stuff. In *An Old Score* and *Charity* (1874) he looked with a satirical eye on the society in which he lived but expressed his satire with an earnestness of purpose that is lacking in his more "Gilbertian" works. He never quite mastered the proper style for these prose dramas: indeed, the hostility with which the public greeted these plays never encouraged him to do so. Despite their faults, these plays might have kept their audience had they not been so very clear in their criticism of contemporary society.

The fairy comedies, on the other hand, were popular in their day: *Pygmalion* and *Galatea* (1871) was Gilbert's most popular non-Sullivan work, earning him around £40,000, according to Hesketh Pearson.[3] Yet, with their blank verse and their mythological symbolism, they stand on their dignity a little too much. After a while, one may be forgiven for yearning for the determined vulgarity of the extravaganzas. Though a bold and in many ways successful experiment, they did not allow Gilbert to explore the full range of his talents.

It was, of course, in the comic libretto, developed at the Gallery of Illustration and elsewhere, that Gilbert's main strengths first came together. As in the extravaganzas, he could combine dialogue and song, thus giving the drama a "lift" that mere words can never give. He could reflect the realities, by the use of exaggeration, parody, and all the wild arsenal of Topsyturvydom, while the conventions of the libretto form provided the much-needed assurance that all this was, after all, not really taking place. Gilbert developed this style over several librettos, and it is difficult to pinpoint a specific moment when everything fell into place, but he had certainly found most of the distinctively Gilbertian style by the time of *A Sensation Novel* (1871).

His style and the vision that he expressed with it were both coming into maturity, and this may be an appropriate point at which to ask what, exactly, Gilbert had to say—relating this in particular to the issues of the age that I highlighted at the beginning of this chapter.

A Sensation Novel is a particularly good example for my purposes. By parodying the conventions and assumptions of sensation fiction, Gilbert was able to laugh at the unexamined morality of the day and to suggest a more realistic view of society. Sensation fiction, modeled on melodrama, saw morality in stark black-and-white terms; it had a suspect fascination with the life of the aristocracy; it demonstrated a naive belief in the provision of happy endings. But Gilbert mixed up good and bad characters, as he was later to do in *Ruddigore*; he made explicit what everyone knows, that the villains are the only bearable characters in this kind of fiction, and the "good" characters are, as a species, stultifyingly boring. By wildly parodying the revelations of high birth that are integral to the genre, he suggested the absurdity of such reverence for rank. And though paying lip service to the convention of the happy ending, here as elsewhere he undermined it with sardonic asides and by ridiculing the convention even in the act of conforming to it.

Gilbert shows us a world in which a virtuous Sunday school teacher may be in love with a yellow-haired villainess; in which virtue is not always triumphant, and indeed it is not always desirable for it to be. As in *An Old Score*, he suggests that it is better to be flawed and human than to pretend to be an ideal being. People are imperfect, and Gilbert rejoices in the fact: but here he speaks as one who is himself human, as he does not seem to do in the fairy comedies.

There is an anti-authoritarian streak in many of these pieces: *The Happy Land* is the most extreme example of this. This tendency may be connected with the idea of preferring the real to the ideal. Respect for authority seemed to involve a sort of half-glimpsed idea that a person in power had to some extent risen above common humanity: for what other reason should he be accorded deference?

As Gilbert had ridiculed and defied the conventions regarding stage morality, so he defied the Lord Chamberlain's rules about "personalities." These things were all of a piece: the stage was still working by rules and conventions that were no longer appropriate in that age of growing discontent. The accepted standards were no longer universally accepted, and Gilbert refused to pretend that they were.

It would be untrue to suggest that Gilbert was some kind of fearless crusader for the new agnosticism: a professional man of the theater, he trimmed his sails according to what was thought acceptable. When his serious prose dramas failed, he saw that it would be safer to speak in his comic voice instead, where, as I have suggested, it was less clear whether the stage action should be taken as "real." Is *Topseyturveydom* a fantasy or a satire? Not even its author seems completely sure of the answer.

As Young noted, the agnosticism of the age was often expressed in oddly dogmatic terms, so that uncertainty itself took on the appearance of being a new certainty. This observation applies very well to Gilbert, whose

barbed wit seems so clearly expressive of a man who knew what he believed and could afford to ridicule anything with which he disagreed but
whose surface confidence is contradicted by an examination of what his
beliefs actually were, as expressed in his plays. His disrespect for authority is clear in a hundred satirical touches, but at the same time he showed,
in his use of a favorite plot structure, his final belief in the established
order. This is the plot structure, used in such plays as *The Palace of Truth*,
wherein the social order is overturned by the intrusion of some other element, often supernatural: at the end of the play, the disruptive element is
banished, and the characters return with relief to the status quo ante. According to this structure, anything that threatens to disrupt the established
order is destructive and to be resisted.

In addition, in the middle years of the 1870s Gilbert was developing his
ironic style and growing comfortable with it but without quite addressing
the question of the ambiguity inherent in irony. In *Engaged*, what is the
object of the laughter? Is it the selfishness of the characters or simply their
pretense at not being selfish? Gilbert's ironic style forbade him to express
his meaning in plain terms, and this makes interpretation a little complex.
Similarly, this kind of irony involves seeming, on the surface, to express
admiration for a point of view that the reader/playgoer then has to reinter-
pret as a condemnation. One must ask whether a writer whose imaginative
world is so firmly rooted in the portrayal of cynical and selfish behavior
does not, by this fact, himself betray a submerged attraction to such behavior.

It took a little time for Gilbert's thought to catch up with his style. He
continued to use his plays—serious and comic—to push single, unambiguous ideas, but the manner of presentation often undermined the primary meaning to some extent. Slowly, he began to come to terms with the
problem—whether consciously or at some more instinctive level is not
clear. In *Princess Toto*, for instance, the Princess's romanticism is made
both ridiculous and attractive. However, it was only with *H.M.S. Pinafore*
(1878) that, whether by accident or design, he was able to create a piece in
which the opposing elements were evenly and attractively balanced.

THE SAVOY FORMULA

This was not the first time Gilbert had parodied the conventions of
melodrama in such a way as to suggest a sneaking affection for them: the
difference lies in the way Gilbert now allowed the melodrama of the

Ralph/Josephine romance to retain its force, despite the parody. The "happy ending" of *The Sorcerer*, *Pinafore*'s predecessor, felt wrong, because its "hero" Alexis was so deliberately unpleasant: he clearly did not deserve to marry the heroine. The defiance of stage convention in his characterization was daring, but it compromised stage effectiveness. Ralph in *Pinafore*, however, retains audience sympathy, despite the mild ridicule given his beliefs, and we can genuinely rejoice at the final fulfillment of his desires. Sullivan's music, which always tends to give "heart" to Gilbert's words, here merely fleshes out something already evident in the structure.

Pinafore succeeded because it appealed to both radical and conservative elements in the audience; because it succeeded in being both witty and romantic; because it managed to hold these opposing elements together without being jarring. It also marked out a space in which Gilbert's skeptical attitudes might properly meet Sullivan's romantic ones.

The opera fitted the mood of the age. Like the audience it addressed, it was not quite sure what, if anything, an intelligent person could hold as a positive belief, but, fearing the desolation of believing in nothing, suggested romantic love as something solid to hold on to. People were still working through the consequences of the Darwinian revolution and continued to clutch at hopeful-seeming alternatives, such as the aggressive patriotism that was one of the moods of late Victorian Britain. In "He is an Englishman" Gilbert and Sullivan ridicule this tendency but also acknowledge its force and perhaps even half-celebrate it. Here and in the later operas Gilbert retreats from using ridicule as a weapon of outright condemnation. Sir Joseph Porter is more unpleasant than the later comic roles will be, but his egalitarian notions are partially vindicated in the opera's ending.

In the sequence of operas from *The Pirates of Penzance* (1879) to *Iolanthe* (1882), Gilbert refined this idea of balanced oppositions, approaching it from different angles apparently instinctively and developing a form of comic theater in which ideas could be ridiculed and behavior rendered absurd without making the butts of these jokes seem hateful. This is a humane form of comedy, nonvicious without being bland, that, if it implies a single positive belief, implies that all human beings are absurd and that we shall be all the better for accepting as much. The satire remains extremely sharp, but these operas have lost the tendency to create scapegoats that is evident in some of the earlier plays, such as *Charity*.

However, the Gilbert and Sullivan operas after *Iolanthe* depart from the single line of development I have traced in the operas that preceded it. Instead, each becomes to some extent a reaction against the previous one, and we sometimes seem to be returning to an earlier style, as in *Princess Ida* and *Ruddigore*. I have related this new unsettled atmosphere to the 8 February 1883 agreement, in which Richard D'Oyly Carte bound Gilbert and Sullivan to produce a new opera at six months' notice. I suggest that the operas became too exclusively a moneymaking enterprise; and while the later operas (up to *The Gondoliers* in 1889) show no falling off of technical quality, some of the early zest has gone out of them. It is also possible that Gilbert had, by the time of *Iolanthe*, reached the farthest point of what he could do with the Savoy formula he had discovered in *Pinafore*. *The Mikado* and *The Gondoliers* fit well into the formula, but they are less daring and are more obviously commercial in intent. Gilbert was a professional and continued to write wittily, inventively, and with variety, but there is something missing. The raw enthusiasm of Gilbert's works of the 1870s, the sense of engaging with living ideas, is almost entirely absent, though these late librettos are much more polished stylistically.

In the 1890s the decline became unmistakable: Gilbert could no longer maintain even his technical expertise, and despite the interesting ideas that are visible in some of these last works, it is clear that the Gilbertian style had run its course. Only in the odd experiment of his last play, *The Hooligan* (1911), are we reminded that he might not have completely run out of things to say.

Gilbert's Continuing Relevance

By the 1890s, the mid-Victorian agnostic balance had been broken: a more pessimistic fin-de-siècle mood had succeeded it. The antithesis was no longer between faith and doubt but between style and substance. And from these seeds grew the distinctive character of the twentieth century, a century of fragmentation in which the doubts born in Gilbert's generation reached their natural, horrifying conclusion.

Today, Gilbert's irony and "cynicism" seem rather genteel, despite the opinion, still sometimes expressed, that Gilbert's words are too bitter without the softening influence of Sullivan's music. What can his works have to say to us now?

It is clear that they do continue to say something to us. The hundreds of amateur productions of the Gilbert and Sullivan operas that occur every year throughout the English-speaking world and their periodic revival by

professional companies are a clear practical demonstration of their continuing relevance. Now, I do not take as a sufficient explanation of this Ian
Bradley's comment that the operas "breathe the innocence, the naïvety and
the fun of a long-vanished age."[4] If the "heritage factor" had been all, the
operettas of Edward German such as *Merrie England* and *Tom Jones*
would have survived as well as Gilbert and Sullivan opera has—which
they have not.

I have been at pains to emphasize throughout this book that almost all of
Gilbert's works relate themselves to deep underlying issues, such as class,
morality, or politics; they have survived because they are not circum-
scribed by the specifics of the day. Many of the jokes remain funny because the assumptions on which they are built still hold true.

However, it must be admitted that part of their continuing relevance lies
in the fact that our society is a natural development from Gilbert's, particularly when it comes to the middle class, which remains what it has always
been, the core audience of the Gilbert and Sullivan operas. Respectability
is still a sacred totem to good middle-class beings such as myself; jokes at
the expense of the monarchy or the peerage retain a slight frisson of daring
for the British bourgeois. And, most important of all, money remains the
vital influence on human behavior that it was in Gilbert's day. The future
of the middle class seems unclear from this vantage in time, but while it
survives the fate of the Gilbert and Sullivan operas seems safe.

It is natural that different aspects of a work of art should be emphasized
in different ages. The Gilbert and Sullivan operas have long been regarded
as genteel, undemanding entertainment for respectable people. This is a
reputation that, it seems, the operas cannot shake off, despite the attempts
of radical reinterpreters such as Max Keith Sutton. The reason is clear: for
there is, after all, some truth in the reputation, just as there is truth in
Sutton's rebuttal of it. The operas could hardly have been viewed in this
way for so long had there not been legitimate reasons for doing so. There
is indeed very little malice and much indulgence in Gilbert's portrayal of
authority figures in the operas. However, it is a distortion to focus *solely*
on this aspect and to ignore the distrust of authority to which it is the compensating reaction. Because the operas seem, on the surface, so simple, it
has perhaps taken people longer to realize their complexities than might
otherwise have been the case. Gilbert's twin impulses toward the respectable and the disrespectful—the common dilemma of the satirist—
have not always been understood, because of people's desire to give his
attitudes a neat internal logic that is, I think, not natural to the human
mind.

This antithesis and others are bred in the bone of Gilbert's mature works. Whether Gilbert put them in deliberately I cannot say, and in a sense it is an irrelevant issue. In these best works thought and expression go hand in hand, as good style demands, and though it may be interesting for us to discover the historical facts of how this was achieved, it is not necessary for us to do so. It is enough if we are satisfied that Gilbert's works do contain these characteristics, however they got there.

The Gilbert and Sullivan operas, and the best of Gilbert's other plays, are highly intelligent investigations of some of the core assumptions of the society in which we still live. It must not be assumed that it was easy to create such works: the theatrical conventions of melodrama, farce, and burlesque were not naturally suited to the propagation of anything other than simple ideas and black-and-white morality. Gilbert bent these conventions to his own ends: by ironizing them and bringing to bear upon them all the techniques of "contradiction contradicted" (in Jack Point's phrase)[5] that we have been examining throughout this book, Gilbert was able to create from these simple elements remarkable complexities.

He was born in an age when these conventions were the theatrical norm; he was incapable of writing in the more natural style of the "New Drama" that succeeded him. He could not create natural characters; he could only play with the established theatrical types. His plot construction was a development from melodrama, and though he laughed at the melodramatic plot devices he could not break free of them. As on so many other issues, he could see that the existing state of affairs was wrong, but he could not see a positive alternative. In this, too, he was a child of his age.

And yet he did point the way forward. Both Oscar Wilde and George Bernard Shaw were influenced by him, though neither was keen to acknowledge the influence. He was bound by limitations, but he used these limitations to his own advantage, investigating ideas that his successors were to pick up and carry as far as *their* limitations allowed them.

If we wish to understand the mid-Victorian period properly—if we want to see beyond the easy dismissal of it as a period of hypocrisy, casual cruelty, and (damning phrase!) "Victorian values"—then Gilbert's plays provide an excellent way of starting to do so. The complex interplay of ideas, the sense of dissatisfaction with the old certainties, and the simultaneous awareness of the dangers of a society from which those certainties have been excised, make us forcibly aware that these were, after all, people like ourselves, struggling with a society not of their making and with assumptions of varying worth, and trying to see their way forward to a better way of life. And if we agree with Gilbert that people are not ideal beings, however much they pretend otherwise, then we may be more inclined to forgive the Victorians for failing in their ambition to be perfect.

The Gilbert and Sullivan operas are an integral part of British national culture. By striving to understand them we may find we have a better understanding of Britain's past, and perhaps we may see more clearly how that past impinges upon the present. Gilbert's writings are nowhere near as simple or simplistic as many commentators have thought: for instance, Hesketh Pearson, though an intelligent man, assumed too readily that the operas were easy to understand. Thus he wrote:

> It must be repeated that the qualities of wariness and daring were mixed in his [Gilbert's] nature in about equal proportions; and also, it may be added, stupidity and insight. . . . He was visited with sudden flashes of reality, but he was not gifted with a steady vision. He had acute perceptions, but no guiding philosophy. . . . Again and again, at the bidding of some powerful intuition, he exposed a social or national absurdity, but as often as not he failed to see the point of his exposure and fell back upon a piece of conventional claptrap which was equally typical of him.[6]

There is much in this with which I must agree. Indeed, that talk of a mixture of "wariness and daring" sounds like a restatement of the major theme of this book. But the overall attitude seems to me false: this airy dismissal of Gilbert as a man "not gifted with a steady vision" simply because there are contradictory elements in his works. Pearson's attitude to Gilbert (uncannily similar to Shaw's, by the way) assumes that any suggestion of ambiguity of attitude is an artistic failure, but I might argue that, on the contrary, the absence of such ambiguities from Gilbert's works would have been an artistic failure. It would have turned his plays into dull, didactic sneers, fixed in their own time like a beetle in amber. Ambiguity is complexity and if properly handled creates great art. Uncertainty begets tolerance, and I believe that such uncertainty, as employed by Gilbert, is a step up from the "steady vision" praised by Pearson, not a step down from it.

NOTES

INTRODUCTION: THE PROBLEM OF GILBERT

1. Isaac Goldberg, *The Story of Gilbert and Sullivan,* or *The 'Compleat' Savoyard* (London: John Murray, 1929), 522.

2. A. H. Godwin, Gilbert and Sullivan: *A Critical Appreciation of the Savoy Operas* (London and Toronto: J. M. Dent & Sons, 1926), 1.

3. Jane W. Stedman, *W. S. Gilbert: A Classic Victorian and His Theatre* (Oxford: Oxford University Press, 1996), 114–18.

4. Paul Turner, *English literature, 1832–90: Excluding the Novel,* vol. II, pt. 1 of *The Oxford History of English Literature* (Oxford: Clarendon Press, 1989), 405.

5. Quoted in Arthur Jacobs, *Arthur Sullivan: A Victorian Musician* (Oxford: Oxford University Press), 1984, 265.

6. See, for instance, the comments of *The Brighton Gazette,* 12 December 1907, quoted in Tony Joseph, *The D'Oyly Carte Opera Company, 1875–1982: An Unofficial History* (Bristol, England: Bunthorne Books, 1994), 139.

7. Ian Bradley, Introduction to *The Complete Annotated Gilbert and Sullivan,* by W. S. Gilbert, ed. Ian Bradley (Oxford: Oxford University Press, 1996), vii.

8. Eric Midwinter, "W. S. Gilbert: Victorian Entertainer," *New Theatre Quarterly* (1986): 274.

9. Ibid.

10. Ibid., 273.

11. Ibid.

CHAPTER 1. 1863–1875—FINDING A STYLE

1. Stedman, *W. S. Gilbert,* 34.

2. Michael R. Booth, *Prefaces to English Nineteenth-Century Theatre* (Manchester, England: Manchester University Press, n.d.), 174.

3. W. S. Gilbert, *New and Original Extravaganzas,* ed. Isaac Goldberg (Boston: John W. Luce & Co., 1931), 9.

4. Ibid., 32.

5. Ibid., 59.

6. Ibid., 132.

7. Ibid.

8. Ibid., 136.

9. Ibid., 117.

10. Ibid., 138.

11. Ibid., 137.

12. Ibid.

13. Ibid., 142.

14. Ibid., 148.

15. Stedman, *W. S. Gilbert*, 71.

16. Gilbert, *New and Original Extravaganzas,* 180.

17. Stedman, *W. S. Gilbert*, 71.

18. *W. S. Gilbert*, "An Autobiography," *The Theatre* 2 April 1883, 220–21.

19. W. S. Gilbert, *Original Plays: First Series* (London: Chatto & Windus, 1925), 135.

20. Ibid., 154.

21. Ibid., 135–36.

22. Ibid., 140.

23. Ibid., 164.

24. Gilbert, "An Autobiography," 221.

25. Stedman, *W. S. Gilbert*, 93.

26. William Archer, "Mr. W. S. Gilbert," in *English Dramatists Of To-Day* (London: Sampson Low, Marston & Co., 1882), 161.

27. Ibid., 163.

28. Ibid.

29. See, for instance, "The Reasons of Decline," in Allardyce Nicoll, *Early Nineteenth Century Drama, 1800–1850,* vol. 4 of *A History of English Drama, 1660–1900,* 2d ed. (Cambridge: Cambridge University Press, 1963), 58–78.

30. W. S. Gilbert, *Original Plays: Third Series* (London: Chatto & Windus, 1923), 374.

31. Bernard Mandeville, *The Fable of the Bees; or Private Vices, Publick Benefits,* ed. F. B. Kaye, (Oxford: Oxford University Press, 1924; reprint, Indianapolis, Ind.: Liberty Classics, 1988), 1:72.

32. Gilbert, *Original Plays 1,* 3.

33. Ibid., 4.

34. Ibid., 9.

35. Ibid., 18.

36. Ibid., 43.

37. Ibid., 43–44.

38. Ibid., 3.

39. Ibid.

40. Ibid., 43.

41. Stedman, *W. S. Gilbert*, 343.

42. W. S. Gilbert, *Original Plays: Second Series* (London: Chatto & Windus, 1925), 15.

43. W. S. Gilbert, *Gilbert before Sullivan: Six Comic Plays by W. S. Gilbert,* ed. Jane W. Stedman (London: Routledge & Kegan Paul, 1969), 51.

44. Ibid., 110.

45. Ibid., 115–16.

46. Ibid., 117.

47. G. K. Chesterton, "Gilbert and Sullivan," in *The Eighteen-Eighties: Essays by Fellows of the Royal Society of Literature,* ed. Walter de la Mare (Cambridge: Cambridge University Press, 1930), 156.

48. See William Archer, "Conversation VI: With Mr. W. S. Gilbert," in *Real Conversations* (London: William Heinemann, 1904), 109–16.

49. Radio interview, quoted by John Lahr, in *Prick Up Your Ears: The Biography of Joe Orton* (Harmondsworth, England: Penguin Books, 1980), 15.

50. Gilbert, *Gilbert before Sullivan,* 133.

51. Luigi Pirandello, *Six Characters in Search of an Author,* trans. John Linstrum (London: Methuen, 1982), 43.

52. Gilbert, *Gilbert before Sullivan,* 141.

53. G. K. Chesterton, "On Phases of Eccentricity," in *"All I survey": A Book of Essays,* 2d ed. (London: Methuen & Co., 1934), 52.

54. John Maddison Morton, *Slasher and Crasher!* (London: Thomas Hailes Lacy, n.d.), 3.

55. Susan Bassnett-McGuire, *Luigi Pirandello,* Macmillan Modern Dramatists (London: Macmillan, 1983), 32.

56. Gilbert, *Gilbert before Sullivan,* 145.

57. Ibid., 144.

58. [W. S. Gilbert], "Jezebel," *Fun,* 24 December 1870, 255.

59. Gilbert, *Gilbert before Sullivan,* 136.

60. Ibid., 157.

61. Ibid., 162.

62. Ibid., 164.

63. Ibid., 42.

64. Ibid., 43.

65. Archer, "Mr. W. S. Gilbert," 172.

66. Goldberg, *Story of Gilbert and Sullivan,* 144.

67. W. S. Gilbert, *An Old Score: An Original Comedy-Drama in Three Acts* (London: Thomas Hailes Lacy, n.d.), 14.

68. Gilbert, *Gilbert before Sullivan,* 145.

69. John Hollingshead, *My Lifetime* (London: Sampson Low, Marston & Co., 1895), 2:20.

70. Ibid.

71. Gilbert, *Original Plays 1,* 105.

72. Ibid.

73. Ibid., 131.

74. Hesketh Pearson, *Gilbert: His Life and Strife* (London: Methuen & Co., 1957), 46.

75. W. S. Gilbert, *Ought we to visit her? A Comedy, in Three Acts, Dramatized from Mrs. Edwardes's novel,* printed as manuscript (London: Samuel French, n.d.), 9.

76. Stedman, *W. S. Gilbert,* 119.

77. E.g., George Rowell, introduction to *Plays by W. S. Gilbert,* ed. George Rowell (Cambridge: Cambridge University Press, 1982), 4.

78. Gilbert, *Original Plays 2,* 105.

79. W. S. Gilbert, *Original Plays 3,* 209.

CHAPTER 2. THE CRAFT OF THE PLAYWRIGHT

1. Quoted in Sidney Dark and Rowland Grey, *W. S. Gilbert: His Life and Letters* (London: Methuen & Co., 1923), 196.

2. Archer, "W. S. Gilbert," 117.

3. W. S. Gilbert, "A Stage Play," in *Foggerty's Fairy and Other Tales* (London: George Routledge and Sons, 1892), 260.

4. Ibid., 260–61.

5. Ibid., 266.

6. Ibid., 261.

7. Ibid., 262.

8. Ibid.

9. Ibid., 265.

10. Archer, "W. S. Gilbert," 110.

11. Patrick J. Smith, *The Tenth Muse: A Historical Study of the Opera Libretto* (London: Victor Gollancz, 1971), 231.

12. Archer, "W. S. Gilbert," 111.

13. Charles Hayter analyzes the "well-made" elements in *The Mikado* in Charles Hayter, *Gilbert and Sullivan,* Macmillan Modern Dramatists (London: Macmillan, 1987), 49–57.

14. John Russell Taylor, *The Rise and Fall of the Well-Made Play* (London: Methuen & Co., 1967), 15.

15. Gilbert, "A Stage Play," 265.

16. W. S. Gilbert, *"The Story of a Stage Play,"* New-York Daily Tribune, 9 August 1885, p. 9.

17. Quoted in Pearson, *Gilbert: His Life and Strife,* 39.

18. Gilbert, "Actors, Authors, and Audiences," in *Foggerty's Fairy,* 229–30.

19. Ibid., 234.

20. Hollingshead, *My Lifetime,* 2:20.

21. Gilbert, "Actors, Authors and Audiences," 231.

22. Review of *The Wicked World* by W. S. Gilbert, *Times,* 6 January 1873, 8.

23. Quoted in Pearson, *Gilbert: His Life and Strife,* 39.

24. George Bainton, ed. *The Art of Authorship: Literary Reminiscences, Methods of Work, and Advice to Young Beginners, Personally Contributed by Leading Authors of the Day* (London: James Clarke & Co., 1890), 213–14.

25. Goldberg, *Story of Gilbert and Sullivan,* 469.

26. Max Beerbohm, "Mr. Gilbert's Rentrée (And Mine)," in *Around Theatres* (London: Heinemann, n.d.), 2:49.

27. W. S. Gilbert, *Original Plays: Fourth Series* (London: Chatto & Windus, 1922), 15.

28. Gilbert, *Original Plays 3,* 408.

29. Gilbert, *Original Plays 2,* 205.

30. Ibid., 226.

31. Mandeville, *The Fable of the Bees,* 2: 297.

32. Gilbert, *Original Plays 2,* 205.

33. Ibid., 224.

34. Ibid., 231.

35. Ibid., 234.

36. Gilbert, *Original Plays 1,* 131.

37. Booth, *Prefaces to English Nineteenth-Century Theatre,* 76.

38. Ibid., 94.

39. William Archer, ed. *'A Stage Play' by W. S. Gilbert* (New York: reprinted by the theater museum of Columbia University, 1916), 7-8.

40. Review of *Foggerty's Fairy* by W. S. Gilbert, *The Era,* 17 December 1881, 5.

41. Gilbert, *An Old Score,* 4.

42. Gilbert, *Original Plays 1,* 106.

43. Gilbert, *Original Plays 3,* 276.

44. Bernard Shaw, *Music in London, 1890–94,* (London: Constable and Company, 1932), 1: 226.

45. Bernard Shaw, *Collected Letters, 1911–1925,* ed. Dan H. Laurence (London: Max Reinhardt, 1985), 445.

46. Bernard Shaw, *Collected Letters, 1874–1897,* ed. Dan H. Laurence (London: Max Reinhardt, 1965), 427.

47. Bernard Shaw, *Music in London,* 2: 75.

48. Archer, "Mr. W. S. Gilbert," 148.

CHAPTER 3. 1870–1877 — THE WORLD TURNED RIGHT SIDE UP

1. Pearson, *Gilbert: His Life and Strife,* 83.

2. *Daily Telegraph,* 6 October 1877, quoted in Michael Booth, ed. *Comedies,* vol. 3 of *English Plays of the Nineteenth Century* (Oxford: Oxford University Press, 1973), 385.

3. James Harding, *Jacques Offenbach: A Biography,* The Opera Library (London: John Calder, 1980), 92.

4. Gilbert, *Original Plays 4,* 466.

5. *Anonymous, 1871–1935* (London: John Murray, 1936), 85.

6. George McElroy, "Meilhac and Halévy—and Gilbert: Comic Converses," in *Gilbert and Sullivan Papers Presented at the International Conference Held at the University of Kansas in May 1970,* James Helyar, ed. (Lawrence: University of Kansas Libraries, 1971), 92.

7. See Edward Righton, "A Suppressed Burlesque: *The Happy Land,*" *The Theatre,* 1 August 1896, 66.

8. See Philip Plumb, "Gilbert and the Censors: *The Happy Land* conspiracy," *W. S. Gilbert Society Journal* 1, no. 8 (1994): 238–40.

9. F. Tomline [W. S. Gilbert] and Gilbert à Beckett, *The Happy Land: A Burlesque Version of "The Wicked World"* (London: J. W. Last & Co., 1873), 18.

10. W. S. Gilbert, *The Realm of Joy: Being a Free and Easy Version of Le Roi Candaule,* ed. Terence Rees (London: by the editor, 25 Nightingale Square, 1969), 11.

11. The title was so spelled in advertisements for the original production; however, in the Licence Copy and in the text of the play published in 1931 the title is spelled *Topsyturvydom.* I have chosen to accept *Topseyturveydom* as the "official" spelling, but have chosen to omit the "e"s when referring to Gilbert's more general use of "topsy-turvy" ideas.

12. W. S. Gilbert, *Topsyturvydom: Original Extravaganza,* ed. Charles P. Johnson (Oxford: Oxford University Press, 1931), 7.

13. Ibid., 9.

14. Ibid., 18.

15. Ibid.

16. Ibid., 19.

17. Ibid., 9.

18. Gilbert, *Original Plays 4,* 447.

19. Ibid., 455.

20. Ibid., 450.

21. Ibid., 452.

22. Ibid., 458.

23. Ibid., 474.

24. Archer, "Mr. W. S. Gilbert," 164.

25. Goldberg, *Story of Gilbert and Sullivan,* 171.

26. Godwin, *Gilbert and Sullivan,* 15.

27. Gilbert, *Original Plays 1,* 242.

28. "The Revolutionary Satire of W. S. Gilbert," *Littell's Living Age* 311 (24 December 1921): 795.

29. Ibid., 798.

30. Gilbert, *Plays by W. S. Gilbert,* 91.

31. Ibid., 95.

32. Ibid.

33. Ibid., 92.

34. Ibid., 132.

35. See, for instance, Leonard C. Pronko, *Eugène Labiche and Georges Feydeau, Macmillan Modern Dramatists* (London: Macmillan, 1982) for a discussion of Labiche's attitudes to the bourgeois society of his day.

36. Gilbert, "Actors, Authors and Audiences," 228.

37. Michael R. Booth, ed. *Farces,* vol. 4 of *English Plays of the Nineteenth Century* (Oxford: Oxford University Press, 1973), 259.

38. Review of *Tom Cobbb* by W. S. Gilbert, *Times,* 26 April 1875, 12.

39. Quoted in Booth, *Comedies,* 391–92.

40. W. S. Gilbert, *Engaged* (London: Samuel French, n.d.), [4].

41. Gilbert, *Original Plays 2,* 42.

42. Ibid., 85.

43. Ibid., 78.

44. Gilbert, *Original Plays 3,* 86.

45. W. S. Gilbert, "A hornpipe in fetters," *Era almanack 1879,* 91–92.

46. W. S. Gilbert, letter to Mrs. Talbot, January 1907, quoted in Dark and Grey, *Gilbert,* 196.

47. W. S. Gilbert, Harrow Speech Day speech, quoted in Ibid., 199.

Chapter 4. Gilbert's "Stage Management"

1. Gilbert, "An Appeal to the Press," *Era Almanack 1878,* 85.

2. Gilbert, "A stage play," 271–72.

3. Ibid., 272.

4. Ibid., 274.

5. Quoted in Stedman, *Gilbert,* 218.

6. Henry Lytton, *A Wandering Minstrel* (London: Jarrolds, 1933), 255.

7. Stedman, *Gilbert,* 216, quoting an undated letter from Gilbert to John Hare.

8. Quoted in Percy Fitzgerald, *The Savoy Operas and the Savoyards* (London: Chatto & Windus, 1894), 14.

9. Gilbert, *Engaged,* [4].

10. Archer, "W. S. Gilbert," 114.

11. *Ruddigore,* in Gilbert, *Original Plays 3,* 235.

12. Quoted in Fitzgerald, *The Savoy Opera and the Savoyards,* 132.

13. Michael R. Booth, "T. W. Robertson," in *Six plays,* by T. W. Robertson, ed. Michael R. Booth (Ashover, England: Amber Lane Press, 1980), xv–xvi.

14. William Coxe-Ife, *W. S. Gilbert: Stage Director,* The Student's Music Library— Historical And Critical Series (London: Dennis Dobson, 1977), 34.

15. Quoted in Ibid., 39.

16. Quoted in Ibid., 32.

17. Pearson, *Gilbert: His Life and Strife,* 49.

18. Stanley Wells, *Literature and Drama* (London: Routledge and Kegan Paul, 1970), 1.

Chapter 5. 1877–1882 — The Land Where Contradictions Meet

1. Richard D'Oyly Carte, letter to Gilbert and Sullivan, dated 8 April 1880, quoted in Leslie Baily, *The Gilbert and Sullivan Book* (London: Cassell, 1952), 97.

2. Jacobs, *Sullivan,* 180.

3. Michael R. Booth, *English Melodrama* (London: Herbert Jenkins, 1965), 62.

4. Gilbert, *Original Plays 2,* 291.

5. Ibid., 249.

6. Ibid., 261.

7. Ibid., 249–50.

8. Quoted in Pearson, *Gilbert: His Life and Strife,* 40.

9. Gilbert, *Original Plays 2,* 300.

10. Ibid., 282.

11. Ibid.

12. Ibid., 284.

13. Ibid., 283.

14. Mary Watkins Waters makes precisely this point in "W. S. Gilbert and the Discovery of a Satiric Method for the Victorian Stage" (Ph.D. diss., Auburn University, 1974), 214, and is very good on *Pinafore*'s satire. However, she says nothing of the opposing influence of melodramatic convention.

15. Booth, *English Melodrama,* 106.

16. Hayter, *Gilbert and Sullivan,* 88.

17. Gilbert, *Original Plays 2,* 289.

18. Ibid., 283.

19. Ibid., 286, alternative pronouns for others to sing deleted.

20. Ibid., 296, alternative pronouns for Josephine to sing deleted.

21. Ibid., 296.

22. Ibid., 283.

23. Ibid., 282.

24. Ibid., 300.

25. See David Russell Hulme, "A note," in *H.M.S. Pinafore* CD booklet (TER, 1987).

26. Booth, *English Melodrama,* 105.

27. Gilbert, *Complete Annotated Gilbert and Sullivan,* 170.

28. Hayter, *Gilbert and Sullivan,* 86.

29. W. S. Gilbert, *The Story of H.M.S. Pinafore* (London: G. Bell and Sons, 1913), 109.

30. Max Keith Sutton, *W. S. Gilbert* (Boston: Twayne, 1975), 84–85.

31. Alan Fischler, *Modified Rapture: Comedy in W. S. Gilbert's Savoy Operas* (Charlottesville and London: University Press of Virginia, 1991), 91–92.

32. Baily, *Gilbert and Sullivan Book,* 351.

33. Goldberg, *Story of Gilbert and Sullivan,* 415.

34. Gilbert, *Topsyturvydom,* 9.

35. Waters, "W. S. Gilbert and the Discovery of a Satiric Method."

36. Sutton, *W. S. Gilbert.*

37. Pearson, *Gilbert: His Life and Strife,* 48.

38. Goldberg, *Story of Gilbert and Sullivan,* 490.

39. Ibid., 491.

40. Gilbert, "A hornpipe in fetters," 91.

41. Ibid.

42. Ibid., 92.

43. Quoted in Dark and Grey, *Gilbert,* 149.

44. *The Era,* 14 January 1872, quoted in Plumb, "Gilbert and the Censors," 238.

45. Samuel Butler, *Life and Habit* (London: Wildwood House, 1981), 306.

46. Harry How, "Illustrated Interviews: No. 4—Mr. W. S. Gilbert," *Strand Magazine* 2 (October 1891): 339.

47. Gilbert, *Original Plays 2,* 187.

48. Ibid., 200.

49. Ibid., 326.

50. Quoted in Stedman, *Gilbert,* 173.

51. Quoted in Goldberg, *Story of Gilbert and Sullivan,* 228.

52. Gilbert, *Original Plays 2,* 306.

53. Ibid., 309.

54. Ibid.

55. Booth, *English Melodrama,* 80.

56. Ibid.

57. Gilbert, *Original Plays 2,* 333.

58. Hayter, *Gilbert and Sullivan,* 105.

59. Gilbert, *Original Plays 2,* 337.

60. Ibid.

61. Ibid.

62. W. S. Gilbert, *The Bab Ballads,* ed. James Ellis, (Cambridge: Harvard University Press, Belknap Press, 1980), 307.

63. Joseph, *The D'Oyly Carte,* 34.

64. Stedman, *Gilbert,* 174.

65. Gilbert, *Original Plays 3,* 102.

66. Ibid.

67. Ibid., 107.

68. Ibid.

69. Ibid., 116.

70. Ibid., 126.

71. Quoted in Baily, *Gilbert and Sullivan Book,* 179.

72. Stedman, *Gilbert,* 183–84.

73. Ibid., 183.

74. Ibid., 184.

75. Gilbert, *Original Plays 3,* 101.

76. Ibid., 124.

77. Ibid., 104.

78. Ibid., 105.

79. Ibid., 128.

80. Archer, *English Dramatists of To-Day,* 172.

81. Goldberg, *Story of Gilbert and Sullivan,* 498.

82. Gilbert, *Original Plays 1,* 245.

83. Ibid.

84. Ibid., 248.

85. Ibid., 250.

86. Ibid., 273.

87. Ibid., 272.

88. Ibid., 268.

89. Ibid., 255.

90. Ibid.

91. Ibid., 256.

92. Ibid., 271.

93. Ibid., 286.

94. Gilbert, *Original Plays 2,* 292.

95. See "The Era of Society Drama," in George Rowell, *The Victorian Theatre, 1792–1914: A Survey,* 2d ed. (Cambridge: Cambridge University Press, 1978), 103–150.

96. Hayter, *Gilbert and Sullivan,* 44.

97. Ibid.

Chapter 6. The Art of the Librettist

1. Gilbert, *Original Plays 3,* 138.

2. Quoted in Craig Zadan, *Sondheim and Co.,* 2d ed. updated (London: Nick Hern Books, 1990), 61.

3. See Patrick J. Smith, *The Tenth Muse,* chapter 6.

4. Ibid., 221.

5. Stedman, *Gilbert,* 212.

6. Stephen Citron, *The Musical: From the Inside Out* (London: Hodder & Stoughton, 1991), 130.

7. Ibid., 47.

8. Ibid., 46.

9. Ibid., 48.

10. Ibid., 149.

11. Richard Traubner, *Operetta: A Theatrical History* (New York and Oxford: Oxford University Press, 1989), 185.

12. Smith, *The Tenth Muse,* 300.

13. Alan Jay Lerner, *The Musical Theatre: A Celebration* (London: Collins, 1986), 26.

14. Ibid., 32.

15. Gilbert, *Original Plays 2,* 318.

16. Gilbert, *The Bab Ballads,* ed., James Ellis, 118.

17. Gilbert, *Original Plays 3,* 179.

18. Ibid., 145.

19. Ibid., 146.

20. Ibid., 177.

21. Ibid., 224.

22. Archer, "W. S. Gilbert," 124.

23. Stedman, *Gilbert,* 244.

24. *The Mikado,* in Gilbert, *Original Plays 3,* 184.

25. Audrey Williamson, *Gilbert and Sullivan Opera: An Assessment,* 2d ed. (London: Marion Boyars, 1982), 129.

26. *Trial by jury,* in Gilbert, *Original Plays 1,* 233.

27. Gilbert, *Original Plays 3,* 198.

28. Ibid., 198.

29. Ibid., 151.

30. Gilbert, *Original Plays 2,* 257.

31. Ibid., 288.

32. Ibid.

33. Gilbert, *Original Plays 3,* 279.

34. Ibid., 280.

35. Ira Gershwin, *Lyrics on Several Occasions* (London: Omnibus Press, 1988), 215.

36. Ibid., 235.

37. British Library, Additional Manuscript 45,291.

38. See, for instance, Citron, *The Musical,* 69.

39. Archer, "W. S. Gilbert," 126.

40. Gilbert, *Original Plays 1,* 279.

CHAPTER 7. 1882–1889 — THE PRESSURES OF POPULISM

1. Jacobs, *Sullivan,* 282.

2. Cheryl Conover Hoffman intelligently explores the ambiguities of Gilbert's portrayal of women in "A Study of the Women in W. S. Gilbert's *Patience, Iolanthe,* and *Princess Ida;* or, The Folly of Being Feminist" (Ph.D. diss., West Virginia University, 1988).

3. Gilbert, *Original Plays 1,* 106.

4. Jane W. Stedman, "From Dame to Woman: W. S. Gilbert and Theatrical Transvestism," *Victorian Studies* (September 1970): 44.

5. Jacobs, *Sullivan,* 180.

6. Arthur Sullivan's diary, 29 January 1884, quoted in Jacobs, *Sullivan,* 187.

7. Arthur Sullivan, letter to Gilbert, 1 April 1884, quoted in Jacobs, *Sullivan,* 189.

8. Review of *Ruddygore* by W. S. Gilbert, *Jack and Jill,* 12 February 1887, 86.

9. Gilbert, *Complete Annotated Gilbert and Sullivan,* 628.

10. Stedman, *Gilbert,* 226.

11. Gilbert, *Complete Annotated Gilbert and Sullivan,* 632.

12. Stedman, *Gilbert,* 234.

13. See Brian Jones, "Ko-Ko's Toe," *W. S. Gilbert Society Journal* 1, no. 6 (1990): 170–74.

14. Gilbert, "The Story of a Stage Play," p. 9.

15. *The Musical World,* 14 March 1885, quoted in Brian Jones, "The Sword That Never Fell," *W. S. Gilbert Society Journal* 1, no. 1 (spring 1985): 24.

16. *The Graphic* (29 January 1887), 107.

17. Quoted in Baily, *Gilbert and Sullivan Book,* 271.

18. Sutton, *Gilbert,* 61.

19. Gilbert, *Original Plays 3,* 238.

20. Stanley Kauffmann, indirectly quoted in in Bert Cardullo, "The Art and the Business of W. S. Gilbert's *Engaged,*" *Modern Drama* 28 (1985): 462.

21. Gilbert, *Original Plays 3,* 249.

22. Ibid.

23. Ibid., 227.

24. Ibid.

25. G. Wilson Knight, *The Golden Labyrinth: A Study of British Drama* (London: Phoenix House, 1962), 302.

26. Edith A. Browne, *W. S. Gilbert,* Stars of the Stage (London: John Lane, The Bodley Head, 1907), 40.

27. Gilbert, *Complete Annotated Gilbert and Sullivan,* 436.

28. Sullivan's diary, [25 December 1887?], quoted in Jacobs, *Sullivan,* 263.

29. Sullivan's diary, 4 September 1887, quoted Ibid., 261.

30. W. S. Gilbert, letter to Mary Leslie, quoted in Stedman, *Gilbert,* 246.

31. Baily, *Gilbert and Sullivan Book,* 281–82.

32. Quoted in Stedman, *Gilbert,* 252.

33. Gilbert, *Original Plays 3,* 285.

34. Williamson, *Gilbert and Sullivan Opera,* 209.

35. Gilbert, *Original Plays 3,* 305.

36. Quoted in Jacobs, *Sullivan,* 282.

37. Williamson, *Gilbert and Sullivan Opera,* 234.

38. Hayter, *Gilbert and Sullivan,* 125.

39. Gilbert, *Original Plays 3,* 325.

40. Ibid.

41. Godwin, *Gilbert and Sullivan,* 35.

42. Gilbert, *Original Plays 3,* 332.

43. Ibid., 334.

44. Ibid., 332.

45. Ibid., 328.

46. Ibid., 346.

47. Ibid., 339.

48. Ibid.

49. Ibid., 340.

50. Gilbert, *Gilbert before Sullivan,* 43.

51. Hayter, *Gilbert and Sullivan,* 124–25.

52. Review of *The Gondoliers* by W. S. Gilbert, *The Echo* (9 December 1889), 1.

53. E.g., Williamson, *Gilbert and Sullivan Opera,* 234.

Chapter 8. 1890–1911 — Last Plays

1. Gilbert, *Original Plays 4,* 134.

2. Quoted in Stedman, *Gilbert,* 283.

3. Arthur Sullivan's diary, 10 April 1884, Quoted in Jacobs, *Sullivan,* 191.

4. Gilbert, *Original Plays 3,* 374.

5. Ibid.

6. Ibid., 387.

7. Stedman, *Gilbert,* 304.

8. Ibid., 305.

9. Gilbert, *Original Plays 3,* 438.

10. Ibid., 408.

11. Ibid., 452–53.

12. Quoted in John Wolfson, *Final Curtain: The Last Gilbert and Sullivan Operas* (London: Chappell & Co., 1976), 203.

13. 11 October 1893, in Shaw, *Music in London, 1890–94,* 3: 62.

14. Gilbert, *Original Plays 3,* 413.

15. Ibid., 409.

16. Ibid., 417.

17. Ibid.

18. Ibid., 443.

19. Ibid., 451–52.

20. Ibid., 452.

21. Gilbert, *Original Plays 4,* 104.

22. Ibid., 103.

23. Max Keith Sutton, "The Significance of The Grand Duke," in *Gilbert and Sullivan Papers,* 224.

24. Gilbert, *Original Plays 4,* 67.

25. Ibid., 74.

26. Ibid.,

27. Sutton, "Significance of The Grand Duke," 221.

28. Gilbert, *Original Plays 4,* 65.

29. Holbrook Jackson, *The Eighteen Nineties* (Harmondsworth, England: Pelican Books, 1939), 114.

30. Walter H. Pater, *Studies in the History of the Renaissance* (London: Macmillan and Co., 1873), 211–12.

31. Gilbert, *Original Plays 4,* 46.

32. Ibid., 48.

33. Ibid., 64–5.

34. Gilbert, Original Plays 3, 437.

35. Gilbert, Original Plays 4, 54.

36. Ibid., 46.

37. Ibid., 56.

38. Ibid., 67.

39. Quoted in Stedman, *Gilbert,* 309.

40. See Stedman, *Gilbert,* 253.

41. George Rowell, ed., *Victorian Dramatic Criticism* (London: Methuen & Co., 1971), 292.

42. Ibid., 229.

43. Gilbert, *Original Plays 4,* 386.

44. Ibid., 424.

45. Ibid., 436.

46. Ibid.

47. Ibid., 440.

48. Stedman, *Gilbert,* 310.

49. Gilbert, *Original Plays 4,* 311.

50. Ibid., 411.

51. Ibid., 400.

52. Ibid., 386.

53. Ibid., 395.

54. Ibid., 437.

55. Stedman, *Gilbert,* 312.

56. Quoted in Dark and Grey, *Gilbert,* 163.

57. Sutton, *Gilbert,* 49–53.

58. Gilbert, *Original Plays 4,* 33.

59. Ibid., 38.

60. Ibid., 35.

61. Ibid., 39.

62. Ibid., 5.

63. Ibid., 21.

64. Ibid., 7.

65. Max Beerbohm, "Mr. Gilbert's Rentrée (And Mine)," 2: 50–51.

66. Gilbert, *Complete Annotated Gilbert and Sullivan,* 573.

67. Gilbert, *Original Plays 4,* 202–23.

68. Edith A. Browne, *W. S. Gilbert,* 54.

69. Quoted in Pearson, *Gilbert: His Life and Strife,* 247.

70. Gilbert, *Original Plays 4,* 484.

71. Rowell, *Victorian Dramatic Criticism,* 324.

72. Gilbert, *Original Plays 4,* 484.

73. Mrs. Alec-Tweedie, *My Table-Cloths: A Few Reminiscences* (London: Hutchinson & Co., 1916), 45.

74. Archer, "Mr. W. S. Gilbert," 110.

75. Ibid., 112.

76. Quoted in Dark and Grey, *Gilbert,* 142.

CONCLUSION: CONTRADICTION CONTRADICTED

1. G. M. Young, *Portrait of an Age: Victorian England,* ed. George Kitson Clark (London: Oxford University Press, 1977), 115–16.

2. Ibid., 344.

3. Pearson, *Gilbert: His Life and Strife,* 39.

4. Gilbert, *Complete Annotated Gilbert and Sullivan,* vii.

5. Gilbert, *Original Plays 3,* 272.

6. Hesketh Pearson, *Gilbert and Sullivan: A Biography* (London: Hamish Hamilton, 1935), 108.

Note on the Texts Used

There is no complete edition of Gilbert's plays, though one has been in preparation in the United States since 1986. The nearest approach to such an edition so far is the four-volume set of *Original Plays*, published between 1875 and 1911, mostly under Gilbert's own supervision. These volumes contain forty of Gilbert's plays and librettos (if we include *The Hooligan* and *Trying a Dramatist,* which were not included before the second, undated, edition of the Fourth Series, and *Iolanthe,* which was not included before the third, 1902 edition of the First Series): the majority of the whole, if only just. I have taken from these four series of *Original Plays* the basic texts of the plays that they include, though there is reason to suppose that these are not the best possible versions of the plays. To take the most prominent instance: the *Original Plays* text of *The Mikado* omits Ko-Ko's famous "Little List" song. There is some evidence in these volumes of unwise editorial decisions and of sloppy proofreading pure and simple, but they remain the most easily available edition of Gilbert's plays, since they were much reprinted in the first decades of this century and are still often found in British secondhand bookshops. Quotations from the Savoy librettos are also taken from the *Original Plays*, though there are better and more easily accessible versions available; I have chosen to do this simply for the sake of consistency. The *Original Plays* texts are, after all, perfectly acceptable in most instances and have the additional advantage of being "authorized" texts: Gilbert proofread every volume except the later portions of the Fourth Series (death having interrupted him before he could finish this task).

Gilbert before Sullivan (1969), Jane W. Stedman's excellent edition of the six German Reed entertainments, fills in one of the areas not covered by the *Original Plays*; *New and Original Extravaganzas* (1931), edited by Isaac Goldberg, provides the five early rhymed extravaganzas with which

Gilbert first earned attention in the theater. *Gilbert before Sullivan* is still relatively easy to obtain; *New and Original Extravaganzas* is much less so: but they remain the only editions of these plays accessible outside specialist theater collections.

One or two of the remaining plays are accessible in modern editions: Terence Rees has published *Uncle Baby* (1968) and *The Realm of Joy* (1969); Stedman has published *The Blue-Legged Lady,* with commentary, in *Nineteenth Century Theatre Research* (1975); George Rowell includes *Princess Toto* in his selection of *Plays by W. S. Gilbert* (1982). Charles P. Johnson's edition of *Topsyturvydom* (1931) is for practical purposes unavailable outside the British Library, and the same applies to the handful of plays published only in Victorian actors' editions by Thomas Hailes Lacy or Samuel French. (For these published single plays I have relied upon photocopies of copies held in the British Library.) There is even a small residue of Gilbert's plays that has never been published: such curiosities as the early one-act farce *Allow Me to Explain.*

To conclude, then, I have chosen the most accessible editions of the plays for reference purposes, though in some instances this is not to imply that the text chosen is "accessible" in the normal sense of that word. This means only that it is the only one available, at least until the Complete Gilbert Edition comes along.

THE PLAYS OF W. S. GILBERT

This list largely derives from those compiled by Reginald Allen, George Rowell, and Philip Plumb. However, I have been able to add one or two extra details of my own. I have tried to give as much information about the plays as I can. The first performance of each play is given wherever possible. It should be assumed that the cited theater is in London, unless otherwise stated. If the piece was published before it was performed, it is placed in the list according to publication date, and publication details are given first.

Uncle Baby (one-act Comedietta): Lyceum, 31 October 1863.

Ruy Blas (burlesque): unperformed; published in *Warne's Christmas Annual 1866.*

Hush-a-Bye, Baby, on the Tree Top; or, Harlequin Fortunia, King Frog of Frog Island, and the Magic Toys of Lowther Arcade [written with Chas. Millard] (pantomime): Astley's, 26 December 1866.

Dulcamara! or, The Little Duck and the Great Quack (extravaganza): St. James's, 29 December 1866.

La Vivandière; or, True to the Corps! (extravaganza): St. James's Hall, Liverpool, 15 June 1867.

Robinson Crusoe; or, The Injun Bride and the Injured Wife [written with H. J. Byron, Thomas Hood, H. S. Leigh, and Arthur Sketchley] (burlesque): Haymarket, 6 July 1867.

Allow Me to Explain (one-act farce): Prince of Wales's, 4 November 1867.

Highly Improbable (one-act Farce): Royalty, 5 December 1867.

A Colossal Idea [period of composition unknown] (one-act farce): unperformed; published 1932.

Harlequin Cock Robin and Jenny Wren; or, Fortunatus and the Water of Life, the Three Bears, the Three Gifts, the Three Wishes, and the Little Man who Woo'd the Little Maid (pantomime): Lyceum, 26 December 1867.

The Merry Zingara; or, The Tipsy Gipsy and the Pipsy Wipsy (extravaganza): Royalty, 21 March 1868.

Robert the Devil; or, The Nun, the Dun, and the Son of a Gun (extravaganza): Gaiety, 21 December 1868.

No Cards (one-act musical entertainment): Gallery of Illustration, 29 March 1869. Music by German Reed/Lionel Elliott?

The Pretty Druidess; or, The Mother, the Maid, and the Mistletoe Bough (extravaganza): Charing Cross, 19 June 1869.

An Old Score [revived at Court (25 November 1872) as *Quits*] (three-act comedy): Gaiety, 26 July 1869.

Ages Ago (one-act musical entertainment): Gallery of Illustration, 22 November 1869. Music by Frederic Clay.

A Medical Man (one-act farce): published in Clement Scott's *Drawing-Room Plays* (1870); performed St. George's Hall 24 October 1872.

The Princess (blank-verse parody of Tennyson's poem in five scenes): Olympic, 8 January 1870.

The Gentleman in Black (two-act musical play): Charing Cross, 26 May 1870. Music by Frederic Clay.

Our Island Home (one-act musical entertainment): Gallery of Illustration, 20 June 1870. Music by German Reed.

The Palace of Truth (three-act fairy comedy): Haymarket, 19 November 1870.

The Brigands [translated from *Les Brigands* by Henri Meilhac and Ludovic Halévy] (three-act comic opera): published by Boosey, 1871; performed Theatre Royal, Plymouth 2 September 1889. Music by Jacques Offenbach.

Randall's Thumb (three-act comedy): Court, 25 January 1871.

A Sensation Novel (musical entertainment in three "volumes"): Gallery of Illustration, 30 January 1871. Music by German Reed.

Creatures of Impulse (one-act musical play): Court, 15 April 1871. Music by Alberto Randegger.

Great Expectations [adapted from the Dickens novel] (drama): Court, 29 May 1871.

On Guard (three-act comedy): Court, 28 October 1871.

Pygmalion and Galatea (three-act fairy comedy): Haymarket, 9 December 1871.

Thespis; or, The Gods Grown Old (two-act comic opera): Gaiety, 26 December 1871. Music by Arthur Sullivan.

Happy Arcadia (one-act musical entertainment): Gallery of Illustration, 28 October 1872. Music by Frederic Clay.

The Wicked World (three-act fairy comedy): Haymarket, 4 January 1873.

The Happy Land [written under the pseudonym of F. Tomline, with Gilbert à Beckett] (two-act burlesque of *The Wicked World*): Court, 3 March 1873.

The Realm of Joy [written as F. Latour Tomline; freely adapted from *Le Roi Candaule* by Henri Meilhac and Ludovic Halévy: title changed after a few nights to *The Realms of Joy*] (one-act farce): Royalty, 18 October 1873.

The Wedding March [written as F. Latour Tomline; translated from *Un Chapeau de Paille d'Italie* by Eugène Labiche and Marc-Michel] (three-act farce): Court, 15 November 1873.

Charity (four-act drama): Haymarket, 3 January 1874.

Ought We to Visit Her? [adapted from the novel by Mrs. Annie Edwardes] (three-act drama): Royalty, 17 January 1874.

Committed for Trial [translated from *Le Reveillon* by Henri Meilhac and Ludovic Halévy] (two-act farce): Globe, 24 January 1874.

The Blue-Legged Lady [no author named; translated from *La Dame aux Jambes d'Azur* by Eugène Labiche and Marc-Michel] (one-act farce): Court, 4 March 1874.

Topseyturveydom (one-act extravaganza): Criterion, 21 March 1874. Music by Alfred Cellier.

Sweethearts (two-act comedy): Prince of Wales's, 7 November 1874.

Rosencrantz and Guildenstern (burlesque in three short "tableaux"): published in *Fun*, December 1874; performed Vaudeville, 3 June 1891.

Trial by Jury (one-act comic opera): Royalty, 25 March 1875. Music by Arthur Sullivan.

Tom Cobb; or, Fortune's Toy (three-act farce): St. James's, 24 April 1875.

Eyes and No Eyes; or, The Art of Seeing (one-act musical entertainment): St. George's Hall, 5 July 1875. Music by German Reed.

Broken Hearts (three-act verse drama): Court, 9 December 1875.

Princess Toto (three-act comic opera): Theatre Royal, Nottingham, 1 July 1876. Music by Frederic Clay.

Dan'l Druce, Blacksmith (three-act drama): Haymarket, 11 September 1876.

On Bail [revised version of *Committed for Trial*] (three-act farce): Criterion, 3 February 1877.

Engaged (three-act farcical comedy): Haymarket, 3 October 1877.

The Sorcerer (two-act comic opera): Opera Comique, 17 November 1877. Music by Arthur Sullivan.

[Ali Baba and] The Forty Thieves [written with Robert Reece, F. C. Burnand, and H. J. Byron; one performance] (pantomime): Gaiety, 13 February 1878.

The Ne'er-Do-Weel [rewritten and restaged three weeks later as *The Vagabond*] (three-act drama): Olympic, 25 February 1878.

H.M.S. Pinafore; or, The Lass that Loved a Sailor (two-act comic opera): Opera Comique, 25 May 1878. Music by Arthur Sullivan.

Gretchen (four-act verse tragedy): Olympic, 24 March 1879.

Lord Mayor's Day [translated from *La Cagnotte* by Eugène Labiche and Alfred Delacour: Gilbert translated the first two acts before abandoning the project, but when it was completed and produced his name did not appear] (three-act farce): Folly, 30 June 1879.

The Pirates of Penzance; or, The Slave of Duty (two-act comic opera): Bijou, Paignton, 30 December 1879; Fifth Avenue, New York, 31 December 1879. Music by Arthur Sullivan.

Patience; or, Bunthorne's Bride (two-act comic opera): Opera Comique, 23 April 1881. Music by Arthur Sullivan.

Foggerty's Fairy (three-act farce): Criterion, 15 December 1881.

Iolanthe; or, The Peer and the Peri (two-act comic opera): Savoy, 25 November 1882. Music by Arthur Sullivan.

Princess Ida; or, Castle Adamant [musicalized version of *The Princess*] (three-act comic opera): Savoy, 5 January 1884. Music by Arthur Sullivan.

Comedy and Tragedy (one-act drama): Lyceum, 26 January 1884.

The Mikado; or, The Town of Titipu (two-act comic opera): Savoy, 14 March 1885. Music by Arthur Sullivan.

Ruddygore; or, The Witch's Curse [retitled *Ruddigore* after a few days] (two-act comic opera): Savoy, 22 January 1887. Music by Arthur Sullivan.

The Yeomen of the Guard; or, The Merryman and his Maid (two-act comic opera): Savoy, 3 October 1888. Music by Arthur Sullivan.

Brantinghame Hall (four-act drama): St. James's, 29 November 1888.

The Gondoliers; or, The King of Barataria (two-act comic opera): Savoy, 7 December 1889. Music by Arthur Sullivan.

The Mountebanks (two-act comic opera): Lyric, 4 January 1892. Music by Alfred Cellier.

"Haste to the Wedding" [musicalized version of *The Wedding March*] (three-act comic opera): Criterion, 27 July 1892. Music by George Grossmith.

Utopia (Limited); or, The Flowers of Progress [retitled *Utopia, Limited* after a few days] (two-act comic opera): Savoy, 7 October 1893. Music by Arthur Sullivan.

His Excellency (two-act comic opera): Lyric, 27 October 1894. Music by Osmond Carr.

The Grand Duke; or, The Statutory Duel (two-act comic opera): Savoy, 7 March 1896. Music by Arthur Sullivan.

The Fortune-Hunter (three-act drama): Theatre Royal, Birmingham, 27 September 1897.

Harlequin and the Fairy's Dilemma [retitled *The Fairy's Dilemma* after a few days] (two-act domestic pantomime): Garrick, 3 May 1904.

Fallen Fairies; or, The Wicked World [musicalized version of *The Wicked World*] (two-act comic opera): Savoy, 15 December 1909. Music by Edward German.

The Hooligan (one-Act drama): Coliseum, 27 February 1911.

Trying a Dramatist (one-act sketch): Published in *Original Plays, Fourth Series* (1911): Performance details not known.

BIBLIOGRAPHY

WORKS BY W. S. GILBERT

"An Appeal to the Press." *Era Almanack 1878* (London) 85–86.

"An Autobiography." *The theatre,* 2 April 1883, 217–224.

The Bab Ballads. Edited by James Ellis. Cambridge: Harvard University Press, Belknap Press, 1980.

The Bab Ballads, with Which are Included Songs of a Savoyard. London: Macmillan, 1924.

The Complete Annotated Gilbert and Sullivan. Edited by Ian Bradley. Oxford: Oxford University Press, 1996.

"A Consistent Pantomime." *The Graphic* (16 January 1875), 62.

Engaged. London, Samuel French, n.d.

Foggerty's Fairy and Other Tales. London: George Routledge and Sons, 1892.

Gilbert before Sullivan: Six Comic Plays by W. S. Gilbert. Edited by Jane W. Stedman. London: Routledge & Kegan Paul, 1969.

"A Hornpipe in Fetters." *Era almanack 1879* (London), 91–92.

"Jezebel," *Fun* (24 December 1870), 255.

New and Original Extravaganzas. Edited by Isaac Goldberg. Boston: John W. Luce & Co., 1931.

An Old Score: An Original Comedy-Drama in Three Acts. London: Thomas Hailes Lacy, n.d.

On Guard, an Entirely Original Comedy in Three Acts. London, Samuel French, n.d.

Ought We To Visit Her?: A Comedy, in Three Acts, Dramatized from Mrs. Edwardes's Novel. Printed as manuscript. London: Samuel French, n.d.

Original Plays: First Series. London: Chatto & Windus, 1925.

Original Plays: Second Series. London: Chatto & Windus, 1925.

Original Plays: Third Series. London: Chatto & Windus, 1923.

Original Plays: Fourth Series. London: Chatto & Windus, 1922.

Plays by W. S. Gilbert. Edited by George Rowell. Cambridge: Cambridge University Press, 1982.

The Realm of Joy: Being a Free and Easy Version of Le Roi Candaule. Edited by Terence Rees. London: by the editor, 25 Nightingale Square, 1969.

"The Story of a Stage Play." *New-York Daily Tribune,* 9 August 1885, p. 9.

The Story of H.M.S. Pinafore. London: G. Bell and Sons, 1913.

Topsyturvydom: Original Extravaganza. Edited by Charles P. Johnson. Oxford: Oxford University Press, 1931.

Uncle Baby: A Comedietta. Edited by Terence Rees. London: by the editor, 1968.

Tomline, F. [W. S. Gilbert], and Gilbert à Beckett. *The Happy Land: A Burlesque Version of "The Wicked World."* London: J. W. Last & Co., 1873.

Works about Gilbert

Allen, Reginald. *W. S. Gilbert: An Anniversary Survey and Exhibition Checklist.* Charlottesville: The Bibliographical Society of the University of Virginia, 1963.

Anonymous, 1871–1935. London: John Murray, 1936.

Archer, William. "Mr. W. S. Gilbert," in *English Dramatists of To-Day.* London: Sampson Low, Marston & Co., 1882.

————. "Conversation VI: With Mr. W. S. Gilbert." In *Real Conversations.* London: William Heinemann, 1904.

Baily, Leslie. *The Gilbert and Sullivan Book.* London: Cassell, 1952.

Beerbohm, Max. "Mr. Gilbert's Rentrée (And Mine)." In *Around Theatres,* London: Heinemann, 2:44–51.

Boyer, Robert D. "The 'Perfect Autocrat': W. S. Gilbert in Rehearsal." *Theatre Studies,* 26–27 (1979–81), 64–78.

Brahms, Caryl. *Gilbert and Sullivan: Lost Chords and Dischords.* London: Weidenfeld & Nicolson, 1975.

Browne, Edith A. *W. S. Gilbert.* Stars of the Stage. London: John Lane, The Bodley Head, 1907.

Cardullo, Bert. "The Art and the Business of W. S. Gilbert's *Engaged.*" *Modern Drama* 28 (1985): 462–73.

Chesterton, G. K. "Gilbert and Sullivan." In *The Eighteen-Eighties: Essays by Fellows of the Royal Society of Literature.* Edited by Walter de la Mare. Cambridge: Cambridge University Press, 1930.

Christiansen, Rupert. "Gilbert and Sullivan and Us." *The Daily Telegraph* (London), 1 August 1997, p. 23.

Coxe-Ife, William. *W. S. Gilbert: Stage Director.* The Student's Music Library—Historical and Critical Series. London: Dennis Dobson, 1977.

Dark, Sidney, and Grey, Rowland. *W. S. Gilbert: His Life and Letters.* London: Methuen & Co., 1923.

Eden, David. *Gilbert and Sullivan: The Creative Conflict.* London: Associated University Presses, 1986.

Ellis, James Delmont. "The comic vision of W. S. Gilbert." Ph.D. diss., State University of Iowa, 1964.

Filon, Augustin. "Chapter 5 [W. S. Gilbert]." In *The English Stage: Being an Account of the Victorian Drama.* Translated by Frederic Whyte. London: John Milne, 1897.

Fischler, Alan. *Modified Rapture: Comedy in W. S. Gilbert's Savoy Operas.* Charlottesville and London: University Press of Virginia, 1991.

Fitzgerald, Percy. *The Savoy Opera and the Savoyards.* London: Chatto & Windus, 1894.

Godwin, A. H. *Gilbert and Sullivan: A Critical Appreciation of the Savoy Operas.* London and Toronto: J. M. Dent & Sons, 1926.

Goldberg, Isaac. *The Story of Gilbert and Sullivan, Or The 'Compleat' Savoyard.* London: John Murray, 1929.

Hayter, Charles. *Gilbert and Sullivan.* Macmillan Modern Dramatists. London: Macmillan, 1987.

Helyar, James, ed. *Gilbert and Sullivan Papers Presented at the International Conference Held at the University Of Kansas in May 1970.* Lawrence: University of Kansas Libraries, 1971.

Higgins, Regina Kirby. "Victorian Laughter: The Comic Operas of Gilbert and Sullivan." Ph.D. diss., Indiana University, 1985.

Hoffman, Cheryl Conover. "A Study of the Women in W. S. Gilbert's *Patience, Iolanthe,* and *Princess Ida;* or, The Folly of Being Feminist." Ph.D. diss., West Virginia University, 1988.

How, Harry. "Illustrated Interviews: No. 4—Mr. W. S. Gilbert." *Strand Magazine* 2 (October 1891): 330–41.

Hulme, David Russell. "A note." In *H.M.S. Pinafore* CD booklet, TER, 1987.

James, Alan. *Gilbert and Sullivan.* The Illustrated Lives of the Great Composers. London: Omnibus Press, 1989.

Jones, Brian. "The Sword That Never Fell." *W. S. Gilbert Society Journal* 1, no. 1 (spring 1985): 22–25.

———. "Ko-Ko's Toe." *W. S. Gilbert Society Journal* 1, no. 6 (1990): 170–74.

Midwinter, Eric. "W. S. Gilbert: Victorian Entertainer." *New Theatre Quarterly* (1986): 273–79.

Orel, Harold, ed. *Gilbert and Sullivan: Interviews and Recollections.* London: Macmillan, 1994.

Pearson, Hesketh. *Gilbert And Sullivan: A Biography.* London: Hamish Hamilton, 1935.

———. *Gilbert: His Life and Strife.* London: Methuen & Co., 1957.

Plumb, Philip. "Gilbert and the Censors: *The Happy Land* Conspiracy." *W. S. Gilbert Society Journal* 1, no. 8 (1994): 238–40.

"The Revolutionary Satire of W. S. Gilbert," *Littell's Living Age* 311 (24 December 1921): 795–98.

Righton, Edward. "A Suppressed Burlesque: *The Happy Land.*" *The Theatre,* 1 August 1896, 63–66.

Stedman, Jane W. "From Dame to Woman: W. S. Gilbert and Theatrical Transvestism." *Victorian Studies* (September 1970): 27–46.

————. *W. S. Gilbert: A Classic Victorian and His Theatre.* Oxford: Oxford University Press, 1996.

Sutton, Max Keith. *W. S. Gilbert.* Boston: Twayne, 1975.

Waters, Mary Watkins. "W. S. Gilbert and the Discovery of a Satiric Method for the Victorian Stage." Ph.D. diss. Auburn University, 1974.

Williamson, Audrey. *Gilbert and Sullivan Opera: An Assessment.* 2d ed. London: Marion Boyars, 1982.

Wolfson, John. *Final Curtain: The Last Gilbert and Sullivan Operas.* London: Chappell & Co., 1976.

GENERAL

Alec-Tweedie, Mrs. *My Table-Cloths: A Few Reminiscences.* London: Hutchinson & Co., 1916.

Bainton, George, ed. *The Art of Authorship: Literary Reminiscences, Methods of Work, and Advice to Young Beginners, Personally Contributed by Leading Authors of the Day.* London: James Clarke & Co., 1890.

Bassnett-McGuire, Susan. *Luigi Pirandello.* Macmillan Modern dramatists. London: Macmillan, 1983.

Booth, Michael R. *English Melodrama.* London: Herbert Jenkins, 1965.

————. *Prefaces to English Nineteenth-Century Theatre.* Manchester, England: Manchester University Press, n.d.

Booth, Michael, R. ed. *Comedies.* Vol. 3 of *English Plays of the Nineteenth Century:* Oxford: Oxford University Press, 1973.

————. *Farces.* Vol. 4 of *English Plays of the Nineteenth Century.* Oxford: Oxford University Press, 1973.

Buckley, Jerome Hamilton. *The Victorian Temper: A Study in Literary Culture.* London: Frank Cass & Co. Ltd., 1966.

Butler, Samuel. *Life and Habit.* London: Wildwood House, 1981.

Chesterton, G. K. *"All I survey": A Book of Essays.* 2d ed. London: Methuen & Co., 1934.

Citron, Stephen. *The Musical: From the Inside Out.* London: Hodder & Stoughton, 1991.

Empson, William. *Seven Types of Ambiguity.* 2d ed. Harmondsworth, England: Penguin, 1973.

Gershwin, Ira. *Lyrics on Several Occasions.* London: Omnibus Press, 1988.

Harding, James. *Jacques Offenbach: A Biography.* The Opera Library. London: John Calder, 1980.

Hollingshead, John. *My Lifetime,* 2 vols. London: Sampson Low, Marston & Co., 1895.

Houghton, Walter E. *The Victorian Frame of Mind, 1830–1870.* New Haven and London: Yale University Press, 1957.

Jackson, Holbrook. *The Eighteen Nineties.* [Corrected edition.] Harmondsworth, England: Pelican Books, 1939.

Jacobs, Arthur. *Arthur Sullivan: A Victorian Musician.* Oxford: Oxford University Press, 1984.

Joseph, Tony. *The D'oyly Carte Opera Company, 1875–1982: An Unofficial History.* Bristol, England: Bunthorne Books, 1994.

Knight, G. Wilson. *The Golden Labyrinth: A Study of British Drama.* London: Phoenix House, 1962.

Lahr, John. *Prick Up Your Ears: The Biography of Joe Orton.* Harmondsworth, England: Penguin books, 1980.

Lerner, Alan Jay. *The Musical Theatre: A Celebration.* London: Collins, 1986.

Lytton, Henry. *A Wandering Minstrel.* London: Jarrolds, 1933.

Mandeville, Bernard. *The Fable of the Bees; or Private Vices, Publick Benefits.* Edited by F. B. Kaye. 2 vols. Oxford: Oxford University Press, 1924; reprint, Indianapolis, Ind.: Liberty Classics, 1988.

Morton, John Maddison. *Slasher and Crasher!* London: Thomas Hailes Lacy, n.d.

Nicoll, Allardyce. *Early Nineteenth Century Drama, 1800–1850.* Vol. 4 of *A History of English Drama 1660–1900.* 2d ed. Cambridge: Cambridge University Press, 1963.

Pater, Walter H. *Studies in the History of the Renaissance.* London: Macmillan & Co., 1873.

Pirandello, Luigi. *Six Characters in Search of an Author.* Translated by John Linstrum. London: Methuen, 1982.

Pronko, Leonard C. *Eugène Labiche and Georges Feydeau.* Macmillan Modern Dramatists. London: Macmillan, 1982.

Robertson, T. W. *Six Plays.* Edited by Michael R. Booth. Ashover, England: Amber Lane Press, 1980.

———. *Plays by Tom Robertson.* Edited by William Tydeman. Cambridge: Cambridge University Press, 1982.

Rowell, George, ed. *Victorian Dramatic Criticism.* London: Methuen & Co., 1971.

Rowell, George. *The Victorian Theatre, 1792–1914: A Survey.* 2d ed. Cambridge: Cambridge University Press, 1978.

Shaw, Bernard. *Music in London, 1890–94.* 3 vols. London: Constable and Company, 1932.

———. *Collected Letters, 1874–1897.* Edited by Dan H. Laurence. London: Max Reinhardt, 1965.

———. *Collected Letters 1911–1925.* Edited by Dan H. Laurence. London: Max Reinhardt, 1985.

Smith, Patrick J. *The Tenth Muse: A Historical Study of the Opera Libretto.* London: Victor Gollancz, 1971.

Taylor, John Russell. *The Rise and Fall of the Well-Made Play.* London: Methuen & Co., 1967.

Traubner, Richard. *Operetta: A Theatrical History.* New York and Oxford: Oxford University Press, 1989.

Turner, Paul. *English Literature, 1832–90: Excluding the Novel.* Vol. 11, pt. 1 of *The Oxford History of English Literature.* Oxford: Clarendon Press, 1989.

Wells, Stanley. *Literature and Drama.* London: Routledge and Kegan Paul, 1970.

Young, G. M. *Portrait of an Age: Victorian England.* Edited by George Kitson Clark. London: Oxford University Press, 1977.

Zadan, Craig. *Sondheim and Co.* 2d ed. updated. London: Nick Hern Books, 1990.

MANUSCRIPT SOURCE

British Library, Add. MS 45,291.

Index

Abbott, Edwin A., 69
à Beckett, Gilbert, 73
Alice's Adventures in Wonderland
    (Carroll), 69
Apple Cart, The (Shaw), 160
Archer, William, 26, 42–43, 61, 65, 66,
    77, 121, 136; interview with Gilbert,
    52, 52, 53, 54, 170, 171
Aristophanes, 165–66
Arms and the Man (Shaw), 65
Art of Authorship, The (Bainton), 57

Baily, Leslie, 109
Bainton, Rev. George, 57
Barker, Harley Granville. *See* Granville-
    Barker, Harley
Barrington, Rutland, 118, 119, 143, 162
Bassnett-McGuire, Susan, 39
Beardsley, Aubrey, 166
Beatty-Kingston, William, 142
Beerbohm, Max, 58, 59, 176–77, 179
Bentham, George, 118
Birth (Robertson), 61
Black-Ey'd Susan (Jerrold), 101, 102
Bond, Edward, 14
Bond, Jessie, 143
Booth, Michael R., 18, 61, 82, 91, 97,
    101, 106, 116
Boucicault, Dion, 88
Bourchier, Arthur, 174
Bradley, Ian, 15, 106, 143, 191
Brecht, Bertolt, 128
Brigand, The (Planché), 116
Brigands, Les (Offenbach), 72, 116, 158
Browne, Edith A., 13, 148, 178
Browning, Robert, 26

Buckstone, J. B., 25, 27
Butler, Samuel, 69, 76, 112, 113

Campbell, Andrew, 102
Carroll, Lewis, 69
Carte, Richard D'Oyly, 86, 95, 119, 141,
    143, 144; "Carpet Quarrel," 154,
    156–57; contract with Gilbert and
    Sullivan (1883), 96, 140, 190
Caste (Robertson), 61
Cecil, Arthur, 35, 36, 43
Cellier, Alfred, 157
Cellier, François, 92
Chapeau de Paille d'Italie, Un
    (Labiche/Marc-Michel), 81, 158
Chesterton, G. K., 36, 39
Citron, Stephen, 129–30
Clark, George Kitson, 184
Clay, Frederic, 80, 130
Comedy Opera Company, 95–96. *See also*
    D'Oyly Carte Opera Company, The.
Cox-Ife, William, 92
Crémieux, Hector-Jonathan, 71
Crimean War, 112, 183

da Ponte, Lorenzo, 127
Darwin, Charles, 112, 183, 189
Dickens, Charles, 61, 65, 139
Disraeli, Benjamin, 75, 103
D'Oyly Carte Opera Company, The, 14,
    89, 140, 144, 149. *See also* Comedy
    Opera Company

Echo, 154
Edwardes, Annie, 48
Era, 112

219